For Brian at

Three score years at ten

with love,

Leslie Beaty

(Leslie)

May '97

The Aristide factor

To my family:
Tim and Jon, born in Port-au-Prince in the days of Jean-Claude Duvalier;
Ruth, travelling companion to Haiti and such an astute observer;
Margaret, who has shared it all with me since the very beginning.

And to the Haitian People
who've suffered so dreadfully and for so long, even though they deserve nothing
but the best.

The Aristide factor

Leslie Griffiths

A LION BOOK

Published by
Lion Publishing plc
Sandy Lane West, Oxford, England
ISBN 0 7459 3647 4
Albatross Books Pty Ltd
PO Box 320, Sutherland, NSW 2232, Australia
ISBN 0 7324 1491 1

First edition 1997
10 9 8 7 6 5 4 3 2 1 0

A catalogue record for this book is available
from the British Library

Acknowledgments
We would like to thank all those who have given
us permission to include quotations in this book.
Every effort has been made to trace and
acknowledge copyright holders of all the quotations.
We apologize for any errors or omissions that may
remain, and would ask those concerned to contact
the publishers, who will ensure that full
acknowledgment is made in the future.

Printed and bound in Great Britain
by Biddles Ltd, Guildford and Kings Lynn

Contents

ACKNOWLEDGMENTS 7

INTRODUCTION 11

CHAPTER 1 The shaping of a leader 22

CHAPTER 2 Aristide throws down a gauntlet 57

CHAPTER 3 'Just who are you, Father Aristide?' 96

CHAPTER 4 Taking the reins of power 130

CHAPTER 5 Seven brave months 164

CHAPTER 6 The army's reign of terror 203

CHAPTER 7 Dealings with America 234

CHAPTER 8 Operation Uphold Democracy 263

POSTSCRIPT 294

BIBLIOGRAPHY 296

INDEX 302

Acknowledgments

My previous book on Haiti (A History of Methodism in Haiti: Port-au-Prince, 1991) was the development of a PhD thesis which I completed at the School of Oriental and African Studies in the University of London. For that exercise, I needed to sit in a number of libraries in cities on both sides of the Atlantic, where I consulted archival and historical material that enabled me to write an account covering the years 1817–1970.

This book, dealing as it does with such very recent times, needed to be approached in a radically different way. For a start, I've lived through the whole period under review and had personal contact with some of the principal actors in the drama I'm presenting. So conversation and discussion has represented a significant 'source' of material in my endeavours to write this narrative. I'm grateful to all those who were prepared to help me understand the complicated affairs of Haiti in this way. In particular, I must mention Freud Jean, Jean-Marie Vincent, Evans Paul, Julio Larosilière, Claudette Werleigh, Jean Angus, Rosny Desroches, Alain Rocourt, Chavannes Jean-Baptiste, Ines Durandis, Gladys Lauture, Yvon Joseph and, of course, Jean-Bertrand Aristide himself. They've all given enormous help (sometimes unwittingly) in the way we've talked together about the problems and opportunities facing Haiti at this moment in time.

In October 1991, a day or two after the coup which ousted Aristide from office, I attended a meeting of non-governmental organizations who were seeking to devise a strategy for maintaining working relationships with their partners in Haiti in the new conditions then prevailing there. I represented no agency and became frustrated at the limited nature of the questions being asked. No one, it seemed, was addressing the essentially political dimension of the problem. Out of my frustration on the occasion, the Haiti Support Group was born and I must pay tribute here to all those gifted and concerned people who have given their time and considerable talents to heighten the awareness of the British public for a country which can count on little basic sympathy and only the most limited (usually voyeuristic) interest. I must mention Charles Arthur, Leah Gordon, Anne and Christian Wisskirchen-McConnell and Philip Wearne. But there are many others in the group whose counsel and energy have strengthened my grasp of issues central to the developing scene in Haiti. I pay tribute to them all. Leah's help with photographs has been invaluable and also shows her sensitivity and skill in this area. Claire Dixon and Tony Dykes have been amazingly generous in opening their home to me whenever they've had Haitian friends staying with them.

Greg Chamberlain is the doughty and inveterate Haiti buff whose ferreting away over many years has given people like me vast amounts of material to delve into. His journalistic skills are married in the most impressive way to a huge personal commitment to Haiti. As well as conversation with Greg, there has been the accumulated documentation for which he's been responsible over the last six years. His work in sending out *Haiti-Hebdo* has been seminal in keeping those of us with other fish to fry really focused on what's happening in Haiti. I certainly could not have embarked on this task without all his hard work. Alongside Greg, I must mention David Nicholls, whose sudden death in the autumn of 1996 was a shock to us all. He brought his brilliant mind to bear upon all that was happening in Haiti. His book *From Dessalines to Duvalier* (Cambridge University Press) remains the finest introduction to Haitian history available in the English language. We were sparring partners; I found myself disagreeing with David as well as sharing his opinions. But he made sure to tell me when he thought intellectual laziness was threatening to affect my judgments.

I'm a Methodist minister with the usual tasks that fall to all such people—pastoral care, teaching, administrative chores, preaching, spiritual leadership. It's really amazing that in the succession of churches and circuits which I've served, my people have given me their warmest encouragement to pursue my extramural interests. In the case of Haiti, this has often meant travelling at very short notice to be present at elections, or at a presidential inauguration, or at some other significant event. It has also involved finding the time to write articles, reports, a thesis, scripts, lectures and, now, this book. So I gladly pay tribute to all my Methodist friends in Loughton, Hinde Street, Golders Green, Mill Hill, and Wesley's Chapel who have been so patient with me and for so long.

Maurice Lyon came up with the idea for this book and has seen to it ever since that I've stuck to my task. His regular contact and encouragement have kept me alert and committed when a plethora of other pressing duties could so easily have distracted me. My family has yet again prepared to share my affections when this book turned up as the latest project to be completed within a ridiculously short timescale. There is no other word to describe their dedication and support than the most hackneyed one of all, love. And that's what they've given me in large doses over many, many years.

With all this support and encouragement, I really should have produced a flawless manuscript. I've no doubt that the end result is rather less accomplished than that. And there's no doubt that it's my bungling and faulty judgment that's to be held accountable. Even so, whatever shortcomings it may contain, I really have enjoyed writing this book and I hope my readers will catch some of the spirit in which it's been written.

Leslie Griffiths

Haiti showing places cited in the text

Introduction

To many of the people who meet him, Jean-Bertrand Aristide is quite simply an enigma. He incites rational people to an anger they themselves feel angry about when they see that same raw emotion in other people. He commands support so passionate that it has all the qualities of religious fervour. He's a dapper little man, well dressed even in casual clothes, yet he seems to create disorder wherever he goes—and his diminutive size seems at odds with his huge personality. His habit of wearing dark glasses is infuriating for those people who might want to gauge his character from what they see in his eyes. His face muscles are often taut and that, together with the hidden eyes, has left many people convinced that he is cold and calculating with a propensity even for cruelty. But when that same face breaks into a smile, those in his company could swear that heaven was beaming undiluted sunshine into the darkest vale of tears.

From time to time he says things that can whip up a crowd into a frenzy of rage at one end of the emotional spectrum or uncontrollable bursts of merriment at the other. As a priest, the sermons he preached to mainly poor congregations were always a heady mixture of powerful ingredients. They were vituperative, funny, sheer poetry, poisoned darts flung with unerring accuracy at people and institutions that deserved them—all by turns, and yet also all at once. They were never received impassively; they sent their listeners home quivering with stirred emotions, angry, self-aware, and radicalized.

He is thought by some to suffer from periodic bouts of depression. Indeed, at the height of a 'disinformation campaign' that sought to tarnish his reputation, he was accused of manic depression, even of being a psychopath. Such talk was shown to be malevolent nonsense, an exercise in character assassination. Even so, many a time he has broken down in fear or shame, especially when faced with wanton violence or the assassin's gun. Often he has missed death by a whisker whilst others within yards of him were hacked to pieces with machetes or had their brains blown out by bullets. Yet he has somehow overcome his trauma again and again before standing defiantly before his would-be assassins, daring them once more to finish him off. He's a man whose strengths and weaknesses have been put on very public display.

I've seen Aristide perform at a number of press conferences and public meetings. He makes a statement in measured phrases, speaking immaculate French or polished English. What he says almost always has a theological or mystical note. For example, he paints a picture of the Haiti of his dreams in terms of a banquet where all God's children will have a legitimate place at the meal table, or he spells out his political programme in the form of a modern-day version of the ten commandments. In some recent speeches, he has summed up his hopes for the Haitian people as being no more lofty than to move forward from the dehumanizing misery with which they're only too familiar to a dignified poverty which, while not much to boast about, will at least respect their integrity. Not for him the honeyed phrases of an all-things-to-all-men politician. Poverty is the destination he promises, honest-to-goodness poverty. But it is a destination that represents progress when compared with the starting point, known to so many of his listeners, that of utter misery.

His interlocutors among the press are often totally at a loss when he speaks in this way. I've seen the glazed look in their eyes. His style of communication defies their need for a soundbite or, at the very least, a coherent and salient plan of action. So they wait for him to finish his set piece, hoping to pin him down in the question-and-answer session that follows. But once again they're disappointed. It is not that Aristide employs the art, well known to politicians, of using reporters' questions to make his own points all over again. That would frustrate them but at least they'd know the rules of that particular game. They simply don't know what to make of it when questions they put to a man who purports to be a politician produce answers that seem to them incomprehensibly theological.

It is important to try to understand just what is happening on such occasions. It seems that hard-nosed questions enter what can only be compared to a 'translation chamber' within Aristide's brain. He speaks half a dozen living languages and has mastered three dead ones to boot. So we know there's some complicated and highly developed linguistic machinery inside his head. In these encounters with the press it is as if a new language, 'journalese', were being processed within his mind in the same way as he'd deal with German or Portuguese. Then a reply is formulated with that slight disjunction which reminds those listening to him that the person they're speaking to is, after all, a foreigner to that language.

For political leaders, the media, officials from non-governmental organizations, and outsiders generally, Aristide has an ability to intrigue by means of what can only be described as mystique. But, for the most part, people abhor the mysterious in the same way as nature abhors a vacuum. Into the void created by mystery rush all kinds of untested assumptions and generalized conclusions. The enigmatic Jean-Bertrand Aristide, far from being understood before generating comment, has been found too complex for soundbite journalism and, therefore, has been assumed to be not worth understanding.

Within Haiti, reactions to the priest-president have been more varied. I recall a dinner-party conversation in one of the grand villas above Pétionville in the spring of 1991. This was during the first few months of Aristide's presidency. The businessmen, politicians and diplomats who made up our company were scathingly dismissive of the efforts being made by their new head of state to govern this, the western hemisphere's poorest nation. They adopted the same sneering tone they employ when complaining amongst themselves about the qualities of their domestic staff, those necessary but servile adjuncts to their households who underpin the lavish lifestyles they enjoy. It was clear from the way they were speaking about him that Aristide couldn't count on the committed support of people like this. On the other hand, there are undoubtedly some elements among Haiti's élite who recognize the new political and social realities which Aristide's election has ushered in. They have risked the scorn of their peer group and thrown themselves heart and soul into his political campaigning. Some have paid for their enthusiasm with their lives.

This same range of emotions can be found lower down Haiti's social scale. On one occasion, at the very worst moment of Haiti's *de facto* years of illegitimate government (1991–94), I persuaded hard-drinking and loud-mouthed thugs gathered outside the Café Normandie headquarters of the fascist terrorist group known as FRAPH (Front for the Renewal and Advance of the People of Haiti) to let me and two journalist friends into their inner sanctum so that we could talk about their feelings and opinions. During the three years of Aristide's exile this organization instituted a reign of terror especially among the deposed president's keenest supporters in the slums around Port-au-Prince. On this occasion, they put on a show for our benefit, boasting and laughing for all they were worth. But I've never met their brand of unadulterated hatred before. They spat at the very mention of Aristide's name. They told me how, if he ever dared to return from his exile in the United States, they'd pull him apart, limb from limb and subject him to the slowest and most painful death they could possibly inflict on him. Those of us listening to this chilling conversation felt as if these people had drunk bile with their mothers' spleen. The atmosphere was odious. I've no doubt this group of malcontents enjoyed some measure of support for their actions and opinions in the country at large, but it was never very much. People at this level in Haitian society were generally to be found in the Aristide camp.

There is one fact that cannot be ignored in any attempt to do justice to the life and times of Jean-Bertrand Aristide. This man embodied in office the hopes and fears of a huge majority of his country's heaving population. The 67 per cent majority he won at the December 1990 election was no fiction. He commanded the affection and undying support of vast numbers of people. For the most part they'd never been enfranchised during the whole of Haiti's independent history. Since being admitted to the democratic process as active participants and invited to help to shape a radically different future, they've shown a clear intention to stay in the frame. These illiterate peasants and urban slum-dwellers have an endurance that beggars belief. They've put up with injustice and economic exploitation since Haitian time began. Their philosophy appears on the surface to be grimly fatalistic. *Bon die bon* (God is good) is a phrase they use to explain away the inscrutable inevitabilities that affect their everyday living. Man proposes—that may be so. But it is a rather grim God who disposes. There's never appeared to be anything they can do to change the lot that's been theirs since the beginning.

But much of that does seem to have changed. The veneer of determinism behind which they've hidden for so long has been swept aside by the arrival of Aristide on the political scene. It is as if he's been able to stand with a people who have lived in 'some dark dungeon's earless den' all their lives and have come to accept its shadowy realities as if there were no others. He's told them there's a way out of their darkness, a way he's found for himself. If they trust him, he'll show them the way to a destiny they cannot even dream of, a world where they can be actors rather than simply the passive and submissive people they've always had to be up to now. This dialogue has never actually been rehearsed in verbal form, but it precisely describes what has happened in Haiti. A whole people has given its complete trust, possibly for the first time since Jean-Jacques Dessalines and Toussaint Louverture (heroes of the struggle for Haiti's independence), to someone who's become almost a saviour figure, someone they look to with expectation for help and hope.

This giving of their trust is not to be underestimated by anyone. The person on whom it is focused carries the enormous responsibility of acting in the best interests of a whole people. Indeed, it is hard in my mind to separate Aristide from the

Haitian people. This fact is both the strongest and the weakest point in everything that's become known as *le phénomène Aristide* (the Aristide factor). On the one hand, it represents new energy available to Haiti on the eve of the two hundredth anniversary of her independence, energy which, if it is channelled wisely, could be used to transform unrelieved chaos and endless night into something radically better. But, equally, it could issue in a dictatorship of the people which would be just as ugly as any of those élitist dictatorships that have so vitiated Haiti's past.

The story of Aristide is the story of a whole people's hopes and fears. So much has been repressed in them for such a very long time that its sudden release cannot come without aberration or distortion. What's surprising is that there has been so *little* wanton violence from this newly enfranchised people. Since there's every prospect that Aristide will be a player in Haiti's destiny for many years yet, it is clearly in everybody's interest to make the effort to understand him and the symbiotic relationship he enjoys with the Haitian people. The international community which has so often shown itself ready and willing to help Haiti with its needs (and yet which imposes such unrealistic and inhumane economic and political targets on its people) could do with learning how to work with the grain of Haitian hope rather than against it, as it has so often done in the past.

The story of Aristide is the story of his people. They belong to each other and they cannot be told apart. But there is one other dimension to *this* telling of the story of Aristide that must be established at the outset. This account of a man and his people will not be done disinterestedly. Of course, I shall try my hardest to give a rounded picture of the good and bad aspects of Aristide's complicated character. He's no saint and I want to portray him as accurately as I can, warts and all. I have no problem with that. My difficulty is of a different order; it issues from my own personal relationship with Haiti and the Haitian people.

It is over a quarter of a century since my wife and I, then recently married, went to live in Haiti. We were there

throughout the 1970s. When we arrived, François ('PapaDoc')
Duvalier was still alive. I met him twice. I'd arrived in Haiti
straight from university studies in Cambridge and was totally
unprepared for what I was to find in this desperately poor
country. Graham Greene's *The Comedians* is still the outstanding
account of what it felt like to live in Haiti during PapaDoc's time
in power. It was an epoch when institutionalized terror, imposed
mercilessly over a period of a dozen years, had yielded a pliant
state totally at the mercy of its dictator's whims. Everywhere, I
met the victims of Duvalier's brutality, people whose loved ones
had disappeared or who had themselves been beaten or thrown
into prison. There were many who had been terrorized by the
Tontons Macoutes, his dreaded henchmen and secret police,
licenced by Duvalier to kill or intimidate at will.

I used to preach from time to time in the main Methodist
church in downtown Port-au-Prince. From the pulpit I could
see one of the pillars of that church, a splendid Christian
woman, whose husband had been snatched by one of PapaDoc's
hit squads many years before. For seventeen years she had no
idea whether her husband was alive or dead. The only word she
had been given by Duvalier's officials was that he'd been taken
into the national penitentiary which, as it happened, was
situated right next to the church she worshipped at.
Throughout the period of his presumed imprisonment, hoping
against hope, fighting against everything her head was telling
her about the likely end her husband had almost certainly met,
she sent food morning and evening to the prison gates with the
instruction that it be given to her loved one. Only when Andy
Young, Jimmy Carter's United Nations ambassador, came to
Haiti in 1977 and demanded the release (by Jean-Claude
Duvalier's government at that time) of all political prisoners,
did this woman discover her husband's fate. It seems that on the
day he'd been picked up, one of eight, he'd been taken into the
jail and lined up with the others against 'the wailing wall' of
execution, and shot. Six of the eight had died immediately. Her
husband was one of the two wounded survivors. They were
taken by boat into the Bay of La Gonâve, with boulders tied to

them, and turned overboard for the sharks. It had taken seventeen years for all this to come out. In that time, she was never officially a widow and was unable, therefore, to inherit her husband's estate or to contemplate re-marriage. She was one of thousands of Duvalier's victims.

In the same congregation, just a pew or two from this woman, I could see a variety of officials and even a minister in Duvalier's administration. They sang the same hymns, listened to the same sermons, said amen to the same prayers as she did. It is clear that there was little scope in such times for social interaction and ordinary association to take place. Those were days of deep despair and all-prevailing fear.

I was sent to live in the rural town of Petit Goâve, some thirty miles from the capital, Port-au-Prince. As a Methodist minister still in training, I was given pastoral charge of forty-eight churches. I was a bishop before I was ordained! The furthest of my churches was a twenty-four hour mule-ride from home over mountains and valleys of inordinate beauty. I had to cross the same river well over a hundred times to reach the town of Bainet on the south coast. And seven of my churches were on the island of La Gonâve. It was most unusual for a foreigner to be given this point of view on Haiti. And especially such an ignorant foreigner. I couldn't speak a word of the Créole language and knew nothing about Haitian culture. I was taught these and also the skills of survival not by educated Haitians in their capital city over cocktails, but by the illiterate peasants and rough country people on whom I was totally dependent.

The Haiti that most people hear and read about in the developed world is the one relayed by reporters at times of political crisis. Theirs is a story of intrigue, assassination, ugly deeds, urban squalor and, of course, the endless fascination of the voodoo religion. The word voodoo deserves to be rescued from some of the more uninformed understandings which prevail outside Haiti. A succession of authors have presented this Haitian religion in terms of cannibalism, the casting of spells, sticking pins into wax dolls, the disappearance and 'zombification' of all kinds of people and other barbarous or uncivilized rituals. In fact, voodoo is a religion that originates in the large variety of animistic belief systems that came with those Africans who were shipped into slavery in the 'new world' during the seventeenth and (mainly) eighteenth centuries. They came from a swath of Africa from Senegal down to the great Congo basin They were deliberately separated from each other and, consequently, never allowed to reconstruct their tribal cultures or faiths on Haitian soil. And so the Créole language and the voodoo relgion came into being as an amalgam of the religions and languages of the slaves. These were, of course, significantly shaped by the planters' own language (French) and religion (Roman Catholicism). For the most part, the voodoo religion is an attempt to seek the help of members of the spirit world, *loas* as they are called, for the living of everyday life. God himself is considered too distant and unbending to approach directly. So the spirits are invoked as intermediaries. The ceremonies where this invocation takes place are lively affairs, with dancing to the accompaniment of heavy drumbeats. At the heart of the administration of this religion are the *bokors* or *houngans* (priests) and *mambos* (women initiates). While there is undoubtedly a dark side of voodoo, it is mostly benign and unexceptional. Most importantly for the purposes of this book, it is a place (like the Créole language) where the deep wells of Haitian identity and culture are to be found.

However, there is another Haiti. Indeed, this other Haiti represents the large majority of its population, a world of gentle people and urbane culture. From this Haiti come calypso and folksong, proverb and story, vivid art and rhythmic dance. It is a world of great generosity of spirit and openness of character. It was into this world that I'd been dropped. And it is through the lens of this Haiti that I've always viewed what happens in that poor benighted land. My time of initiation in the Haitian countryside lasted a year. That period gave me a wider view of Haitian society, a complete fluency in Créole and a huge respect for the dignity of the Haitian peasant.

After my year in the hills and countryside, I was called back into the capital city where I became deputy director of a large High School in Port-au-Prince, the prestigious Nouveau Collège Bird. This was the school to which François Duvalier sent his children after his excommunication from the Roman Catholic Church. It was here, a mixed school, that Jean-Claude Duvalier had first met his future wife Michèle Bennett. More importantly, this was for a number of years the only secondary school in Haiti where the children of the rich (the business élite, Tontons Macoutes, army officers, diplomats and professional people) sat in class alongside the offspring of the poor, children who heard no French at home, had no electricity, slept on a straw mat. It was my responsibility to develop a Religious Education curriculum and to train teachers to apply it. When that curriculum raised social and ethical questions I knew we were going to be exploring the very frontiers of acceptable thinking in those paranoid times. It was a great place to be and I made many friendships then which have lasted to this day.

I did this job for a few years before moving out of Port-au-Prince to take charge of seven churches and some fairly progressive community development work in and around Haiti's second city (and ancient capital) Cap Haitien. This put me back in touch with rural populations and their needs, as well as their potential. Together, we planted thousands of trees, sank wells, developed literacy schemes and primary schools, organized co-operatives, built windmills and established irrigation schemes. What's more, we set up a mobile clinic that served a number of scattered outposts and, from time to time (in the aftermath of natural disasters) we organized relief programmes. We taught people the elements of the Christian faith too, and always in a way that linked our theology and spirituality to the world where those under instruction had to live their everyday lives. It was while I was in Cap Haitien that I got to know Monsignor François Gayot, the recently consecrated bishop of that diocese. We enjoyed each other's company enormously and I found his intellectual prowess both intimidating and stimulating. I mention this because Gayot was to be identified repeatedly by Aristide as an opponent to the kind of progress he believed in. Indeed, 'enmity' wouldn't be too strong a word to describe Aristide's view of the prelate.

Haiti received me as someone with deep internal wounds and in dire need of healing. I'd spent the previous ten years of my life in the world of British higher education—learning, doing research and teaching. I'd greatly enjoyed all of it but education, whilst conferring so many benefits and offering untold opportunities for social mobility, can also have an alienating effect on its beneficiaries. In my case, it took me further and further away from my beginnings in life. I arrived in Haiti cut hopelessly adrift from the abject poverty of my childhood and using my education as a kind of mask behind which I could hide myself. It was the Haitian people who put me back in touch with my deepest self, the parts of me I'd preferred to hide from for some years. In fact, they did for me what all the king's horses and all the king's men *couldn't* do for Humpty Dumpty; they put me back together again and made me as near as can be a complete person. It was in Haiti that my wife and I began our married life, here that our two sons were born and here too that I was ordained to the Methodist ministry. So it should be clear by now that what follows can by no means be an objective account of matter-of-fact happenings in faraway Haiti. It will be *une oeuvre engagée*, a piece of committed writing. If it is true that Jean-Bertrand Aristide cannot be understood apart from the Haitian people, it is no less true that *my* telling of his and the Haitian people's story is likely to find me persistently present, rather than a detached observer, in what unfolds.

1 The shaping of a leader

Jean-Bertrand Aristide was born on 15 July 1953 in Port Salut, in the far south-west corner of Haiti. He was only three months old when his father died and his mother took him and his two-year-old sister Anne-Marie to live in Port-au-Prince. And that's where he's lived for virtually the whole of the rest of his life to date. But it would be hopelessly simplistic to assume that the town of his birth could be so easily summed up and dealt with. For Port Salut is far more than merely the place where he was born. It has always been an important clue for any understanding of this complicated man. It is a tiny place, but one that has managed more than any other entity or experience to furnish his mind with its myths and give him the visionary gleam that never allows him to forget his country's glory or her dream.

It is not easy to get to Port Salut. Travellers must first of all take a huge inter-city bus from Port-au-Prince to Haiti's third city, Aux Cayes. That's about a hundred and fifty miles of pot-holed and twisty roads, negotiated with apparent disdain by drivers who seem to be either as sensitive as bulls in china shops or as mad as hatters. There are two types of bus: the passenger vehicle that roars its way along the road for five hours, filled with its complement of passengers from the outset and stopping only for refreshments, and the converted truck that takes human beings as extras to the vast amounts of market produce and household effects that constitute its main cargo. Every bus is heavily decorated and sports some kind of slogan, usually religious, that makes it seem like a mini-sermon on wheels. *Qui est comme Jehovah?* (Who is like Jehovah?) or *Ceconçalavie* (Life's like that) or *Puissance Divine* (Divine Strength) they proclaim with bravura.

The road passes at first through the towns of Grand Goâve, Petit Goâve and Miragoâne, which are spaced out like stepping stones along the Bay of La Gonâve on the northern coast of the long peninsula that runs out to Jérémie at its westernmost tip. Along this first leg of the journey, there's still plenty of evidence of the sugar plantations that made Haiti (then known as St Domingue) the richest of all France's colonies in the eighteenth century. Then, with about seventy miles done, the driver turns inland, crossing the mountain range that runs like a spine along the whole length of the peninsula. Scrubland and eroded hills now make up the scene. But soon the Caribbean Sea appears enticingly in view and the remaining miles into Aux Cayes take travellers alongside lovely beaches and weary fields with occasional pockets of lush countryside. The bus passes through the old French towns of Aquin, St Louis du Sud and Cavaillon. Local specialities here are various kinds of sugar-based *douce*, sweets that come as fudge or jelly. Rum, in a number of its variants, is also readily available. The city of Aux Cayes is dominated by its cathedral, built at the beginning of the twentieth century. The grid format of its city centre is still perceptible, though the rest of the city is an ugly sprawl. It all looks as if it needs a fortune spending on it. But there are some lovely gingerbread houses hiding coyly here and there and one or two of its wide streets carry an air of undoubted (though faded) elegance.

A gaudy little local bus takes travellers on the final leg beyond Aux Cayes, though how it survives the harsh road with which it does daily battle is anybody's guess. Such a route would be flattered to be called a cart track; but there it goes, snaking its way across the low hills before it eventually drops down into Port Salut, a town which squats on the very edge of the sea. The journey from Aux Cayes is little more than twenty miles but it opens the door to a different world. The little town lies far from the madding crowd and is hidden on the blind side of a promontory which is, in fact, the last fading outcrop of the vast mountain range known as *Massif de la Hatte* whose highest peak rises to 7,500 feet. Apart from the ever-present Coke, Pepsi and 7-Up signs, the communities that dot the wispy littoral road from Port Salut to Les Anglais are off the beaten track and beyond the reach of visitors. It is hard to imagine that much ever changes here. Or even that much ever happens.

And yet a great deal has happened here in the past. In colonial days, Port Salut was one of the handful of ports that linked St Domingue with Europe. It seems scarcely credible now. One or two place names link the present-day town with an eighteenth-century mayor, the Marquis Barbé de Marbois, who owned a small sugar plantation in the area. More astonishing, perhaps, is evidence that links Haiti with Poland. In 1802 Napoleon Bonaparte, to show how determined he was to suppress the Haitian rebellion which was by then already ten years under way, sent an expeditionary force of considerable size under the command of his brother-in-law General Leclerc. Included in that army was a contingent of almost 5,000 Poles. During the campaign they became disaffected from the French cause and transferred their allegiance to the Haitian army, fighting alongside the former slaves. When independence was declared in 1804, a number of them returned to Poland, but many stayed. They should have been in some danger. Almost all the white people who didn't leave were killed. It was one clear way of making a firm statement about the intention of the Haitian people to make a radical new beginning. Further, Haiti's first constitution of 1805 made one or two things quite clear. Article 12 stated that 'no white man, of any nation whatsoever, shall set foot on Haitian soil either as a master or as a property owner'. But then the very next article goes on specifically to exempt Poles from these exclusions. According to Article 13, they had been 'naturalized' by the Haitian government, a tribute to their support in the struggle for independence.

It seems that a colony of these naturalized Poles settled in

Port Salut. Some ethnological fieldwork has brought to light folk memories of Polish music and dancing, the polka and violins, to say nothing of some physiological features, such as blue eyes and lighter skins among the local people. There's also a proverb: *chajé kou Lapologn*, weighed down like a Pole, which means 'carrying more than a fair share of responsibility'. Commentators suggest that this saying dates back to the time the local population saw the first Polish people come into their communities carrying all their worldly goods on their backs. Who knows? What's of far greater interest is that this ethnological mix and these trace memories of belonging to a larger world continue somehow to exist in this little backwater of a town. Just a few miles further up the coast, the little town of Les Anglais (again a nowhere of a place) was the port used by another expeditionary force which, in the years 1793-98, sought to appropriate St Domingue for the *British* crown. As many as 20,000 British soldiers were lost in that little episode, a military campaign that rarely gets a mention in our history books. All memories of that ill-fated business seem to have been utterly (and deliberately?) forgotten. And that might have been the fate of the Polish links with Port Salut too. But they were resurrected quite recently when Pope John Paul II, himself a Pole, paid his fleeting visit to Haiti in 1983.

It was in this little place that Aristide was born and to which he returned regularly as a child to spend his summer holidays with his maternal grandfather. He describes the countryside vividly. There are no trees or roads, neither water nor electricity. The soil remains difficult and ungrateful even when a great deal of care and hard work have been lavished upon it. There are no draft animals and nothing more sophisticated than rough-and-ready hoes or machetes to use in the constant battle to wrest a harvest from the unwilling earth. Aristide's grandfather owned some land and this gave him standing in the local community. But his land lay outside the township in the *mornes*, the hills, in conditions similar to those lived in by the vast majority of the Haitian population.

Aristide refers to his grandfather's life in terms of a perpetual struggle, not only with the land but also with corrupt officials from the town. And yet, the picture he gives is not painted gloomily in varying shades of grey. On the contrary, it is vividly multicoloured. Aristide looks back on his grandfather's life and the peasant communities around Port Salut in what can only be called an idealized way. He praises his grandfather's wisdom, this man who would answer his grandchildren's questions and play with them too. He was a man who burned with a sense of justice and knew that many of the petty thieves who were brought before him (he was a Justice of the Peace) were in no way criminals. So often it was their poverty or hunger that had driven them to steal some produce from a neighbour. As often as not, he'd place them in custody and release them that same day before nightfall. He shared with his grandchild the conviction that real thieves were rarely brought before him, people who exploited others and used their official position for their own advantage. He was a champion of the poor. Though illiterate himself he insisted that education was the key to personal empowerment and sent all his children to school. Nor did he discriminate against his daughters. They had the same opportunities as their brothers.

Aristide's summer visits to Port Salut were elemental in fixing within his deepest self an identification with Haiti's peasant people and also in giving him an early sense of social justice. His grandfather, aware no doubt that the youngster would be viewed as a privileged stranger by the neighbours, ensured that Jean-Bertrand slept out with poor peasant families in the neighbourhood as well as in his own home and that he treated his hosts with the deference that belonged to them. He and his sister were also put to work with peasant groups in their *konbits*, the co-operative labour schemes, where two or three dozen people from a locality were called together by a blast on the *lanbi* (conch-shell). This gave Aristide a sense of the peasant's readiness to work and of his inbuilt capacity to work with others for common objectives. He is adamant that the peasant people he knew from his earliest days never succumbed to resignation: 'No matter how hard life was, or death, they tried to transform it.'

Jean-Bertrand and his sister Anne-Marie were, without doubt, considered rarefied people by those who lived in his grandfather's neighbourhood. From the time they were small children, they would write letters and read stories for the illiterate people of the village. They formed a clear picture of these rural people as being fair-minded, egalitarian and living in solidarity with each other. In them the future president of Haiti saw a natural spirituality and an equally natural 'socialism', a readiness to share their labour and resources. What's more, he saw both these qualities—religious and social—as belonging inseparably together in the order of things. No amount of high-powered theology learned later in his life could shift him from this early perception of the way the spiritual and the socio-political are but two aspects of the same lived reality. His liberation theology, with its stress on social context as the starting point for all religious analysis—a school of thinking he learned academically from the writings and teachings of Latin America—was picked up first under a Haitian sky by the simple observation of the lives of the poor peasant people of Port Salut.

Aristide is well aware that in describing his early impressions in this way, in seeing Haiti's rural poor in terms of some kind of archetypal, primordial goodness, he is opening himself to the accusation of idealizing them and turning the Haiti of his earliest memories into some kind of uncorrupted paradise. He can be accused of being just like those artists whose pictures can be bought in any gallery or from a roadside vendor and who depict Haiti as if it were the Garden of Eden, all green and golden, its vegetation lush with all the animal species imaginable (including many that have never even been seen in Haiti, like lions and giraffes) roaming its rich fields peacefully and with impunity. He's afraid that his critics will think him some kind of latter-day Jean-Jacques Rousseau. God forbid! His utopianism is far removed from that of the eighteenth-century Frenchman with all his talk of 'the noble savage' and his appeal to the universality of human goodness. But Aristide is undoubtedly tapping into a deep vein of idealism in the almost prelapsarian way he views the world of the Haitian peasant. He claims to be well aware of quarrelling and selfishness among the peasant people he met in his childhood. They had their bad side, he admits. But all this is as nothing compared with 'the quintessence of goodness and the spirit of justice which appeared to me to be joined [in those people] in a paradise of simple and honest morals'.

The rural world that shaped a future Haitian president's mind was one that predated the depredations of François Duvalier. PapaDoc came to power in 1957. He extended his absolute rule to the south-western corner of Haiti only in the mid-1960s. During Duvalier's years of power, well-nigh absolute social control was imposed on even the most remote populations by the appointment of *chefs de section*, rural police, and by the establishment of the notorious Tontons Macoutes, a kind of personal militia force. The essential ingredient in the power exercised by both these bodies was freedom to control the affairs of their communities. Absolute obedience to Duvalier and a readiness to keep the president informed of malcontents and anything that could be construed as 'subversion' was the only price that had to be paid for the power granted to them. These institutions regularly set neighbour against neighbour, generation against generation, and destroyed communal trust and freedom of association almost completely. In these ways François Duvalier, virtually alone, wilfully injected Haiti's body politic with carcinogenic cells whose destructive course has still not been fully checked. It was Duvalier, after all, who again and again used to quote an old Haitian proverb *depuis nan Guinée nèg ap trayi nèg*: since they were in Africa black people have been betraying each other. For him this became an axiom on which to base his political strategies of divide and rule. By contrast, Aristide appealed to an entirely different stratum of experience, *ampil main chaj pa lou*: when everyone pulls together burdens become light. For him, the myth of a Haitian Eden, so much part of the furniture of his mind, owes far more to the memories of his childhood and adolescent visits to Port Salut than to any empirical assessment of rural life in the post-Duvalier years.

But this myth-making is by no means peculiar to Aristide. The intellectual climate of his youth, the cultural air that he breathed, was filled with a tradition which, though petering out by then, still carried great emotional weight. And something of this needs to be understood if we're to probe the mind of Jean-Bertrand Aristide.

Until 1915, Haiti's intellectual life was wedded to that of France. It was conducted by a super-educated élite whose highest hopes were that their children might be educated in Paris. When in 1912 the poet Etzer Vilaire was awarded the prestigious Prix Archon Despérouse by the French Academy, Haitian literature seemed to have reached its apogee. But the American Occupation changed all that. No event has shaped Haitian sensitivities more than this military invasion which lasted nearly twenty years; the Americans didn't leave Haiti until 1934.

To justify the invasion, the US government pretended to be overseeing the return to an ordered society in a nation that had undergone some traumatic and turbulent political events. History has indicated, however, that the real reasons were not nearly so altruistic. The overriding objective in sending in the Marines was, in fact, to safeguard the approaches to the recently constructed Panama Canal. To achieve this, a determined effort was made to bring a France-orientated Haiti firmly within the American sphere of influence. The national debt was paid off in France and redirected towards Wall Street. The Constitution was re-written (Franklin D. Roosevelt, then assistant Navy Chief, seems to have played a major part in this) and, for the first time since independence, the right was conceded to foreigners to own land in Haiti. This allowed large American corporations to move in and buy substantial tracts of land for the growing of bananas, sisal, sugar and tobacco. While there were some sensible capital ventures, others (like an abortive plan to build a national railway) were expensive failures with the Haitian state picking up large bills. The Americans exercised a total control over Haitian finances. They also abolished the Haitian gendarmerie and set up a model army whose officers were trained in the United States. This army was also the main intelligence-gathering machine for the Central Intelligence Agency and maintained that role until Aristide disbanded it (the army, not the CIA!) in 1995. Its part in destabilizing Haiti and fuelling an American disinformation campaign aimed at Aristide will be examined in a later chapter.

The Americans set up puppet governments and favoured Haiti's business class. The heirs and successors of these beneficiaries of the American presence, the business élite and the armed forces, formed the coalition of interests that ousted Aristide and put an end to the first experiment in democracy in September 1991. But the American Occupation had other, and very radical, effects on the Haitian consciousness too.

For health care, education, church leadership, literature, architecture, engineering, and social developments, successive Haitian governments looked towards the old metropolis. An unexpected consequence of the American Occupation was the re-examination by Haiti's intellectuals of their national culture. Redneck racist marines were unable or unwilling to differentiate between the various strands that constituted Haitian society. To them, all Haitians were black, all 'gooks' and 'niggers'. When local people protested against the American presence or resorted to guerrilla warfare, the Americans adopted 'hunt-and-kill' methods against a people they obviously despised. It was by such methods that Charlemagne Péralte, a kind of Haitian Che Guevara and the most celebrated of all his country's insurrectionists during this period, was found and killed on 1 November 1919. A photograph of Péralte's body, attached in the shape of a cross to a door that had been used to transport it, became the supreme icon of the Haitian resistance. One of Aristide's most brilliant rhetorical devices, quite lost on most foreigners who have heard him use it, but one which never fails to win a huge and emotional response from Haitian crowds, involves a reference to Charlemagne Péralte. When challenging his listeners to find deeper reservoirs of courage for any aspect of their daily struggle, he calls on them to behave *Charlemagne Péralte-ment*,

Charlemagne Péralt-ly. It is a nonsense in English and rather limp when explained. But this turning of a martyr's name into one huge adverb is always dynamite when used on the hustings or to rally the faithful to dig deep and summon extra reserves of determination.

The presence, attitudes and goading of the American occupier pushed Haitian intellectuals to examine the strand of their ethnic identity which, until then, they had tended to ignore. They turned their attention away from Europe and America to Africa. They had been offended and humiliated by white culture. As a result, they began to investigate their black roots instead. Unlike Rastafarians in nearby Jamaica whose dreams of a distant Africa played such an important part in shaping their inner universe, Haitians were almost surprised to discover an Africa-in-their-midst, in the form of the culture of their own peasants, just waiting to be discovered. The energy with which they gave themselves to the study of this aspect of their own previously suppressed history bore fruit far beyond Haiti. It played an important part in raising the awareness and engaging the solidarity of black Americans with their cause and in focusing the idea of Negritude and black consciousness which was to be such an important intellectual phenomenon for black people everywhere in a later generation. It also laid a foundation for what became known as Pan-Africanism.

All this intellectual ferment was given impetus by the seminal work of Jean Price-Mars whose *Ainsi Parla l'Oncle*, Thus Spake Uncle, appeared in 1928. This was a field study of peasant people and, amongst many other aspects of their culture and psychology discussed within its pages, it took the voodoo religion with the utmost seriousness. In looking at the peasant culture Price-Mars glossed over the misery and disastrous poverty of rural communities and instead speculated about *le substratum psychologique d'où dérive la mystique nègre*, the hidden subconscience from which comes the black mystique. His search for the black soul, or the soul of blackness, gave impetus to a flurry of intellectual activity. People like François Duvalier, then a young doctor, committed themselves to what became a great national effort. Ethnology, social psychology, painting, poetry and the novel flourished in the following twenty-five years. Even foreign social historians and anthropologists like Melville Herskovitz, James G. Leyburn, C.L.R. James and Alfred Métraux entered the fray. The Haitian peasant was centre stage. He was portrayed with Christ-like dimensions in the person of Manuel, hero of Jacques Roumain's 1944 posthumous novel *Le Gouverneur de la Rosée*, Lord of the Dew. Manuel sacrificed himself in order to reconcile feuding factions in his rural community. Here, indeed, was someone who had acted Charlemagne Péralte-ly.

Another voice that championed the Haitian peasant was Carl Brouard. He belonged to Haiti's mulatto élite and worked with François Duvalier on the influential journal *Les Griots* for many years. Brouard wanted to portray the power of the peasant people, a power untapped mainly because it remained unrecognized (especially, of course, by the peasants themselves). This is a translation of his poem *Vous*, You:

> *You,*
> *the rabble,*
> *the filthy,*
> *the stinking:*
> *peasant women coming down from our hills,*
> *baby in belly,*
> *horny old men, toilers on the land,*
> *feet drilled by vermin,*
> *whores,*
> *and you*
> *the decrepit, dragging yourselves along*
> *in the stench of your wounds, thick with flies.*
>
> *You,*
> *all of you common people,*
> *stand up!*
> *Now for the clean sweep.*

You are the pillars of society,
you get out
and it all collapses, like a house of cards.

One day
you will know you are a tidal wave
whose power has remained hidden.

So then, wave:
gather yourself,
boil up,
roar,
till under your shroud of foam,
nothing remains, nothing
but what is clean through and through,
scoured, well washed,
bleached right down to the bone.

For Brouard, national healing and cleanness can only come from those who are denigrated by the powerful as being dirty. Power rests not with those who have money and prestige but with the ostensibly powerless peasants who are prevented from shaping Haiti's destiny only by their ignorance.

These same notes have been struck again and again by Aristide in his sermons and political speeches. From his earliest years he formed an identification with peasant people and read widely in the ideological writings of people like Brouard, Roumain and Price-Mars. It was all part of a heady brew that would one day overflow in the thinking of Aristide's political group known as *Lavalas*, the Avalanche. The essential spirit of this 'movement' (even 'movement' is really too formal a word to describe it) can be readily understood from a frequently repeated litany, a kind of platform patter, that never fails to evoke animated responses wherever he uses it: 'Alone we're weak,' he declaims and continues, 'together we're strong,' before reaching a climax with, 'and *all* together we are the avalanche.' More and more voices are added to this little formula as it develops and, by the time he reaches the end of the sequence, a surging roar is rising from the whole vast crowd in front of him. It is his capacity to engage the raw energies of large numbers of the politically inexperienced that's so greatly feared by his opponents. And, in spirit, it is not so very different from Brouard's 'Gather yourself, boil up, roar, till under your shroud of foam, nothing remains, nothing but what is clean through and through.'

Aristide's widowed mother had to make the best of her lot in the years when her children were young. She bought and sold cloth. That sounds a simple enough activity, but there's far more to it than appears at first hearing. She would buy her cloth in Port-au-Prince and travel to rural markets across the southern peninsula, working the market days of a number of small, remote communities. There are markets in the towns, of course, and they're open every day of the week. But the rural markets are set up on fixed days of the week and at places that seem very bewildering to the stranger. They seem to take place in the middle of nowhere. When investigated, however, they're always found to have their own logic, being held where significant routes (usually mere footpaths) meet or else near a communal clothes-washing spot on a river bank. Hundreds of merchants arrive from many different directions. They display their wares by spreading them on the ground. Fruit and vegetables, charcoal and household utensils, machetes and soap, and cloth in a hundred hues and patterns strike the eye in a cacophany of colour. This, together with colourful noise and constant bustle, gives to these rural markets an air of industry and breathless activity.

The women who sell their wares at these markets, who have a backbreakingly ceaseless itinerary week after week after week, are popularly known as *Madame Sara*. Theirs is an important cornerstone in the commercial life of the whole republic of Haiti. Their energy is prodigious. On the day of his inauguration as president, Aristide chose a group of just such women, clothed brightly in dresses of blue and red (the national colours)—garments that might well have been made of cloth straight from one of his mother's market pitches—to sing the National Anthem before the great crowd of VIPs gathered on the lawn of the presidential palace. His predecessors had tended to choose some well-trained, musical literates to give a neo-classical rendition of the anthem. But as the rough voices of these women sang lustily of their national pride and determination to be worthy of the sacrifices made by the heroes of Haiti's independence, it was hard not to think just how personally the president understood their contribution to the day's proceedings.

His mother had engaged in her cloth-vending activities in order to bring up her children, send them to school, and pay the rent. The family moved from one house to another and always seemed able to take in lodgers for shorter or longer periods—cousins, friends, people from back 'home' in Port Salut making their way in the capital city's confusing life. Aristide now reckons that this experience of living perpetually in the company of an extended family gave him a taste for community which he's never lost. He's even grateful for it, calling it 'biblical'. Sometimes the house his mother was able to rent was near the slums of downtown Port-au-Prince whilst at other times they ended up in more well-to-do areas.

From a very early age, while his mother was to-ing and fro-ing with her merchandise, Aristide learned to enjoy two pursuits which have continued to give him deep consolation and pleasure; he learned to play the guitar and he became a voracious reader of books. But he took little interest in the details of his mother's buying and selling: already he was acquiring an academic bent and, by his own admission, took little interest in the practical side of his mother's life.

Aristide went to school from the age of five. He attended a primary school run by the Salesian brothers in Port-au-Prince and remained there for eight years. He always refers both to his schooldays and to the Salesians with great affection. It is clear that his family was devoutly Roman Catholic. There were aunts who gave themselves assiduously to preparing for various feast days and liturgical rites. As often as not, there would be a priest among those enjoying the hospitality of his home. Wherever they lived, his mother would invariably set up a little shrine in some corner of a room and the family would say its prayers together every day. Conversation frequently touched on the question of God. So it was always clear that Aristide's mother would want to send him to a Roman Catholic school. In choosing that run by the Salesian brothers, however, she little knew how deeply she would affect the whole of her son's subsequent life.

The Salesians are an order named after St François de Sales who was Roman Catholic bishop of Geneva in the early part of the seventeenth century. But most of the work done by the Salesians in Haiti was a response to the example of the prominent nineteenth-century Salesian St John Bosco in Spain. He had worked with destitute children and managed to season his spirituality with a commitment to social action. The Salesians in Haiti tried to keep to this formula and had schools—both classical and vocational—as well as working with street children and in the realm of agriculture. Their churches tended to be in poor areas of the town or countryside. Their large campus in Port-au-Prince is at the northern end of the city's main road, the Boulevard Jean-Jacques Dessalines. It is just where that wide street readies itself to leave the commercial life of the capital in order to meet the less salubrious realities of the desperately poor area known as La Saline, named from the fact that it is largely built on land reclaimed from the sea. This would become a place of cardinal importance in Aristide's later life.

The boy Aristide was blissfully happy at school. In view of the rather bookish mien he came to acquire later on, it is important to note his love of sport whilst at school. He enjoyed table tennis and swimming, but his love of football was even more passionate. He also joined the school clubs and discussion groups and tended to end up as their leader. His sister remembers all this and reckons it was early evidence of her brother's understanding that if you want to get things done there are few better ways than to get your peer group to elect you as their leader.

There are some key memories that Aristide retains of his days at primary school. Firstly, there was the tone and temper of the school itself. Classes were fifty in size and discipline was severe. Pupils were expected not only to behave themselves but also to do justice to themselves. Aristide was obviously a brilliant scholar, but he was punished as severely as anyone else if he failed to live up to his own standards. He was usually head of the class but this only raised expectations of the level at which he ought to be performing. If he failed to meet the exacting targets his teachers set for him he was beaten. The fact that he'd outperformed his classmates was irrelevant to this exercise. And it seems that a beating was the accepted way of imposing discipline.

Aristide's fondness for the Salesians cannot disguise his unhappiness with their paternalism. But, for all that, he admires the way they managed to raise their pupils' awareness of the social and political realities then reigning in Haiti. François Duvalier was tightening his grip on the country and, while it would have been considered subversive to discuss his policies and his actions openly in class, the Salesians found a way of exploring the social dimensions of the nature of good and evil. Often they did this by debating some social and observable phenomenon, for example the relative merits and demerits of Haiti's national lottery, the *borlette*. The national addiction to gambling gave them opportunity to describe the causes and the nature of misery and to hint at the deeper issues which underlay Haiti's poverty at that time.

Pupils were not allowed to speak their native Créole in school. They all accepted this at the time but Aristide has come to view this matter more critically with the passing of time. When he entered primary school he spoke no French, yet he found no escape from it at school. This, the language of those who colonized Haiti and enslaved her people, was the only permitted mode of expression for all pupils. If someone offended against this rule in the school playground they were given a lump of wood to carry. They held on to it until they heard someone else speak the offensive language of their

37

fathers. They then passed the piece of wood on to the new offender. This pass-the-parcel routine continued until the bell rang for classes to resume. The person in possession of the dreaded talisman when the bell rang was soundly thrashed. Yet for all this, Aristide and his fellows came to love the French language and would study its finer points for hours in their attempt to perfect their knowledge of its contours and nuances.

The whole question of the status of Créole has always been a highly political one in Haiti. There's long been a movement for giving Créole *de facto* as well as *de jure* equality with French. One of the obstacles in the way of such a logical step has been the simple matter of spelling. Créole is a child of Haitian history. The African slaves who worked on the plantations spoke a variety of languages. They heard their masters' French and learned some of its more necessary phrases from their daily battle for survival. Then, in the white heat of the struggle for independence, two instruments were forged which were going to play an important part in the whole of Haiti's subsequent history. Or, to use a different metaphor, the newly liberated Haiti, after an eleven-year period of gestation, gave birth to two children, twins but not identical twins. These were the voodoo religion and the Créole language. They carried Haitian identity, were vehicles for the deepest experience of her people, and offered instruments for the shaping of the national achievement. But such was the early desire of Haitian leaders to prove themselves French that neither the religion nor the language was allowed to serve in its positive sense. Both were sidelined. Everybody spoke Créole, almost everyone was touched by the world of voodoo. For reasons of fashion and good standing in society, however, they were both considered 'primitive' and consequently marginalized.

Whenever the question of raising the status of Créole cropped up, everyone agreed that it would be a sensible and honourable thing to give it greater standing in the life of the nation. And then they quarrelled about how precisely to do it. In the late 1930s, a Methodist missionary, an Irishman named Ormonde McConnell, appealed to the world-renowned champion of literacy Dr Frank Laubach to come over to Haiti to direct his considerable skills and experience at this problem. Together, Laubach and McConnell devised a spelling system for what was still largely at that time an oral language. Their system was based on the International Phonetic Alphabet and sought, as its overriding objective, to give each sound in the spoken language one, and only one, written symbol. Field tests were held and the results seemed exceptionally good. But it proved almost impossible to raise a head of steam and bring the benefits of this work to the whole population in a concerted literacy campaign.

There were two reasons for these difficulties. Firstly, the Haitian élite knew full well that its most important tool in keeping the people compliant was their ignorance. Literacy would not only confer reading and writing skills but would also raise self-awareness and sharpen a sense of curiosity among its beneficiaries. This was hardly what Haiti's wealthy business class needed. So self-interest on their part meant a withholding of resources from any possibility of a national literacy campaign. The second obstacle had more to do with the actual spelling system devised by McConnell and Laubach. It was considered by its critics to be too *English*. They thought they detected a hidden agenda in these proposals, that of bringing Haiti unconsciously nearer to full incorporation in an Anglo-Saxon hegemony. These critics argued vehemently for a spelling system that would more honourably reflect the essential relationship between Créole and French. This quarrel effectively kept the whole question of Haiti's *lingua franca* (delicious pun!) on the back burner until Aristide's own time as president. Of course there were enlightened groups and organizations that made their own contribution to this debate and committed considerable resource to providing reading materials and teaching outlets for the Créole language. But without government support and commitment the whole question remains marginal and progress can only be intermittent.

From his earliest school-days, Aristide became aware of the

role and status of Créole in the life of the nation, and also, in those days before the Second Vatican Council, of the role of the Roman Catholic Church in keeping French as the predominant language. (I once knew an English nun who belonged to a French order in Haiti. For seventeen years she'd taught in élitist schools and couldn't speak a word of Créole. We had to act as interpreters for her when she came to tea or when we took her shopping.) Not only that but, with Latin still rampant in liturgical life, Aristide experienced the role of language as a tool of social control from a very early time. In the 1980s, when the Council had ushered in the vernacular mass and when the Roman Catholic Church seemed at last to be ready for a committed attack on illiteracy, Aristide was in the van of the efforts being made to conduct the campaign. When he became president, he made literacy one of his first priorities. His sense of urgency on this matter stretches back to his earliest days at school.

If, through oblique reference, pupils of the Salesians were made aware of the fraught political realities then prevailing in PapaDoc's Haiti, they had every opportunity to discover those realities directly for themselves in the world which lay just outside the school gates. The school was only a short distance from Fort Dimanche, the dreadful prison where François Duvalier consigned his political prisoners and where some of the worst atrocities of his dictatorship were committed. Schoolchildren were able to see with their own eyes the brutal way in which the Tontons Macoutes treated those they were hauling off to the prison. Arbitrary arrests and wanton beatings took place on the main road outside the school. This was how the régime dealt with anyone suspected of offending the dictator. Aristide saw, marked and inwardly digested this evidence of state terrorism. He drank in the oppressive atmosphere of those times. Twenty years after leaving the St John Bosco Primary School, in the final throes of the struggle against Duvalierism, Aristide, now parish priest in the church located alongside his old school, took an active part in some highly emotive demonstrations outside Fort Dimanche. One of the first things he did as president was to have the place demolished and its remains turned into a memorial for all those who'd lost their lives there. It is clear that the memories of despair retained from his primary school years continued to disturb him all those years later.

Aristide was thirteen years old when he ended his primary school-days in Port-au-Prince and entered the Salesian seminary in Cap Haitien. It is important to recognize just how important and radical a step this was for the future president. It meant leaving home and the direct influence of his family for the first time in his life. Of course, the Salesians became a kind of substitute family, or at least an extension of his family. But no longer did he enjoy the constant nearness of his mother and sister. And, what's more, he moved from one culture to another, from Haiti's south to the north, from the capital Port-au-Prince to the second city, Cap Haitien, 160 miles away.

Since the very earliest days of her independence, there has been a perceptible difference of culture between Haiti's northern and southern departments. Cap Haitien was the colonial capital. It was called Cap Français in those days. Despite repeated arson attacks during the battles for independence, a severe earthquake in 1842, and the negligence of so many years, it retains something of its old-world charm to this day. Its narrow streets, historic and sometimes monumental buildings, and seaside location, give it an undoubted attractiveness.

It was just outside Cap Haitien, at Bois Caïman, that a ceremony took place on 14 August 1791 which is commonly agreed as marking the birth of the voodoo religion as well as the beginning of the struggle against the French. This brought forward a number of local slaves who formed an extraordinarily charismatic leadership, people like Boukman, Jean François, Biassou, and Jeannot whose very names, incomplete as they remained, identify them as someone else's property. Drinking the blood of a sacrificed cockerell and calling on the voodoo spirits, they committed themselves to the supreme effort of gaining their freedom and destroying the white planters.

Standing tall among this disparate bunch of leaders was the brilliant Toussaint Louverture, who combined the best qualities of field commander, subtle statesman and simple human being in a very remarkable way. The final battle against the French took place at Vertières, just outside Cap Haitien, in November 1803 and this led to the creation of the new nation a few weeks later. Toussaint had been tricked into captivity by this time and the leadership of the new nation was entrusted to one of his officers, Jean-Jacques Dessalines, who held office until he was himself assassinated in 1806.

His death, an ominous beginning for the new republic, brought two contenders for the succession into opposition with each other. In the south, mulatto Alexandre Pétion became the republic's new president. But increasing enmity from black leader Henri Christophe led to a secession of the northern part in 1810. The north took on monarchical government and Christophe was pronounced to be King Henri I. He ruled his people with a rod of iron, getting his soldiers to build the imposing Citadel Laferrière, a huge fortress in the mountains which could garrison 10,000 troops at one time as well as offer luxurious quarters to the king and his court. This was built to defend the kingdom from any possible return of the French. As well as building the Citadel and other monumental edifices, the king made valiant efforts to regenerate the agricultural life of his kingdom. But here he was working against the grain. After all, people who have thrown off the yoke of slavery can hardly be expected to want to return to plantation life. The move towards subsistence farming was irreversibly taking place. However, Christophe's disciplinary methods are commonly held to have given the north of Haiti an entirely different 'feel' from the south.

So Aristide left home, entered a different culture, began life in a new school and also joined a couple of dozen other young Haitians who'd committed themselves to the priesthood. All this at thirteen years of age.

The Salesian seminary is a couple of miles out of Cap Haitien, and there the seminarians lived together and received their priestly formation. For their first year they were kept on campus. Thereafter, there was more liberty and they pursued their secondary studies at the Notre Dame high school, which looks grandly down on the old city from its lofty site on the steep hillside which wraps itself around the southeastern flanks of Cap Haitien. Aristide's memories of these days are happy ones. Every day there were lectures, an evening mass and a talk from the director, either of admonition or encouragement. It all created the sense of belonging to a new family. In particular, Aristide remembers some of the summer camps with their long, carefree days and plenty of time for swimming and fun.

Was it really as blissful as it now seems with hindsight? He'd already experienced the joy of his summers in Port Salut as a small boy. In the presence of his grandfather and the peasant people of his neighbourhood, he'd caught what he called 'the priestly virus' which he defined as being 'nothing but a concern for others'. His recollections of life in Port-au-Prince, times when his home seemed always full of people, are equally rosy. That's where he gained, he says, 'a sense of, a taste for, community'. He argues that he was even then being weaned from the idea that one's family was limited to the biological sense of that word. 'They were all my brothers and sisters,' he wrote, 'just as my companions in struggle would later be, both the young intellectuals and the starving people from the slums.' In that same home, where there was much talk about God and daily reading from the Bible, Aristide had come to ask himself whether the spirituality being learned from the Salesians was 'a flight from politics' or a 'theological consideration of the subject'. He felt that he was given 'a theological strength' that allowed him to love the poor, to share with them, and to resist the dictator.

When referring to his admission to the St John Bosco seminary in Cap Haitien, he seems most anxious to show that it didn't in any way cut him off from real life. He emphasizes that he still came across hungry people and shared food with them. He still saw injustice and the victims of oppression. The essence of the priestly vocation for Aristide, to which he refers again and again, is the vocation and the capacity to transcend self and to forge bonds of solidarity with others, actions which turn a mass of individual human beings into a community of brothers and sisters. The very centre of his priestly formation, he argues, could be found in one overriding concern, 'to encounter and serve the poor'. He even attributes the exceptional skill in foreign languages which he developed in these years to his 'fascination by the other'. Even when he moves from these humanistic principles to a consideration of theology, defined in part as 'speaking of God', he couples that half-definition with a 'concern for other people' which he holds to be an essential part of any fully rounded understanding of theology.

This way of thinking was buttressed by a number of developments taking place at that time. The focusing of theological questions on the plight and the potential of human beings, an understanding of theology that starts with real life in the here-and-now, was hugely underpinned by the teachings of the Second Vatican Council which were beginning to rock the Roman Catholic Church during his years in Cap Haitien. It is not putting it too strongly to say that the worship of the church was democratized and that the humble poor enjoyed new levels of participation in the mass. The changes that occurred went further than the simple move away from Latin to the vernacular Créole. Suddenly indigenous musical instruments and modes of expression were brought into worship too. Drums, pipes, shakers sounded their tunes and throbbed their rhythms, while singing and dancing worshippers responded bodily to their beat. The sense of mystery which was part of the experience of worship in Latin was replaced by a spirituality that was a more appropriate reflection of the local culture. Transcendence became more a statement of the human capacity to discover solidarity with one's brothers and sisters than a matter of standing in awe in the presence of the majesty of God. In keeping with many other developments in the field of theology in the 1960s, the human was emphasized rather more than the divine. And this was meat and drink for Aristide.

François Duvalier died in April 1971. This event also gave

rise to feelings which, however temporarily, led Haitians to hope for better days of freedom and improved human rights. This was a false dawn. It didn't take long for Jean-Claude Duvalier, who succeeded his father as Haiti's president-for-life, to make it crystal clear that things would go on much as usual. I was living in Haiti at that time and remember the general release of long-suppressed feelings which greeted the death of PapaDoc. I was teaching in a large high school in Port-au-Prince and well recall the questioning looks on the faces of many of my pupils. The question I seemed to read on their faces was a simple one. Could this be the beginning of a new kind of future? On the other hand, the sons and daughters of those people who'd benefited from Duvalier's rule formulated a rather different question. They wondered whether this might be the end of a lucrative past. Aristide was seventeen years old at that time and I'm clear which of these questions he'd have been asking. But he had to wait another generation for an answer to it.

In the late 1960s Liberation Theology began to make its mark. The Vatican Council had encouraged theologians to inculturate Christian teaching in their particular situations and guaranteed them freedom in their efforts. The 1968 Medellin Conference of Latin American Bishops was a key event that focused on the plight of the poor and committed the church to the integral development and liberation of the people of the whole continent. This work was done with zeal, and the Uruguayan Jesuit Juan Luis Segundo, the Peruvian Gustavo Gutiérrez and the Brazilian Franciscan Leonardo Boff led the way with important books and articles. Indeed, Gutiérrez's book *A Theology of Liberation* became the most influential response to this thrust and canonized the use of the label 'liberation theology'. The fundamental methodology of this school of thinkers is to allow the concrete experience of poverty and oppression to pose questions to the doctrinal tradition and to elicit responses that are spelled out in locally appropriate ways within the specific Latin American situation. Aristide devoured these writings as they appeared and there can be no doubt they played a very important part in his intellectual and spiritual growth.

The Vatican Council, the death of Duvalier and the rise of liberation theology, all happening at a critical phase in Aristide's formation, ensured a social and left-of-centre bias to his theology. What we don't get from listening to Aristide's speeches or reading his books is much sense of the traditional doctrines of the church. There isn't much about the nature or the existence of God, little about Christ's atonement or even his resurrection. The person and gifts of the Holy Spirit are hardly mentioned. The Trinity, the church, the afterlife, the Virgin Mary may all have entered his mind. But they scarcely figure in such thinking as he's given us. On the other hand, the humanity and ministry of Christ are well represented. The Sermon on the Mount is often enough referred to. The centre of gravity for his theological thinking is undoubtedly humanistic. As he himself points out, he found Gabriel Marcel's thinking about the unity of body and soul to be germane to his deepest thoughts. He read Boff, Rudy Erès and other American writers. Meanwhile he became 'very critical' of those two pillars of traditional Christian theology, Plato and Aristotle. He claims to have read the Bible dozens of times and says he enjoys reading it in a variety of translations. It continues to be a fundamental tool for his theological work.

During his secondary school years he also drew a great deal of inspiration from other, more secular, fields. I've already mentioned his linguistic abilities. He mastered Latin and Greek whilst at school and went on to study Hebrew (in its modern and biblical forms) when he was given the opportunity to spend time in Israel. French, English and Spanish he learned at school. He taught himself Italian when his sister Anne-Marie went to study in Italy. When Aristide visited London in August 1992, I accompanied him to Bush House where he was interviewed by various people from different language groups at the World Service of the BBC. Rather than take him around the various departments of a very complicated building, we sat him down in one place and a variety of interviewers came to put their questions to him. It was truly amazing to see him move so easily from one language to another on that occasion.

And so his school-days in Cap Haitien drew to their end. In an interview given in 1990, one of his teachers gave a very perceptive resumé of Aristide's character at school: '[He] was a brilliant student but what was most remarkable was his seriousness. The exact word would be mature, he was more mature than his little friends. Why is he so popular? Because he has always taken people in hand. He's struggled with them, taken an interest in children and their families. He's looked for money, distributed medicines. You know, the hungry are hard of hearing even when it's God's word that's being spoken. That's liberation theology in a nutshell. But God isn't neutral and Aristide has always thought him to be on the side of the poor.' It is clear from this account and so much else that his vocational, intellectual, social and political sensitivities all developed greatly in these eight years. It is clear that he was thought to be a very brilliant student and it is impossible to disagree with that judgment. His brilliance was not limited, however, to matters academical. He was captain of the school soccer team, patrol leader of the scouts and leader of the school orchestra. He admits to the occasional abuse of his natural authority when he placed himself 'too often at the head of different groups'. This fragment is worth hanging on to and may be useful when looking at some of the ways he used his power as head of state twenty years later.

Aristide was twenty-one when he left Cap Haitien to continue his priestly formation in the neighbouring Dominican Republic. There, for a year, he studied the history and spirituality of the Salesian Order before ending his time as a novice by taking his first vows. It is difficult to find any record from this time of his feelings or experiences about the country that shares an island with his native Haiti. This may be because he had little opportunity to leave his own religious community in what must have been a pressurized year. At the end of the year, in late 1975, he returned to Port-au-Prince where he entered the state university to study philosophy and psychology. These were separate courses and he did them in parallel, one in the morning and the other in the afternoon. He noted the fact that his fellow students tended to be from middle-class families who often struggled hard to provide this opportunity for their son or daughter. Meanwhile, the children of Haiti's richest families were to be found studying in foreign universities. The régime kept a special watch on the university, fearing that the students might prove subversive. Indeed, PapaDoc had had to come down hard on students, many of whom lost their lives, in his attempt to impose his rule on all sectors of the country in the 1960s. Aristide found everything rigidly controlled but, even so, there was an unmistakable feeling of greater freedom among the students on campus than it was usual to find in Haiti at that time.

By the time he took his degree in psychology in 1979, Aristide had begun to launch out towards a wider public. He'd had some musical compositions broadcast on radio. Now he began to contribute to the speech output of *Radio Cacique*. There were a number of radio stations in Haiti, very few of them able to reach the whole nation. *Radio Cacique* was typical of those which concentrated their output on Port-au-Prince and its hinterland. Aristide and his companions would write short plays and talks, usually based on the Bible, but with a lively commentary intended to raise listeners' awareness of issues of current interest. He confesses to having a particularly fertile imagination through these years and that this taxed the wit and patience of the station director who was responsible for everything the station put out and accountable to the government itself. There were tussles between the director and his audacious contributor. Often there were requests to change a script and sometimes the poor director had to cut something out of a piece while it was going out on the air. It is clear that Aristide was pushing conventions to their limits. He describes his attitudes in these broadcasts as 'impertinent and accusatory'. He kept up this barrage not only on radio but also within the life of the church and earned the criticism of his superior, Monsignor Kébreau, who told him in no uncertain terms that what he was saying was 'political' and would get them both into trouble. 'You are going too fast,' he's reported to have said, 'don't go driving two hundred miles an hour: fifty is fast enough.' Kébreau became one of the bishops whom Aristide accused of going at fifty when they should have been going at least twice as fast! In *In The Parish of the Poor*, a little book published in 1991, he wrote as follows:

> *You who have plotted against me,*
> *You who have plotted against the Haitian people:*
> *Bishop Paolo Romeo, Bishop Gayot, Bishop Ligondé,*
> *Bishop Kébreau and the rest,*
> *Let me look you in the eye,*
> *Please, don't be ashamed,*
> *Look me in the eye.*
> *I have come to tell you: I love you too.*
> *Because I love you, I must tell you the truth.*
> *Truth and love are the same.*
> *Truth and love are Jesus in the midst of the poor.*
>
> *The church is rich thanks to us, the poor,*
> *Who have stopped certain bishops*
> *(Hidden behind the sins they commit)*
> *When they try to tell lies,*
> *To conspire together*
> *And to create silence.*

For Kébreau to be lined up with Romeo, Gayot and Ligondé is as clear an indication of Aristide's dislike of the man as can be and also of his conviction that the bishop has been an obstacle to the aspirations and proper progress of the Haitian people. This dislike developed out of a conflict of personalities stretching back to Aristide's days as a priest-in-training.

In 1979, the Salesians sent Aristide to Israel to pursue a course in biblical studies. Looking back some fifteen years later at the likely reasons why he was sent away, he remained torn between two different possible explanations. On the one hand, he was undoubtedly a good student and would have been considered an excellent prospect for future preferment. But, on the other, his superiors recognized only too clearly his impetuosity and they could conceivably have been hoping that a protracted period of study away from home would allow him to mature and calm down somewhat. In Israel he could develop his biblical knowledge and build on his linguistic skills. A future posting as a seminary teacher or even a bishop might mark the culmination of this experience.

Aristide has never been able to rid himself of the idea that some of what he called the 'Macoute' bishops had already had enough of him and, by the simple ploy of sending him away, were planning to get shot of his turbulent presence, possibly for good. The chief amongst this little group within the Haitian hierarchy was Monsignor Wolff Ligondé, Archbishop of Port-au-Prince. He had been consecrated in 1966, the first Haitian to achieve such high office. François Duvalier had sent the French and Canadian bishops whom he found in office packing and the Vatican had excommunicated him for doing so. Duvalier insisted that the time had come for indigenous leadership to take the reins of the Roman Catholic Church in Haiti. It was clearly a bid on his part to gain control of the church as he had already done with the army and the business community. In all discussions between his government and the Vatican, he held out for his right to make nominations when a diocese needed a new bishop. At first, this was strongly resisted by Rome. But, through a strange irony, Duvalier was aided by the deliberations of the Second Vatican Council then taking place in Rome and which came down strongly in favour of finding local leadership for churches that had previously been considered 'missions'. No longer were their activities and development to be overseen by foreigners. For the sake of inculturating the gospel, an indigenous clergy was considered necessary. So the Council found itself recommending precisely what Duvalier had been demanding all along. Even so, there was a world of difference between the Vatican's decision to choose local bishops and Duvalier's desire to have rights of nomination granted to himself. In the end, after protracted negotiation, a protocol was agreed that gave precisely this power to Haiti's president-for-life. Duvalier's account of this process (in his book *Mémoires d'un Leader du Tiers Monde*, Memories of a Third-World Leader) still makes sickening reading. Included in the first batch of bishops whose nomination by Duvalier was endorsed by the Vatican were Claudius Angénor, whom Duvalier described as 'my friend whose wide experience and intelligence make him suitable to exercise an efficient oversight of the southern diocese of Aux Cayes', and Emmanuel Constant, former chaplain to the army barracks and the Port-au-Prince prisons. Constant's brother was Duvalier's army chief. His nephew, the general's son (nicknamed 'Toto'), was later to head the anti-Aristide neofascist group FRAPH which sprang up during the *de facto* years of military rule in the years 1991–94. Angénor and Constant clearly enjoyed Duvalier's unquestioning trust.

Ligondé was even more closely allied to his political patron. In his citation to the Vatican, Duvalier identified him as a 'young and brilliant prelate from a prestigious family'. In his turn, and by way of expressing his gratitude, the archbishop-designate lauded the president's beneficial contribution to the wellbeing of Haiti. The young and brilliant prelate soon appeared to be taking some leaves out of Duvalier's book when he banished the Jesuits and Holy Ghost Fathers from Haiti. He was widely believed to enjoy close links with the Tontons Macoutes and was connected with the Duvalier régime right through to its bitter end. His role in making it possible for Jean-Claude Duvalier to marry divorcee Michèle Bennett—against the teaching of the Roman Catholic Church, which does not allow remarriage after divorce—showed him ever ready to stretch the rules and provide support for the dynasty. Ligondé's contribution to the relationship between the newly-elected Jean-Bertrand Aristide and the Vatican will be examined in a later chapter.

Aristide feels (though his arguments seem to have benefited somewhat from hindsight) that from as long ago as his student days these Duvalierist bishops definitely wanted him out. There was some degree of truth in this which, combined with a clear readiness of his Salesian superiors to develop his undoubted intellectual gifts, led to his departure from Haiti in 1979 for a three-year sojourn in Israel, 'the land of Christ'.

Twelve years after the six-day war, Israel was living in a constant state of 'red alert'. Aristide lived with his community in Bethlehem and would have had daily encounters both with Israeli troops deployed in the city and also with resentful Palestinians, Moslem and Christian, who lived their subjugated lives and cherished their secret hopes in the face of political realities that offered little but endless pain and deprivation. He made the regular journey into Jerusalem for his Hebrew language classes. These were the years when Israel changed from defensive military attitudes, responding to Palestinian 'terrorism' or Arab aggression with immediate and deadly effect, to a more expansionist conduct of its zonal policies. This included a development programme which saw ever larger numbers of Jewish settlers establish themselves in previously Palestinian areas. And it also saw the Israeli army cross the border into south Lebanon, an act which led to vociferous protest among Israeli Jews as well as by Arabs. Aristide would have been aware of this society in turmoil.

He wanted to study both Arabic and Hebrew but time limited him to the latter. For him, learning another language is an important key to understanding the people who speak it. He was well enough aware of the tragic hostilities that were raging in the society that surrounded him. He regretted his inability to learn the two languages because he was anxious to maintain and develop relationships with members of both communities. He saw how Jews and Palestinians suffered under the same kind of oppression as Haitians, a heavy weight whose main elements were racism and colonialism. He doesn't seem, however, to want to ask the question begged by his own analysis. He might have asked himself just how it came about that two peoples who'd both experienced such wickedness at the hands of external bodies could in their turn become so oppressive and bestial to each other. What is it that makes a people that has known such depths of suffering capable of inflicting truly terrible suffering on others? He is quite right in suggesting that some of the lessons he learned in Jerusalem could readily be applied in Port-au-Prince, but not just those that relate to non-violence and cultural awareness. The depths of human depravity and the capacity of human beings to act without compassion were also a clearly visible reality in the everyday life of the Holy Land.

Just a few months short of completing a doctoral dissertation in theology, he made the decision to return to Port-au-Prince. There were those who felt he should stay for a further year to complete his studies. But Aristide felt that he was now ready for ordination and returned home in the summer of 1982 to prepare himself for this important new step. On 3 July he was ordained to the priesthood by Willy Romélus, who had been bishop of Jérémie since 1977. Romélus was related to Aristide on his mother's side. In his autobiography, he suggests that Romélus was the one and only member of the nine-man episcopal conference who seemed 'truly acceptable' to him to officiate at his ordination. But this really does seem like special pleading. Other bishops who became 'unacceptable' to him just a few years later had hardly had time to fall into that category at this early date. It seems far more likely that Aristide's preference for Romélus had more to do with family ties than anything else.

After his ordination, and together with his friend Arthur Volel, he was appointed to the downtown Port-au-Prince parish of St Joseph. This is in a part of the capital city that positively heaves with life. I often take people visiting Haiti for the first time to a vantage point above St Joseph's Church. The view is unforgettable. A sea of human beings moves and bustles below, like rolling waves forming and re-forming endlessly whilst heading to pound some unknown shore. Port-au-Prince's principal market lies within the parish boundaries, as does the landing area for a lot of Haiti's coastal shipping. It was in this part of Port-au-Prince that the slave traders used to disembark their human cargoes in the days of the colony. From those days to the present, this has been a part of the city alive with activity and the ant-like movements of people in perpetual motion. And, from the word go, Aristide showed what he was made of. With reckless abandon, he launched into an attack on Haiti's political overlords. A report in a newspaper of the time, *Haiti-Observateur*, ran thus:

> From his lofty pulpit in St Joseph's Church, a priest denounces the Duvalier-Bennett régime. On 13 September, the Reverend Father Jean-Bertrand Aristide, a Franciscan priest, in a sermon broadcast by the Roman Catholic radio station '*Radio Soleil*', stated that official government ideology had turned the word of God into a philosophy of resignation. To a congregation of some 500 people, Fr Aristide recalled that 'Christ is a synonym of liberation. In Haiti,' he said, 'white exploitation has been replaced by black exploitation.' This was a clear reference to the Duvalier dynasty and he didn't mince his words in denouncing Jean-Claude Duvalier as 'the person mainly responsible for the misery of the Haitian people'.

This is the first of Aristide's fiery sermons of which a record was made. He was a Salesian of course rather than a Franciscan, but he had touched a raw nerve. Such outbursts against the prevailing authority were very rare in 1982. A hasty meeting between church and government leaders saw speedy action. After a few short months as a parish priest, Aristide was put back on a plane leaving Haiti. But this time he didn't head for Jerusalem where he might have finished his doctoral thesis. Instead, he found himself en route for Canada. In his pocket was a sealed letter to be handed to the Salesian superior in Montreal. He'd been sent there to undergo theological reprogramming, or pastoral reorientation. His hosts hardly knew what to do with him. So, in order to use his time to some profit, he signed up for a psychology course in the University of Montreal. In the next two years he completed a master's degree in biblical theology and also the course work for a doctorate in psychology. He also had time to look around at the state of the church in Quebec.

Aristide found strange resemblances between life in this Canadian province and some aspects of Israeli society. Two communities were obliged to co-exist. One of them, the French-speaking Québecois in this case, were struggling to claim their rights. The church stood in the midst of social tension and seemed utterly dead. Very few worshippers were to be seen at its services. Indeed, the liveliest moments of church life revolved around the bingo sessions that seemed to take place with great regularity. 'In that society,' wrote Aristide, 'the institution [of the church] was regarded as utterly unbearable by all the forces tending towards progress and emancipation. In that society, the church had finally succeeded in killing God.' Having delivered this damning indictment of the Canadian church, he offered a word of warning to people nearer home. 'Without the prophetic irruption of the excluded,' he thundered, 'Haiti might see the same end.'

As a special project within his degree studies, he chose to look at 'neurosis' in the Old Testament. This led him to read Freud, amongst others. It is interesting to note this preoccupation with psychology and neurosis. Just over ten years later, when as president of Haiti he found himself languishing in exile, those seeking to ensure his permanent exclusion from Haiti purported to have discovered a psychologist's report dating from these years in Canada. The report was supposed to have indicated that Aristide suffered from psychopathic tendencies and that he showed depressive symptoms of an alarming nature. According to his accusers, this was sure proof that he was unfit to be allowed back to Haiti and the presidency. No evidence has ever been found to substantiate such allegations and, as we shall see in a later chapter, they seem to have been invented as part of a carefully orchestrated piece of character assassination. It is ironic to note that, while he proved to be innocent of the charges of psychological imbalance levelled against him, he was in fact heavily preoccupied with psychology at this time and was delving deeply into its findings. This may have made him more fitted to pass comment on the state of mind of his denigrators than they on him!

After a period of more than two years in Canada, topped by a study tour to Greece, Aristide finally returned home to Haiti in January 1985. He'd been away from home (apart from a brief return for his ordination and the curacy at St Joseph's) since 1979. But the Haiti of 1985 was very different from that of 1979; indeed it was quite unlike the country Aristide had last seen in 1982. Haiti was on the move and the church was taking a leading part in developments for change that were soon to reach fever pitch.

2 *Aristide throws down a gauntlet*

By January 1985, it was clear that Haiti had reached the end of an era. The Duvalier years had run their course and the disintegration of the dynasty's hold on power seemed simply a matter of time. It is arguable that the marriage of Jean-Claude Duvalier to Michèle Bennett in May 1980 sent the first shock waves through the land and portended the imminence of change. So much of François Duvalier's struggle to retain power had been waged against the business élite, dominated by mulattos (lighter-skinned Haitians of mixed descent), whom he'd fought tooth and nail. Few families could have epitomized that class better than the Bennett family. So the Duvalier-Bennett marriage was a frontal challenge to the prevailing political and ideological orthodoxy. PapaDoc's widow, Mme Simone Duvalier, was known to be furious at the match, forecasting that it would inevitably lead to disaster. Indeed, there had been widespread reports that she had consulted voodoo priests in her attempt to strengthen her son's hold on power. One published report spoke of the priests arranging a 'marriage' between her and her son and of their assurance that the young president could expect a further 22 years in office (the number 22 was held in superstitious awe by the Duvaliers). This was a prospect that clearly delighted her and caused her to exclaim: 'After Duvalier, Duvalier!'

But Jean-Claude had other ideas. He wanted a more conventional marriage and chose as his partner a woman who'd been a classmate many years previously. In 1962, his father had been excommunicated from the Roman Catholic Church for ousting the church's foreign hierarchy from Haiti. To show his contempt for this decision, PapaDoc had withdrawn his children from the single-sex, Roman Catholic schools they'd been attending and sent them instead to Nouveau Collège Bird, a co-educational Methodist school in downtown Port-au-Prince. Michèle Bennett had had a failed marriage before her union with Jean-Claude Duvalier. Indeed, her first husband was the son of a man who'd attempted a *coup d'état* against PapaDoc, a detail that fuelled the already incandescent anger felt by the Duvalierist old guard. But neither her divorce nor the fact that she was an Anglican got in the way of an extravagant $3m wedding. The ceremony in Port-au-Prince Cathedral was led by Archbishop Wolff Ligondé who'd dug up some of the small print from the proceedings of the sixteenth-century Council of Trent to provide the sophistry necessary to meet the normal church requirements in such cases. He maintained that since Bennett's 'marriage' had been performed by a clergyman of another confession and no Roman Catholic priest had been in attendance, then the union was not valid and the president's marriage could proceed. It is always good to have a friendly archbishop when facing such tricky moments in your life.

But if the partner chosen by Duvalier shocked the whole political class in Haiti at that time, a far more important consequence came from the widespread feelings of disgust which the style of the wedding generated among ordinary people. The Haitian people had put up with Duvalierism with great stoicism. They'd found ways of coping with the injustices and depredations it had imposed on them. But there was something gratuitously offensive about this wedding. Container-loads of flowers had been shipped in from Miami. Bennett had brought a Parisian jeweller to Port-au-Prince with a large store of precious metals and stones from which she proceeded to make up ornaments of her choice for her and her friends. The cathedral was filled with several hundred people from the bourgeois class who all passed through the poor populations of Port-au-Prince in their finery in order to get to the cathedral. The reception at the president's ranch put the lid on a disgusting day of self-indulgence. The people had got used to a playboy president who moved from one luxurious mansion to another, who seemed constantly at the wheel of one of his dozens of flashy cars, or else showed off his large yacht in the waters around Port-au-Prince. But this was different. Revulsion for the wedding welled up from deep within the Haitian soul. Something changed in the attitudes of the people to their president that day. Passive indifference would no longer be enough.

Far removed from the world of the president's wedding, though not so far from his political agenda, something else was happening at this time, something that took Haiti's peasant population several steps beyond the already existing poverty they knew too well into sheer, soul-depressing misery. It all had to do with swine fever.

There had been an incidence of African swine fever in the Dominican Republic in 1978. This had spread to certain parts of Haiti by the early 1980s and gave rise to fears among American agriculturalists that the disease could threaten the US pig industry. So the Haitian government was pressurized into mounting an operation that would eradicate the country's entire pig population. No account seems to have been taken of the fact that instances of the disease had been limited to a relatively small part of the republic, nor of the tiny proportion of pigs that had died. The perceived threat to the American interest was sufficient to ensure nothing less than the total eradication of the indigenous, disease-resistant, cheap-to-keep pig population of Haiti. The programme began in May 1982 and the slaughter ended in June of the following year. Haiti was declared free of the fever in August 1984 by which time there were no pigs left at all.

The devastation which this measure caused to Haiti's poorest people can scarcely be exaggerated. Bernard Diedrich (*Caribbean Review,* 14(1), 1985 p.16) put it very succinctly as follows:

The peasant subsistence economy is the backbone of the nation, and the pigs were once the main components of that economy. With no banking system available to him, the peasant relied on hog production as a bank account to meet his most pressing obligations: baptism, health care, schooling, funerals, religious ceremonies, and protection against urban-based loan sharks who would grab his land at the first opportunity.

The Iowa pigs that were brought in for the 'replacement programme' proved useless for the purpose. They were expensive to keep, had no resistance to disease and produced very small litters. They proved unable to take the place of the tough Créole pigs that had been eliminated. And meanwhile, the very heart had been taken out of Haiti's rural economy.

The way in which American interests dictated the slaughter of the entire local pig population, followed as it was by the imposed programme to replace it with pigs from the American mid-west, made it less than surprising that Haitians perceived a deliberate US policy to undermine their economy and find yet another way of making profits at their expense. But their wrath was not aimed simply at their rich neighbour to the north. It was also directed at their own government. After all, within a very short period of time responsibility for the special centres set up to distribute the American replacement pigs seemed to pass from USAID officials into the hands of officials in the Duvalier power-system, army officers and rural chiefs of police. To the peasants this smacked of indecent haste and revealed a relationship between those who implemented American aid and their own government that was too cosy for words. It fuelled deep anger and resentment.

The presidential marriage and the loss of the Créole pigs disturbed the normally resigned population deeply. But there were other forces at work too. The Roman Catholic Church was shaking itself out of a torpor that had lasted right through the Duvalier years. Its hierarchy had been hand-picked by PapaDoc and could be counted on to buttress his régime. The archbishop of Port-au-Prince, Wolff Ligondé, and the bishops of Gonaives and Aux Cayes, Emmanuel Constant and Jean-Jacques

Claudius Angénor, were 'first generation Duvalierists' and had always been loyal to their political masters. As we've already noted, Constant's brother was Duvalier's army chief of staff. Ligondé's sycophancy has also been noted. A further illustration of its tone can be gathered from part of the sermon which he preached at Jean-Claude Duvalier's installation as Head of State in 1971. 'You know,' he said, 'that you derive your authority from God... As Head of State, your Excellence, you aren't simply the representative of the community, you are its guide in the pursuit of its highest goals. You have understood that God is the supreme master and that the work accomplished by you as Head of State, called to lead the people, is in fact God's work.'

But some new bishops had been appointed since the death of François Duvalier. François Gayot, Willy Romélus and Franz Colimon were appointed to the dioceses of Cap Haitien, Jérémie and Port-de-Paix in the years 1975–78. Their arrival injected new life and ideas into the Conference of Bishops. Suddenly the church was encouraging activities that would represent a new force in national life and empower the poor people of Haiti for their eventual participation in shaping their country's future. I was living in Cap Haitien through these years and became a good friend of Bishop (later Archbishop) François Gayot. I had unbounded admiration for him. His doctorate in sociology from Strasbourg University, together with his humble origins, promised a new capacity for analysis and readiness for action. He blew away the cobwebs that had stultified relations between the Catholic and Protestant churches. I preached in his cathedral and he preached and taught courses in my little Methodist chapel. He convened a diocesan synod which put a heavy emphasis on the need for social as well as spiritual development. I attended several sessions of this synod. Armed with its findings, fired by the way it had captured the imagination of his people, Gayot made ready to address the national agenda. And, with Romélus and Colimon alongside him, he made a splendid beginning.

Three documents were put out by the Bishops' Conference in the period 1980–82. There was a distinctly challenging tone to all of them. They identified and listed Haiti's ills, recognized the 'bias towards the poor' that must be the hallmark of the church's response, and provided a focus for the unity of the whole Roman Catholic Church of Haiti—bishops, priests, members of religious orders, and lay people alike. The most searching of these documents *Legliz se nou. Nou se legliz* (The church is us. We are the church) has a distinctly prophetic note. It was based on the results of a consultative exercise which allowed people in the parishes to identify their anxieties, hopes and dreams for the future. It insisted on the unity of all sections of the population in the search for a new kind of future. 'With its bishops,' it thundered, 'the whole church is up and moving, seeking to give its backing to a "people on the march".' This was stirring stuff and it is worth emphasizing it in view of the tragic developments that were to occur just a few years later.

This awakening of the Catholic Church wasn't merely a matter of congresses, synods and fine documents. In 1982 a grassroots movement was launched within the church. It was called *Ti Kominote Legliz*, Little Church Communities, a title which soon gave way to the simpler *Ti Legliz*, Little Church. Small groups of lay Christians began to meet across the length and breadth of the republic to address questions that related the gospel to the social realities around them. This was liberation theology pure and simple and it was present in Haiti long before the return of Jean-Bertrand Aristide. These groups encouraged lay people to claim their rights and urged them forward to play a part in Haiti's political life. This was a startling development. Such people had never taken an active part in public affairs before. The government soon got worried by what was happening and, in December 1982, arrested Gérard Duclercville, leader of the *Ti Legliz*. There was an outcry. As a result of sustained and concerted pressure, the church succeeded in getting Duclercville released. This was a very significant reversal for the régime.

And then the Pope came. He stayed a mere matter of hours, a tiny part of a tour of a number of Central American countries he was undertaking at that time. But, for all its brevity, his visit of 9 March 1983 will long remain an important landmark in Haiti's vicissitudinous history. At a mass held on the runway of the international airport he delivered a speech in the Créole language. This Pope, who had criticized priests whose ministry got too political, delivered a sermon which galvanized all the progressive forces in the land, even the bishops and the papal nuncio, for the last throes of the struggle against the Duvalier régime. 'There must be a better distribution of goods,' he declaimed, 'a fairer organization of society with more popular participation in its affairs, a more generous concept of service on the part of those who direct society.' This was heady stuff. But the Pope continued: 'I appeal to all those who have power, wealth and culture, to understand their urgent responsibility towards all their brothers and sisters.' He spelled out his message under the general theme: 'Things must change', and nobody missed the point.

The Pope was accompanied by Jean-Claude Duvalier who made a speech in which he revoked that part of the protocol negotiated so painstakingly by his father and which gave the Haitian president the right to nominate bishops. This right now reverted to the Vatican. It was another deadly blow for those who'd fought to build the Duvalierist programme. One of their most significant victories had been frittered away with nothing but a hole in the head by way of thanks. For the Pope's visit (and speech) gave courage to the whole Haitian church, bishops included, to fight against the oppression and injustice of the régime. It was as if the Holy Father had given his cohorts permission to fight with their gloves off. And that's pretty much what they did.

Barely a month after the Pope's visit, in April 1983, the Bishops' Conference issued a document entitled: 'Reasons for the church's intervention in the social and political domain'. In it, the bishops refused to accept the limited role of overseeing people's spiritual needs. They spelled out how impossible it was to preach the salvation of people's souls while allowing their physical and human rights to be denied. 'The political dimension is a fundamental element of human existence,' they argued. And then, *mirabile dictu*, they quoted the Puebla Conference of Bishops of 1968, the event that gave wing to the teachings of liberation theology. 'Politics has a global dimension since it envisages the Common Good. But it's not only political scientists who have something to say about the needs and values of society.' After all this theory, the bishops went on to spell out a list of duties with which they challenged the government. A concern for human rights, they urged, must mean that certain courses of action must be avoided at all costs. Then they listed some of these, including the abuse of basic human rights, the illegal dispossession of peasants (especially of their land), the violation of the justice system, torture, arbitrary arrest and illegal detention.

One further weighty document needs to be mentioned at this stage. In December 1983, the bishops issued a Charter spelling out a development programme for the citizens of Haiti. It had all the marks of a political manifesto, with sections devoted to Human Dignity, The Development of the Family, the Role of the State, and detailed programmes for Health, Education, Work, Agriculture, Rural Life and Industry. This massive and important document ended by spelling out a list of projects with a clear priority being given to the need for a Literacy Campaign. This was to be the ground on which the Roman Catholic Church later found itself divided. But, by the end of 1984, the church was united and committed to a programme of spiritual and social development, unafraid to address reprimands and directives to the government, and able to articulate the needs and aspirations of Haiti's previously submissive and suffering population. A giant had awoken from a long slumber. It is worth taking the time and space to spell this out. For when Jean-Bertrand Aristide arrived back in Haiti in January 1985, he found a country in turmoil, a politicized church, a disintegrating régime, and an uncertain future. Some commentators have suggested that it was Aristide who singlehandedly brought together all the factors and forces which eventually disposed of the Duvalier régime. It wasn't. He discovered a situation in 1985 that was totally unlike that of

1982 and light years from the one he'd left behind in 1979. There was a spirit in the air that exactly matched his own inclinations. And, as the church leadership began to falter before the enormity and the complexity of the responsibilities facing it, he became the natural focus for all the energies that had been released in the period prior to his return. It was as if history had given him this moment. He knew he must not waste it. There was no going back.

That's how it looked and felt from his point of view. As for those awaiting his return, there was confusion in the ranks right from the start. Aristide had been given to understand that he would be teaching biblical studies in the Port-au-Prince seminary. His arrival on 5 January gave him a bare three or four days before the opening of the new term. But his nervous superiors got cold feet at the last minute. Instead of allowing him to hold down a key post with its possibilities of influencing a whole generation of new priests, they decided to send him to the distant outpost of Aux Cayes and to give him some demanding but humdrum duties there. Aristide knew the city well. It was little more than a stone's throw from Port Salut where he was born. But the last thing he wanted at this time was to be banished to a backwater, deliberately kept away from the action. The biblical word *kairos* would have been in his head, a word that means 'opportune moment' or 'a time charged with possibilities'. He argued with his superior, Father Louis Kébreau, urging him to keep to the original decision. When Kébreau refused to budge, Aristide sought some concessions and, a true mark of his perseverance, ended up with a tiring compromise which, while it kept him in Aux Cayes for much of his time, allowed him to return to Port-au-Prince every week to give some classes to the seminary students there. He kept up this exhausting régime for several months.

During one of his visits to the capital, he was asked to preach in the cathedral. It was the week before Easter and he chose to speak on the theme of holiness. The city was full of talk about the possibility of a general strike. Opposition to the régime was intensifying. Aristide's sermon is an early indication of his readiness to go for the jugular. He began by tilting at Pope Paul VI's preference for Spaniards and Italians amongst those he'd proclaimed as saints of the church, wondering why places like Haiti seemed never to figure in such considerations. After all, he argued, there are plenty of people in Haiti whose courage and faith are tested in the most extreme conditions. Then, seizing on the biblical concept of Jubilee (defining it as a divinely ordained general strike!), he launched into a savage attack on those who oppressed and stood in the way of Haiti's saints. He attacked 'capitalist bosses' who took in four dollars for every one they put out, enriching themselves at the expense of the poorest of the poor. 'Is it right,' he asked, 'for these unholy ones—who supposedly invest in our country—to stop us from living?' He continued in this vein, calling for justice for Haiti's poor, until he reached his peroration. At this point, we have to imagine his excited audience in a Haiti still unused to open criticism of the powers-that-be. And we must picture Archbishop Wolff Ligondé, Duvalierist to his fingertips, in whose cathedral Aristide was preaching. The increasingly self-confident priest reached his climax by developing the words of Psalm 1 in this way: 'Hallelujah for men and women in Haiti who do not join forces with the malevolent régime. Hallelujah for the Haitians who do not enter into the gluttonous pillaging by a band of the bloodthirsty, in whose midst brother sells brother, in whose midst a brother is not his brother's keeper. Hallelujah, because the path of those Haitians who reject the régime is the path of righteousness and love, and that is what the Lord requires. Where there is beating, breaking, and destruction, the righteous man is not. The way of the Lord is the way of justice, and justice blooms on the banks of Deliverance.' No one would have misunderstood these words. Aristide was throwing down a gauntlet.

Then, in September 1985, he was unaccountably recalled to Port-au-Prince and given responsibilities in the parish of St John Bosco where he'd spent his schooldays. In addition to that, he was allowed to hold on to his teaching position at the seminary. Perhaps his superiors thought that the overwhelming needs of this poor parish, with its slum populations and endless problems, would keep Aristide quiet, but it was exactly where this young liberation theologian would have chosen to be. As well as offering him a platform for his own theological views, it made him a rallying point for all the progressive priests of a previous generation who, when they'd appeared troublesome to their bishops, had been banished to distant parishes. One such priest, Father Freud Jean, ended up in the remote parish of Belladères in the Artibonite Valley where he'd long been an active proponent of the *Ti Legliz*. Later he was to become head of the Roman Catholic Church's Justice and Peace Commission. He's told me just how well placed Aristide was to focus the energies of out-of-town priests like himself who were working hard with grassroots groups in a nationwide programme to raise public consciousness. And so, as dissatisfaction with the Jean-Claude Duvalier régime mounted, Aristide found himself in the ideal position to play an active part in the decisive events which led to the ending of a twenty-nine-year period of dynastic dictatorship. And he threw himself into the action with relish.

In the months since his return, the church had been pursuing its newly-unfolding programme of social change with barely-disguised enthusiasm. In May, the Conference of Bishops, under its president, François Gayot, had secured the release of a number of agriculturalists who'd been working on diocesan development programmes when they were arrested the previous November. Their work—of stimulating peasant communities into identifying ways of improving their standards of living—was considered threatening by the Duvalier government, so they'd been put into prison where, five months later, no charges had yet been brought against them. The bishops had also submitted to the government a statement about the desirability of forming political parties. They'd also had to protest loudly at the deportation of three missionary priests. On this matter, in order to reinforce their point, they announced that a '*Te Deum*'—part of the church's liturgy—would no longer be sung on the 22nd day of certain months in the year, a day of superstitious importance to the

Duvalierists. And finally, since April, the bishops had announced an ambitious literacy programme, including detailed proposals concerning orthography, teaching methods, and application. An appeal was made to all sections of the population, including the Protestant churches, to give their collaboration to this scheme. In the event, Duvalier had already been ousted before the literacy campaign (called *Misyon Alfa*) was officially launched. But it caused a great stir right from the outset. It was intended to be the first practical contribution to the church's national development programme which had been announced eighteen months earlier.

It is interesting that Aristide makes no mention of all this positive action being undertaken by the church in these first months of his return. What he recalls of this time in his autobiography are the oppressive acts and arbitrary arrests of the Duvalier government in its dying months. And also the demonstrations that seemed to multiply as people became more and more confident in their opposition to the régime. For him, this was the decisive phase in the overthrow of the dictator, it was the culmination of what he called a 'revolutionary process' that would bring victory to the people. Unprecedented freedoms were being claimed by political leaders and journalists, especially radio reporters, who kept the whole population informed of events across the republic. For Aristide, the end of Duvalier's reign had become inevitable. Now the larger question was how to keep him in the country and bring him to justice. He was sure the Americans would want to get Duvalier out without first settling his accounts with the Haitian people. Aristide's preaching became a focal point for anti-Duvalierist feeling. Huge crowds came to hear his sermons. He became less and less inhibited, naming those who'd misused their power, however highly placed they might have been, and calling for an end to macoutism and the power of Duvalier's secret police.

But the incident which brought the end of Jean-Claude Duvalier's rule into sight had nothing to do with Aristide, nor indeed with the ambitious programmes of the Roman Catholic

Church. On 27 November 1985, an anti-government demonstration was organized by students in the city of Gonaives. Members of the armed forces patrolling the streets assassinated three of the demonstrators, Jean-Robert Cius, Mackenson Michel and Daniel Israel. These young men, all from different schools in the city, were shot down in cold blood and their death unleashed a tidal wave of anger that surged from the hearts of a whole people. Even the bishop of Gonaives, arch-Duvalierist Emmanuel Constant, was fiercely critical of those who'd done this dreadful deed. So passionate was the outburst of grief, and so open the denunciations of journalists and others, that the government responded by curbing the already limited freedoms of the press and by closing down a number of radio stations. In early December, the Catholic *Radio Soleil* was shut. Throughout December, the whole nation was in mourning for the three young people who'd died. Aristide took a leading part in orchestrating young people's protests and he kept on reminding them of the promises they'd made at a Youth Congress held earlier that year in Jérémie: 'If one young person is unjustly attacked,' their communiqué had read, 'then all young people are attacked... and all must express their solidarity.'

Aristide clearly saw himself as a focus for this solidarity among young people. His services at St John Bosco were packed out, largely with young worshippers. And he travelled to various parts of the republic to stiffen the nerve of all those yearning for their liberation from Duvalierism. He found in the *Ti Legliz* a network of activists already formed. It was a network he could use to spread his message of opposition to the government. He worked tirelessly for the cause. And, inevitably, he made enemies.

On 31 January 1986, a man named Stephan Joseph (described by Aristide as a Tonton Macoute) turned up at a church service intending to kill him. As he was drawing his revolver, he made eye contact with the priest. His resolve weakened and, instead of shooting his intended victim, he took the bullets out of the gun and gave it to Aristide. Or at least, that's one version of the story. Another suggests that it was some of the young people in the congregation who spotted what was happening and disarmed the would-be assassin. They discovered a passport and visa and a large amount of money in his pockets: he clearly had his departure from Haiti already well planned. Outside the gates of the church there were military trucks and Tontons Macoutes waiting to whisk their colleague away and deal with any possible consequences of the assassination. This was the first attempt on Aristide's life. There were to be many more in the following months and years.

The young people who'd seized Stephan Joseph gave him a thrashing. Meanwhile, the Tontons Macoutes who were still at the gate were soon at work beating up the worshippers as they tried to leave the church premises for their homes. It was a savage display of brute force. In his autobiography, Aristide makes a grave allegation. 'Neither the hierarchy,' he writes, 'nor the apostolic nuncio, Bishop Romeo, uttered a single word of solidarity or even of simple comfort on this occasion.' Aristide may have been right to expect some such message from his superiors. But it is possible to question whether this negligence on their part was quite as deliberate as he implies. The whole country was in turmoil by this date. There had been demonstrations in many cities. In Cap Haitien, three people had been killed by the city police just four days earlier. On 29 January, death threats had been served against the Bishop of Cap Haitien and two of his priests. Fr Freud Jean was beaten almost to death by a gang of Tontons Macoutes. And that very day (31 January) *Radio Soleil*, which had been briefly re-opened after its December shut-down, was forcibly shut again, as was the Cap Haitien *Voix Ave Maria* station. What's more, there was a rumour that Jean-Claude Duvalier had left Haiti. Everything was in turmoil and it is perhaps too severe to blame the hierarchy at this early date for attitudes they hadn't yet formed.

Having made that observation, however, there were signs that a chasm was beginning to open up between the church's hierarchy and its popular base. A statement by the Conference of Bishops, dated 6 January 1986, criticized groups who were using language that sounded as if it had come from the church to incite people to violence and political activism. The bishops were thinking of those who had infiltrated the *Ti Legliz* in order to use it for political ends. Amongst others, they may have had Aristide in mind. They argued that while 'base ecclesial groups' (a rather ugly title for 'grassroots groups') operated across the land under the leadership of lay leaders, these still came under the authority of the local priest who himself was obedient to his bishop. 'The *Ti Legliz*,' they declared, 'is not a parallel church nor a political movement.' Clearly these were the first cracks heralding what was later to become a huge rupture. And all this was occurring during the extremely turbulent times that preceded the downfall of Jean-Claude Duvalier.

Bishop Willy Romélus of Jérémie, the most progressive of Haiti's bishops, in a long letter written to Pope John Paul II, is clear that the church was a principal actor in the overthrow of the dictator. And, in his view, the bishops and the people achieved that act together. According to Romélus, the disintegration of the church's solidarity didn't begin until 1987. To Aristide's mind, however, it had already begun as early as January 1986. What is certain is that the period from January 1986 to July 1987 is the time when the gains of the early 1980s dissolved and the church lost a historic opportunity to give shape to the as yet inchoate forces seeking to mould a new Haiti.

At 3.47am on 7 February 1986, a page of Haiti's chaotic history was turned. Jean-Claude Duvalier left the country over whose affairs he'd presided for fifteen years. He was accompanied by his wife and close members of his family and a few hangers-on. The US Air Force C-141, which had flown in from Guantanamo to pick them up, took off towards an unknown destination. The dreadful Duvalier years were over. A military group known as the CNG (National Council of Government), under the leadership of Lieutenant General Henri Namphy, took over the running of the country. Everything around them was in turmoil. Huge crowds thronged the streets of Haiti's cities, exhilarated by their first taste of freedom. People genuinely believed that the years of torture and suffering, arbitrary arrests and sudden disappearances, fear and dread were finally over. I remember making telephone calls to my friends in Haiti and the sense of liberation was palpable; we were able to speak without restraint, joke and express opinions, laugh and be merry. It is so hard to explain the sense of inebriation that comes to those who are able at last to drink at the wells of freedom after so many years of enforced abstinence.

But the mood was not wholly joyous. Gangs formed and moved towards known macoutes and collaborators with the Duvalier régime. Property was destroyed and people put to death on the streets. One man, caught whilst still wearing his uniform, had his legs hacked off with machetes before being 'necklaced'—burned to death with his head encircled by a blazing rubber tyre filled with petrol. This particularly grim method of dealing with the people's enemies was to come back to haunt Aristide at a critical moment in his presidency.

In the aftermath of Duvalier's departure, the mood was dominated by the need for vengeance. It was a time of cleansing. The red and black Haitian flag, imposed on Haiti by PapaDoc, was replaced by its red and blue predecessor. The François Duvalier International Airport became the Port-au-Prince International Airport. Avenue Jean-Claude Duvalier was renamed Avenue Jean-Paul II while the great heaving slum known as Cité Simone (named after PapaDoc's wife) was given the euphemistic and singularly inappropriate name Cité Soleil (Sun City).

Just a month after the ousting of Jean-Claude Duvalier, in the presence of General Henri Namphy and his government, a huge popular mass was sung in the capital's football stadium. This was held to launch *Misyon Alfa*, the literacy campaign announced a year earlier by the Catholic bishops. It would cost $24m and be one of the most ambitious campaigns of its kind in the world. The bishops, meanwhile, were pleading with the government that the people's voice should be respected and listened to, that freedom of speech and participation should be encouraged for everyone. They were also urging the people to be calm and patient and to show a spirit of forgiveness. It was certainly too early to ask for this last commodity. No one of any consequence in the old régime had been brought to justice; all the leading macoutes and members of Duvalier's secret police had gone into hiding or been allowed somehow to leave the country. The bishops were asking their people to take part in the rebuilding of the country; but they weren't demanding justice or helping people deal with their anger. It is hardly surprising that people took justice into their own hands, nor that radical priests found themselves orchestrating the people's struggle.

The one word which best summed up the mood of these days was *dechoukaj* which means 'uprooting, weeding out, sorting'. Bands of men and women roamed the city streets and the country lanes searching for collaborators, anyone who'd given uncritical support to Duvalier and his henchmen. *Dechoukaj* was a word which appeared strongly in the textbook produced as part of the literacy campaign *Misyon Alfa*. This was one reason why the military junta began to condemn the campaign, accusing all those giving it their unqualified support of being communists.

Aristide was active in all this ferment, travelling the length and breadth of the country to add his weight to the work being done by grassroots groups. An agenda which had previously centred on 'consciousness-raising' now moved on to 'organization', and a commitment to a far more militant phase in the quest for justice and human rights. The fiery priest was clear that there could be no question of accepting 'reconciliation' (understood as an uncritical papering-over of the past) without a clear recognition of the demands of 'justice'. This distinction would come back to haunt him in the last days of his presidency when he seemed to his erstwhile friends to be asking for precisely the undifferentiated notion of reconciliation he'd previously savaged. But in 1986, in those early days of the post-Duvalier era, there was a different atmosphere. Aristide was clear that 'a new and genuine state could not be built without the *dechoukaj* of all the machinery of a corrupt régime that had embedded itself down to the roots of society'. The trouble with Aristide's uncritical use of these buzz words is that no one can ever tell whether he has a clearly restricted and sanitized view of their possible meanings or whether his use of them is deliberately ambiguous. It is impossible to tell whether his advocacy of this uprooting metaphor, for example, included a silent approval for some of the barbaric things that were happening in its name and under its banner. Necklacing was one of these and his critics were clear that Aristide's refusal to condemn those resorting to such actions was tantamount to an approval on his part. This was another issue that would return to haunt him when he became president.

On 25 March, 4,000 students demonstrated in the streets of Port-au-Prince. The previous day had seen another large demonstration during which there had been some violent incidents. Soldiers had fired on the crowd who, in their turn, had defended themselves by throwing stones. The student demonstration was, by contrast, wholly peaceful. The marchers headed for a downtown church, where their proceedings culminated with the singing of a mass. The object of the demonstration was to show solidarity with agricultural workers and with fellow-Haitians enduring virtual slavery in the neighbouring Dominican Republic. Aristide, by now the idol of the young, was the preacher of the day. He denounced the military junta. 'We are serving an apprenticeship in democracy,' he declared. 'The army has been trained in the art of repression and those it represses are the ordinary people.' Then, referring to the previous day's events, he went on: 'They tell us we mustn't throw stones at them. It is certain that stone-throwing isn't the best way to make our point. But we will only stop throwing stones when they stop using their batons and revolvers against us.' By compounding details from these two demonstrations in this way, by using illustrative material from the previous day's event that served his purposes better than the more pacific happenings of that day, it is clear that Aristide was using every opportunity that came his way to address issues that were general rather than particular and to reach the widest possible audience.

Aristide's fiery sermons were becoming more and more focused and ever more popular. But his courage (some would say foolhardiness) was not restricted to mere rhetoric. He showed this by the way he stormed the Haitian equivalent of the Bastille, Fort Dimanche, in April 1986. Very few of those committed to its dank interior had ever regained their freedom. Every kind of human misery was known in this foul place during the years of PapaDoc's dictatorship. Many a prisoner was executed against its walls; cruellest torture was systematically used to extract information or confessions from its internees; and a lack of sanitation and overcrowded cells, together with a grimly inadequate diet, saw the resistance of many of its inmates yield to the attacks of disease and infection. Only the strongest-willed survived. Beyond any doubt, Fort Dimanche was the clearest symbol of everything Duvalierism stood for. And it was kept in use long after the flight of Jean-Claude Duvalier.

A huge demonstration had been planned for Saturday 26 April to commemorate a massacre that had taken place in Fort Dimanche on that same date in 1963. On that occasion, in the aftermath of an assassination attempt on PapaDoc's children, hundreds of people were arrested and interned within this ghastly place. They were never seen or heard of again. 'It has never been confirmed,' wrote Al Diedrich in 1970, 'whether they were quickly executed... or kept in prison and liquidated whenever Duvalier was seized with the urge to kill someone.' Two days before this anniversary, a mock funeral for the prison was organized in the slum area of La Saline within the St John Bosco parish. Aristide described its purpose graphically in his little book *In the Parish of the Poor*, which he published a few years later. 'It was [to be] a funeral for death,' he wrote, 'for all symbols of death, for all the places where there is death, crime, murder, torture, assassination. We performed the funeral in the name of our Christian faith.' Before the demonstration had got under way, soldiers from Fort Dimanche intervened, disrupting the procession and making a number of arbitrary arrests. That day, the infamous prison mocked those who thought they were celebrating its funeral rites. Instead, like an insatiable beast, it swallowed up those who'd dared to declare it dead.

When Aristide heard of this he was furious. We only have his account of this incident but he doesn't hide his feelings. It was ten o'clock at night when he telephoned the prison chiefs and told them he was coming to secure the release of his parishioners. It was a dangerous thing to do. He had no idea what might happen to him, but he felt driven to go. Increasingly at this time, he seems to reveal a recognition that it was his destiny to lead the people's struggle and he seeks to justify these feelings theologically. As he put it: 'It was not really I who lived... but Jesus Christ who was living through me, as I still wish [this was 1991] for him to go on living though me... I felt myself to be a missionary, completely a servant to the Spirit, completely in the hands of God, on a mission that 'went beyond my own weaknesses or strengths, that went beyond what I myself am, and I obeyed, and went to Fort Dimanche, because the Lord commanded me to go.'

He was allowed in by heavily armed, taunting soldiers who threatened and goaded him. Once within the prison, he was left for a moment in total darkness before being led to the prison governor Franck Romain, one of François Duvalier's closest collaborators, to whom he explained the purpose of his mission. Romain was a cultured and urbane man and he held a polite and accommodating conversation with Aristide in textbook French.

There's an air of the surreal about this encounter. Yet I remember having just such a discussion in London with Hervé Boyer, Haiti's chargé d'affaires in the 1970s and one of PapaDoc's faithful henchmen. For the whole time we were together, he drank the finest whisky and smoked expensive cigars. And what did we discuss? We considered the merits of French, English and Haitian literature. I was clearly in the presence of an intellectual who was thoroughly at home in the world of *belles lettres*. But I couldn't drive from my head the knowledge of what this man had done. As Rector of the University he'd seen to it that any student who showed the slightest evidence of 'subversion' paid for it, often with his life. He'd overseen many a torture session and ordered many an execution. Yet here we were, the two of us, discussing culture. The weird co-habitation within one and the same person of Dr Jekyll and Mr Hyde strained my credulity to breaking point. Yet it helps me understand the Fort Dimanche governor's reasonable and cultured tones as he listened to this upstart priest asking politely to be allowed to take the whole batch of that day's prisoners home with him when he left. There was no shouting or posturing by either of them. They might have been two city gents of the old school concluding a deal with a firm handshake. And so it was conceded to Aristide that, after he'd gathered the names of his terrified flock and noted their injuries, he was allowed to take them away with him. For all the calm that prevailed on the surface, however, Aristide was furious with this further evidence of the barbarous treatment meted out to his fellow-Haitians by the Duvalierist system. He railed inwardly at the arrogance of the prison governor who pretended he'd ordered the arrests simply in order to protect lives and property. ' "To protect lives and property",' I thought to myself. 'This is a mantra for such men, "to protect lives and property". Whose lives? Whose property? Such phrases on the lips of these men make me want to set fires in the streets and burn down buildings and erect walls of righteous fire to protect the lives of the people and the property of the people from such men.'

Two days later, the planned demonstration took place. After a mass at the Sacré Coeur Church in the Turgeau suburb of Port-au-Prince, the procession wound its way through the city centre towards the prison. More and more people joined the demonstration as it neared its destination. Aristide rode in a jeep with another priest and a journalist, giving a live commentary for listeners to the Roman Catholic *Radio Soleil*. Thousands gathered in front of the prison. There was no attempt to be militant. The people were there to mourn and they knelt in an attitude of prayer. Then, with no warning, the soldiers inside the prison opened fire on the crowd. Bullets flew and tear gas cannisters burst amongst the people spreading a sense of panic. Aristide refused to lie low or take cover. He kept his head up, relaying a constant commentary to his radio audience. He told them he might be shot before he got to the end of his sentence but they must hear the details of what was being done to innocent people. It was battlefront broadcasting of the highest order. He told his listeners how he could see Franck Romain, the same man who'd engaged him in polite conversation a couple of days earlier, turning his gun on fleeing demonstrators as if he were hunting wild animals. Aristide pleaded with the people not to resort to throwing stones, largely because it was clear they were a poor weapon against the soldiers' guns. Meanwhile, groups of armed men were running out from the prison to haul in the dead and the wounded. No one was ever able to count the number of casualties that day. But Aristide was certain he'd been an intended victim; this was his second close brush with death. And it was incidents like this that not only secured his position as a focus for the popular struggle but also strengthened an impression being formed by those who'd seen him in action that he was divinely protected from his enemies' bullets.

The bishops were less impressed. They put out a statement which, when it had offered routine sympathy to the friends and families of the victims, went on to address a word of stricture to those who organized demonstrations. Crowds are sometimes difficult to control, the bishops said. They can be infiltrated with agitators and imbued with a spirit of revenge. And when people claim their legitimate rights, they need to remember to measure those rights, however just they may be, against the general good. Those who lead demonstrations need to know something about crowd psychology! It is clear from this statement that the bishops had become nervous about the way popular sentiment was developing. But, apart from a non-specific appeal to the police to show more discipline, they showed little readiness to criticize those who'd shot and killed unarmed people holding a peaceful demonstration outside one of the most fortified places in Haiti. It is not difficult to understand how this kind of episcopal utterance would fan the flames of mistrust amongst those who were now ready to demand and fight for their rights.

Aristide's role in the Fort Dimanche demonstration made him the darling of all those forces, especially the young, who were striving for liberation from an ever more oppressive military régime. He was now centre stage and this became a source of real concern for his superiors in the Salesian order. They were pressurized by the bishops to crack down on this priest who had by now begun to make his presence felt beyond Haiti's borders. On 16 May he received a letter from his Salesian superior, Father Angelo Sotto, ordering him to desist from taking any further part in activity that could be construed as political. There were to be no further words on public events. He was to shut up and keep quiet. News of this got out and people jumped to the conclusion that the Catholic hierarchy were looking for the earliest opportunity to get Aristide out of Haiti. There was widespread opposition to this move. Political groups like *Komite Inite Demokratik* (Committee for Democratic Unity), and young people's organizations like *Lave Je* (Wash Your Eyes) sent petitions to the Salesian superior reminding him it was the *duty* of his order to serve the needs of the poor. There were demonstrations, telegrams, open letters galore both in Haiti and amongst the Haitian diaspora in the United States and Canada. The pressure grew to such a point that the Father Superior, from Santo Domingo, had to go back on his instructions and announce that everything had now been resolved satisfactorily.

Instead of going into exile, Aristide went on a retreat in Jérémie under the eye of Bishop Willy Romélus. This gave him time to think about the position his order had put him in. He'd had a particularly bad experience during the time he was banned from speaking out. On one occasion, he'd gone to comfort people who were suffering from an outbreak of fire in the miserable slum of La Saline. He was convinced that it was a case of arson but, when challenged by reporters from the national TV station to offer his opinions, faced with the responsibility of ignoring the banning order, he just turned and fled. It was an action that shamed him and he resolved never again to behave in so cowardly a fashion even if that did mean disobeying his superiors. His overriding duty was to the poor; he was clear about that.

A few months after this event, I helped edit and dub some film for Channel Four's 'Bandung File'. This was my first glimpse of Aristide, my first awareness of his oratorical skills. There had been a flood in another of Port-au-Prince's teeming slums and Aristide was once again on the spot within minutes. And yet again there were TV cameras present too. Cameras of any kind are normally a very inhibiting factor in these poor places, but on this occasion they did nothing to hold the people back from speaking with openness and patent trust. His own utterances to camera were sharp, even shrill, as he denounced the transitional government for its deficiencies and heartlessness. He called for a concerted effort to get rid of macoutism and state terrorism and for humane programmes aimed at relieving the misery of the people surrounding him.

Through all these months journalists were pushing the régime's tolerance to the limits. They began now to turn on the Haitian bishops. 'Are the bishops betraying us?' a headline in *Haiti Progrès* demanded. They were especially critical of Bishop François Gayot, whom they accused of abandoning the people and giving support to the military government—who by now had shown themselves wedded to Duvalierist programmes and oppressive styles of imposing their power. Indeed, the Bishops' Conference (under Gayot's presidency) published a huge document at the end of June 1986 that purported to map out Haiti's passage to a democratic future. But it had some interesting disclaimers in it. Just three years earlier, these same bishops had resisted any idea that the church's role could be limited to merely spiritual matters. They'd quoted a Puebla document to insist that 'the political dimension is fundamental to human existence' and that the church cannot preach its message without addressing the world of politics. Now, they wanted to emphasize the fact that 'the church is not a force in politics' but rather wields its influence in a specifically 'religious' area of national life. This was a clear volte-face and shows a hierarchy in full flight from its earlier idealism.

Aristide had not been leading the life of a normal parish priest for some time. His sacramental ministry was irregular and his pastoral role greatly diminished. Now it was clear he must keep a lower profile on the social and political fronts too. He found himself somewhat aimless for the first time since he'd returned to Haiti a year and a half earlier. He chose this moment to found an institution for the care of children and young people. A little child was picked out at random from a Sunday morning congregation to make a presentation to a visiting priest. Aristide interrogated the nine-year-old, a boy named Selavi ('*C'est la vie*'—'that's life'). The little session went as follows:

> Aristide: How old are you?
> Selavi: I don't know.
> Aristide: Who is your mother?
> Selavi: I don't know.
> Aristide: What do you do on the streets?
> Selavi: Sometimes I wash cars.
> Aristide: How do you eat?
> Selavi: When I get work, I eat.
> Aristide: And if not?
> Selavi: I don't eat.
> Aristide: Where do you sleep?
> Selavi: Sometimes I am so hungry that I can't sleep.

Out of this conversation was born a community called *Lafanmi Selavi* (either: Selavi's Family, or: The Family Means Life). It attracted support from a number of agencies including Caritas and France-Libertés and the personal interest of Danielle Mitterand, wife of the French president. A house was bought and children who'd only ever seen the slums were taken into a

better-off area in an up-market district of Port-au-Prince. A
number of doctors gave their services free of charge and
members of the bourgeoisie began to give their support to what
was becoming a rapidly developing charity. For Aristide this
innovative piece of work achieved two important purposes.
Firstly, it allowed him to put his theology into practice. The
waifs and strays he found at his church door were given an
opportunity to live a secure life, go to school, learn a trade,
enjoy someone's affection. He was able to show that the
children of the slums, given a different perspective, could
become contributing members of society. But a second
advantage that came indirectly from *Lafanmi Selavi* was no less
important. It gave Aristide contact with good-hearted
members of Haiti's better-off classes, people who'd previously
tended to be on the receiving end of his tongue. It is from this
time that he began to enlarge his social network and build the
platform from which he'd launch his presidential bid three
years later.

Aristide's withdrawal from commenting on social and
political events, imposed on him by his superiors, eventually
came to an end. He came out of purdah in September with a
magnificent oration protesting against the arrest of Charlot
Jacquelin, a teacher in the *Misyon Alfa* literacy programme.
Even in its printed form (it appeared in the *Misyon Alfa* bulletin)
it spits and splutters on the page like hot fat in a frying pan.
Aristide gave this speech in Créole, a vivacious language which,
unlike French, isn't worn out with centuries of carrying the
intellectual baggage of a whole civilization. In a staccato style,
words fired like machine-gun bullets, Aristide picks his targets
and shoots them down with a torrent of verbal ammunition. He
begins by addressing the Haitian soldier who'd arrested Charlot
Jacquelin: 'You, my brother, you chose to enter the army;
remember today, my brother, that it is your own brothers who
are under the table (Aristide frequently uses the metaphor of a
table to refer to Haiti's national life and the way its resources are
shared out); you, my brother, are also the brother of Charlot
Jacquelin, Jacquelin is your brother. So then, what can be done?

Today, I plead with you, in the name of Charlot, hold back the gun they've put into your hand, hold on to it, keep a firm grip on it, put it to one side; just think a little, consider your country...' And then, after an amazingly poetic, strikingly bold, stirringly incantatory passage he rounds on those who were responsible for Charlot Jacquelin's disappearance, claiming the whole incident to be against all God-given notions of justice. With that he rises to a climax:

> 'Valiant Haitian men and women, valiant boys and girls, wash out your eyes, rinse them, open them, take a look at the table. See how the cards are dealt; they've been badly dealt so let's shuffle the pack, shuffle it and re-shuffle it; the cards are crooked, let's shuffle, re-shuffle and shuffle them again and again... And take heed of all these accusations of communism going about. Around the table you'll find capitalists living in vice, small vices and large vices too. In the way they do wrong things they're like the Americans, they've become sharks who eat the little fish around them; through injustice, to protect capitalists, they say that every nationalist is a communist. Turn around, they say, and there's a communist; just go down the road and there's another communist; wherever you pass you find a communist; crack your fingers and you conjure up a communist. Only Duvalierist capitalists and CNG-ist [these letters refer to Haiti's then military government] capitalists have kept off the list of all those communists... My brothers, the cards have indeed been badly dealt.'

The energy released in his listeners, the assonance, sibilance, firepower were astonishing. And the symbiotic relationship this repetitive style forged with his audiences, their participation in its litanies, the sheer joy, inspiration, danger of it all, is hard to wring out of a translation from a printed version of what must have been an utterly brilliant rhetorical event. But it was through his simply magical oratorical skills and his undoubted personal courage that Aristide was making himself a force in the land, someone who simply couldn't be ignored or marginalized.

The military government meanwhile was blundering on. General Henri Namphy proved to be an irascible and ill-tempered man with an alcohol problem. Whatever hopes he might personally have had of a civilian government shaping policy and running the affairs of state, they were sabotaged again and again by his head of staff Colonel Jean-Claude Paul. Paul had fastened on to the drug trafficking business which had been developed by Michèle Bennett's family. Her brother had been jailed by the US courts and her father had used his own personal airline to carry drugs to the US mainland. Her own private homes and a hospital she was associated with were found, after the ousting of the Duvaliers, to contain large amounts of cocaine and marijuana. Paul maintained and indeed strengthened the links with Colombian drug barons and also developed his own line in contraband. He was pulling in a lot of money fast and wasn't at all anxious that Haiti should move towards accountable government. In all this activity, he was hand in glove with elements in the business community. They were happy enough with the status quo. So the junta lurched from one crisis to another while Haiti lacked any coherent form of government. Every week saw one organization or another demonstrating on the streets. One week saw 30,000 women in a huge parade; they were followed in successive weeks by students, trades unionists, and peasant groups. There were also strikes that enjoyed varying degrees of success. It was clear that the Haitian people, having tasted liberty, were not going to rest until they'd got rid of military rule and gained some form of democratic government. Meanwhile, the junta just managed to keep the lid on a seething cauldron through the period of dechoukaj that followed the Duvaliers' hasty departure, and then through the demonstrations, the penetrating criticism of young journalists in the written and spoken press, and through the strikes. But there was a cost. The régime resorted again and again to wanton murder, arbitrary arrest, intimidation and torture. The bright light of freedom that had shone in February

1986 had soon been extinguished. No one could predict what would happen next.

The next few months, during late 1986 and early 1987, were draining for Aristide. He travelled ceaselessly to speak to meetings and to preach at services across the length and breadth of the republic. In addition, he preoccupied himself with the work of establishing *Lafanmi Selavi*. It was exhausting work, yet it began to establish him as the leading voice in the land. The army, the world of commerce and business, the hierarchy, political aspirants and ordinary people waited for his next word. And many of these were wondering just what they could do to get rid of him. He allowed himself little time for recreation or relaxation. He enjoyed singing to his guitar and reading, but these months gave him little time for either of these. Around him were all those priests on whose work he was building, to whose concerns he was giving focus. For years priests like William Smarth, Freud Jean, Jean-Marie François, Gilles Danroc, Max Dominique and Antoine Adrien had beavered away in remote places to raise the self-awareness of peasant communities. There were hundreds of such priests, mostly Haitian, whose working agenda was soon to become Aristide's political programme. In his travellings he often had occasion to visit some of these collaborators. No doubt they'd pass an evening in animated conversation. But there weren't too many times like that.

In the early months of 1987, Aristide seemed to be a man driven by some inner sense of purpose in search of his destiny. Even his closest friends and collaborators confess to being unable to fathom his deepest thoughts. There is an impenetrability about him which leaves those he's with wondering how to assess just what he's really thinking. And yet it was this very mystique that set him apart from his fellows and attracted the crowds. Increasingly it became obvious that he was the man whose hour was about to come; there was something messianic about it. Yet even after talking to many of those who were closest to him at this time, I'm not at all sure of the extent to which he imposed his thinking on the current of events as opposed to letting the stream carry him along. It is against this whole area of unreachable and undefinable mystery that some of his questionable words and actions are to be judged. Those who meet Aristide, even those who know him best, would all feel there was some unresolved ambiguity in the deep centre of his being. Curiously, Aristide may be just as bemused by his own inner tensions (and contradictions) as anyone else.

Since late 1986, the Commission on the Constitution were working away at a new Constitution for Haiti. This was published in early March. It appeared in French and Créole and radio stations began at once to educate a public who'd never previously been aware of their constitutional rights in its various provisions. A referendum was held on 29 March1987 and 1,496,210 people, voting in 215 polling stations throughout the land, gave it their overwhelming support. Nothing like this had ever happened before in Haiti's turbulent history. It was astonishing that there was such a good turnout; it was another indication that the Haitian people could never again be pushed back into the shadows. The results of the referendum were published at the end of April and, a couple of weeks later, a Provisional Electoral Council (CEP) was established to prepare for elections later in the year. The Council was made up of people representing a dozen sectors of national life. But it ran into trouble almost at once. The ruling junta took exception to the Roman Catholic and Protestant representatives, who had to be replaced. The Rev. Alain Rocourt was the head of the Methodist church in Haiti and he became the Council's treasurer. When the CEP headquarters were attacked and its staff intimidated, only resolute action by Rocourt kept the operation on the road. He personally had all the election matériel moved into the Methodist buildings in the centre of Port-au-Prince. This edifice had been built by an English missionary and its thick walls and heavy steel shutters were specifically planned to withstand fire, earthquake, revolution and flood. There was no further difficulty on that score. But some members of the CEP were threatened by the Tontons Macoutes. Rocourt came under savage attacks, he was vilified and accused of misappropriating large amounts of money. Like Aristide, Rocourt is a little man who has the courage of a giant. In view of what happened, however, he must many a time have wondered if it might have been better had the whole 1987 electoral exercise folded up in its early days. But that wasn't to be.

The summer of 1987 was a torrid time. Terror stalked the streets and popular neighbourhoods. Death, arson and gun battles were everywhere in evidence, with most incidents taking place under the cover of darkness. The country was descending into chaos. Then on 30 June, Willy Romélus spoke out. He'd had enough. Addressing the National Government Council, he urged them to go. But the Créole metaphor he used became a watchword for the next stage of the struggle. *Rache manyok ou, bay tè a blanche* (Pull up your manioc roots. Give us a clean patch). The manioc plant sits in the ground for years at a time. The lively image would not have been misconstrued: get out, it declared, give the country back to us clean, ready for a new start. This was startling coming from a bishop. But Romélus had become increasingly unhappy at being pressurized into signing the official documents emanating from the Bishops' Conference. He had a rare relationship with his priests and members of religious orders in the Jérémie diocese and was finding it more and more difficult to share their dreams and feel their frustrations while still belonging to a body of hierarchs whose every utterance was opening an ever-widening chasm between them and the church-on-the-ground. His imaginative and impatient demand for a new beginning indicates that this tension had reached breaking-point.

Demands on Aristide intensified. Sunday by Sunday he preached at the St John Bosco mass and could expect as many as 3,000 young people in his congregation. In the account of one of his sermons from this time, we read that he denounced the military and its exactions, the role of the United States in arming Haiti's oppressive régime and also those opportunists who were using the people's struggle to further their own sectional interests. His sermon ended with another of those inspiring (yet frightening) sentences that were his trade mark. 'We swear 70 times 7 times,' he promised, 'that the blood of the victims hasn't flowed for nothing.' With such sermons Aristide had become an icon for a whole generation of Haitian youth. They were raring to go.

An event occurred at the end of July 1987 that proved to be a defining moment in Haiti's post-Duvalierist history. Nearly three hundred peasants were massacred 150 miles away from Port-au-Prince at Jean Rabel in the remote North-West Department. There had been disputes over land for many years. Duvalier's law enforcement officers had appropriated the land of peasant families and they sensed that at last the time had come to reclaim what had been taken from them. For a number of years Father Jean-Marie Vincent had worked with them to make them aware of their rights. Under his leadership they'd formed an association called *Gwoupman Tèt Ansanm* (Heads Together Group) whose membership had risen above 10,000. Vincent had been recalled by his bishop who suspected him of moving in too 'political' a direction. Even without him, the peasants sensed that the state of near anarchy prevailing in the land gave them their opportunity to act. They marched in protest against the landowners carrying only their machetes. They were met by heavily armed men and were savagely shot down in cold blood. The Roman Catholic *Radio Soleil* reported some thirty deaths while the Haitian government drove this down to a derisory ten. The journalist for *Agence France Presse* reported at least fifty deaths while the BBC correspondent put the figure at 'hundreds'. The *New York Times*, quoting a Protestant missionary, gave a more specific total of 235, which seems likely to be the nearest we'll ever get to an accurate figure. It wasn't only information about the number of casualties that was doctored, however. Official Haitian channels were equally keen to attribute blame for the calamity to anyone but their own officials and sympathizers. Thus they put all the troubles down to internecine factions among the peasant population; or else to a religious dispute between Catholics and Protestants; and, for good measure, they also suggested that the subversive work of communists might have had something to do with it too.

The Bishop of Port-de-Paix who'd replaced the activist priest Jean-Marie Vincent with someone more pliable found that Vincent's work survived his departure. In his sermon after the massacre, therefore, Monsignor Colimon took up a clear position against the *Gwoupman Tèt Ansanm* and in favour of the powerful landowners. He accused the peasant organization of communism and promised to bring them under control. He brought in agents of the Care Foundation to distribute food, a measure that the *Gwoupman* had always strongly resisted. They'd preferred to stimulate local farmers' production rather than undermine their markets by dumping vast quantities of surplus grain from the United States. When the bishops put out a statement two weeks later, they 'deplored the killing and the violence of individuals and groups such as in Jean Rabel, la Gonave and Léogane'. Yet that's the only specific reference to this massacre that appears in what is quite a lengthy document. Jean Rabel is lumped together with places where other far smaller incidents had taken place. The bishops then went on to ask the question 'Who are the perpetrators of these crimes?' before refusing to answer their own question, offering instead an anodyne exhortation: 'Let everyone search their conscience,' they advised, 'and ask what they themselves have done to bring all this violence to an end.'

Throughout this period the bishops were being demonized by Aristide and like-minded priests, and grassroots church members too. A lot of the criticism they received was over the top. But they didn't help themselves. They lost their nerve at crucial moments. They continued to allow arch-Duvalierists like Ligondé and Constant to play an active part in their deliberations. And they too readily gave the appearance of backing the régime on matters like Jean Rabel and the readiness of workers to go on strike. Perhaps the history of the Roman Catholic Church since the French Revolution, with its traditional defensiveness against the inroads of modernism and anti-clericalism, has left it with an impossible legacy. It seems to lead the church to offer instinctive and inflexible support for anything that smacks of the status quo. This means that too often it has little to contribute to rapidly changing situations such as it has encountered in Haiti since 1986.

Within days of the Jean Rabel massacre, news of another attempt to marginalize Aristide filtered out. This time it came direct from Rome. Father Varesco, one of the Salesian high command, faced Aristide with a decision to take him out of the St John Bosco parish and send him instead to Croix-des-Missions. The significance of this move was not lost on anyone. This new parish was situated on the plain some twenty miles to the north of Port-au-Prince, where a number of wealthy members of Haitian society and many Tontons Macoutes lived. Aristide would suffer internal exile in a place where he'd have no natural following and where there would be severe constraints on his now clearly established role as a national leader. Already certain sectors of the national press had carried an appeal for a provisional government headed by Gérard Gourgue, a veteran human rights campaigner, and Aristide himself. The leaders of ten grassroots organizations had signed an open letter calling for such a move. Rome was worried. The fourteen months that had passed since the last attempt to gag Aristide had seen him rise inexorably in people's minds as the undisputed champion of the voiceless. But, in the view of his superiors, it was at least possible that he himself was a factor in instigating the troubles and violence breaking out across the land.

For a much briefer moment than in May 1986, the question of obedience seems to have crossed Aristide's mind. He prepared to go to Croix-des-Missions but saw to it that as many people as possible got wind of the change well before it took place. The outcry was predictable. But less expected was the takeover of Port-au-Prince Cathedral by a group of young people who went on hunger strike in protest. Aristide avows that he knew nothing about this initiative, that he was well away in the north at the time it happened. And so he was. In fact, soldiers and their accomplices broke into the huge congregation who'd come to hear him preach in a Cap Haitien church and broke up the service with tear gas and bullets. Wherever he went at that time feelings ran very high. But despite his distance, it seems more than a little disingenuous of him to deny all knowledge of the hunger strike. A whisper from him about his forthcoming move was soon public knowledge, he saw to it that everyone knew of the church's move to oust him from his city parish. So it is inconceivable that such a brilliant plan to focus opposition to his removal should not have been communicated to him. But his handling of the incident was even more astute than the way he gave the appearance of knowing nothing about it in advance. He kept away from the cathedral. He claims that to have called the strike off would have played into his opponents' hands. He'd have opened himself to the accusation that if he had the power to call off a strike then he also had the power to instigate one; so he kept away. For six whole days news of the hunger strike dominated the news. Pictures of the three young women and four young men involved filled the front pages and also the television screen. Doctors came and pronounced their condition to be lamentable. A hundred other young people conducted a sit-in in the rest of the cathedral and no services took place during this time, which included one of the highest festival days in the Catholic calendar, the Feast of the Assumption. What's more, a sit-in was also taking place at St John Bosco where a 'surveillance committee' had been established to maintain a round-the-clock watch against the possibility of some kind of reprisal on the part of the authorities. Everything had reached crisis point. The auxiliary Bishop of Port-au-Prince, Joseph Lafontant, paid the hunger strikers a visit and his report to his fellow bishops was grim. And still Aristide didn't show his face.

It was only when the bishops backed down and when, in addition, they'd made a statement regretting the horrors of Jean Rabel, that Aristide felt he was able to enter the cathedral. Just before he did so, however, a man carrying a gun was arrested outside the cathedral. He admitted intending to kill Aristide and, if he'd kept his cover for just a few more minutes, he'd have had excellent opportunity to fire on his target. This was the third brush with death that Aristide had had in the eighteen months since he returned to Haiti. But now the stage was set for a 'triumphal entry'. Aristide's arrival at the cathedral doors had an almost messianic feel to it. This little man walked quietly into the sanctuary. The crowds may not have been waving palm branches but their cheers certainly sounded like 'Hosannah'. He didn't hurry. The strikers, weak after their six-day ordeal, were lying on their rush mats waiting for their hero. He entered the free space surrounding them and went to each in turn, embraced them, sat with them and talked quietly. No one heard what was said. This was pure spectacle rather than a press conference. It was a clear message to the bishops, to the government and to the people.

The sheer awesome power of this dignified, heavily symbolic, piece of theatre was overpowering. The church's hierarchy (and Rome itself) had been made to eat its words. All their huffing and puffing had simply reinforced the people's opposition to them. Nor had the might of a military government achieved anything. And the money of the wealthy business élite had been powerless too. Seven young people and an infuriatingly obstinate priest had out-manoeuvred them all. Aristide had won this battle hands down. But he'd also made some implacable enemies who didn't take long to strike back.

The Sunday following the end of the hunger strike saw an enormous celebration in and around the St John Bosco Church as Aristide returned to his parish. Later that day he travelled north to Port Sondé, a little town in the Artibonite valley about seventy miles from the capital. He and some friends went to join in a memorial service for the victims of Jean Rabel. At the very moment Aristide got to his feet to speak, gunmen moved in to destroy the meeting. There was indiscriminate shooting and Aristide came face to face with an armed man pointing his weapon directly at him. For some reason the armed man backed off and the priest escaped near death for the fourth time. He was hurled to the ground and lay there with a number of other people until it was safe to get up.

Aristide took counsel with his friends. They formed a little group of five priests, the others being Antoine Adrien, William Smarth, Jean-Marie Vincent and a Canadian named Burg. They decided to wait for nightfall and then attempt to return to Port-au-Prince. They got as far as Freycineau, a tiny place on the edge of St Marc, where they found a police barrier in place. It was pouring with rain and pitch dark. They had to get out of their car and became aware of a number of men armed with machetes, rocks and guns. Aristide remained in the car and hid on the floor beneath the back seat. Those conducting the search picked on one of the priests and beat him severely, but it was clear they were looking for Aristide. They broke the windscreen and punctured the tyres of the car he was hiding in. Rocks flew and Vincent and Burg were hit on the head and face. When, several years later, Jean-Marie Vincent sat in my front room and told me the details of this ambush, his eyes still welled up with tears at the memory of it. And he showed me the long scar that ran down the side of his face, the remains of the injury he received during that incident. But it was Vincent who saw an opportunity to get away, a small gap in the rocks that had been used to bar the road. He urged Burg to put his foot hard down on the accelerator and make a run for it. Miraculously, without headlights and in driving rain, they got away to the safety of a Protestant missionary's house in nearby Montrouis. Early the following morning, a delegation from Port-au-Prince (including the papal nuncio, Monsignor Paulo Roméo) arrived to escort the group back to the capital. A fifth escape for Aristide, two in one day (and three in a week) simply served to impress people with a sense of his invincibility. The army and Tontons Macoutes had made a bid to regain the initiative after Aristide's triumph in the hunger strike a few days earlier. They failed abysmally and now had to face a barrage of outrage directed at them at home and from the international community. This was a heavy blow for the government forces.

Aristide was rapidly acquiring legendary stature, creating the impression that he was 'untouchable'. From deep within the Haitian mind-set a folk-memory survives of the heroes of their independence, men who rushed against French guns armed only with their high spirits and a few rocks. Some of the earliest leaders—Jean-François, Biassou, Jeannot and the mighty Toussaint Louverture—gained a reputation for being immune to their enemies' bullets. *Yo gen pwen pran bal* (they've got the power of absorbing bullets) was how their contemporaries thought of them. They seemed superhuman. And many people were beginning to bracket Aristide with these mighty men of yore. His succession of escapes from death, sometimes from close-quarter encounters with armed men, began to inspire awe. People thought he was divinely protected.

He himself put it all a little differently. He wrote in *In the Parish of the Poor:*

> Even if we had died at that barricade, we would have lived on in the memories of the people because our spirit is their spirit. What moves them moves us too. We speak the words that the spirit of the poor breathes into us. That is our humble role, a simple role, one that requires no learning, no pride, no cassock, no mitre. It requires faith only, and of faith we have plenty. It requires a willingness to serve the people, and no machete, no fusillade of rocks, no bullets or rifles or Uzis, no tear gas or bombs, will ever dissuade us from that willingness, from that faith. We are unshakeable. Like the poor, we will always be with you. Kill one among us, and we rise up again, a thousand strong.

This last ringing declaration is a clear echo of Toussaint Louverture's word that even if the tree of liberty should be cut down, new shoots galore will spring up from its roots, for freedom is an unstoppable force.

As a matter of fact, Aristide turned out to be just as human as anyone else. He needed a couple of days' treatment in hospital. 'My wounds were only superficial,' he wrote, 'but, as it turned out, I needed several hours to recover my spirits.' That confession of vulnerability is an important one. It points to a side of his character rarely seen. His enemies were to make much of this during his presidential years, turning a natural despondency into something bordering on the wildly psychotic in their attempts to discredit him. Meanwhile, the failed assassination attempt at Freycineau gave an undoubted boost to his march towards national leadership.

3 'Just who are you, Father Aristide?'

In February and March 1987, the Port-au-Prince weekly *Haiti en marche* (Haiti on the Move) ran an extended interview which stretched over three consecutive issues. They appeared under the collective title: 'Just who are you, Father Aristide?' It was precisely the question everyone was asking and this was the first in-depth interview he'd been submitted to. It offers some intriguing insights into the character and personality (as well as the views) of this complex man.

He was first of all questioned about his well-known opposition to Haiti's bourgeois class. In his reply he described the bourgeoisie as an oligarchy caught up in a class war against the poor. Whilst distinguishing between individual members of the bourgeoisie whom he felt he could get on with as collaborators and even as friends, he was categorical about being with the poor in their struggle against the bourgeoisie as a class. 'But,' his questioner added, 'these people are afraid of you and think you have a troop of commandos at your beck and call, people ready to shake them out (*dechoukaj*) and destroy them.' Aristide gave short shrift to this comment and its implications. Even so, it is interesting to note from the way the question was put just how his opponents were already beginning to categorize him. In his reply Aristide pointed out that, far from having shock troops at his command, the only thing he was in fact armed with was *good news*. 'But when I announce this good news,' he said, 'I must say that I do expect a practical response. This might well be some form of action which, though non-violent, will even so be considered by certain people to be violent. There is such a thing as institutional violence, of course, and that's something the bourgeois class direct against the poor all the time.' He went on to point out how, in its entrenched and privileged position, the Haitian bourgeoisie not only had the Haitian Armed Forces under its thumb but could always count too on the help of American imperialism. These, he concluded, were the various strands of the multi-layered oppression under which the Haitian poor were suffering.

'How would you respond to General Henri Namphy's reported criticism that priests like you have turned the mass into a political meeting or even into a black mass?' Once again the question is revealing, showing as it does the perceptions being formed by his opponents. His populism is once more seen as cause for concern; but this time something even darker is being hinted at, a diabolical perversion of his spiritual authority. But the question doesn't only show up possible ambiguities in Aristide's character. It is equally revealing of the paranoia beginning to invade the minds of his opponents. Aristide didn't waste much time on a direct answer to this question. 'Those who come to church expecting to have their consciences salved or to be drugged into submissiveness are living on the wrong planet,' he avowed. 'The God they invoke isn't the God of the Bible. It's the living God who waits to meet his people in the celebration of the Eucharist. This is the God who has revealed himself in history and who has shared our suffering and misery, the God who struggles with us now. *This* is the God of the Bible.'

'But what about your last Christmas Eve mass?' his interviewer persisted. 'You called it a *Kanzo* (voodoo) ceremony. How on earth do you explain that?'

'The word *Kanzo*,' replied Aristide, 'comes from a cultural and anthropological source close to the very centre of our identity. We couldn't speak as Haitians without somehow recognizing the deep and personal links with our own voodoo. *Kanzo* focuses the change which a person experiences when he has contact with a spirit in touch with a force it calls God. The individual feels stronger, better, for this contact. I don't use words like *Kanzo* all that often, but we have to be able to use concepts capable of leading us nearer the source of our identity. The word *Kanzo* doesn't belong exclusively to voodoo; nor are voodoo adepts somehow excluded from the Haitian people as a whole... sooner or later our liturgical language will have to embrace the totality of our being, our whole identity as Haitians.'

At this point the questions turned towards differences within the Roman Catholic Church. Aristide spoke frankly about the attempts that had been made by his congregation (the Salesians) to transfer him to other duties. He went on to express his regret that Monsignor Willy Romélus, Bishop of Jérémie, had failed to become president of the Bishops' Conference. Instead, Bishop François Gayot, whose voice had become increasingly conservative since the departure of Jean-Claude Duvalier, had been re-elected when his own term had come to its end. This was to be regretted. The church leadership was calling for democratic government in the country at large while denying all forms of it within the church. This could be nothing other than hypocrisy.

Asked if he was prepared to admit to being a 'liberation theologian', he gave a clear and immediate yes before continuing with an intriguing passage that's worth quoting extensively:

We must work to clean up our society. That means a class struggle. Once upon a time we avoided speaking of such things. Today we have to. That doesn't mean we must preach class struggle but it has become a reality we must lean towards. In order to repair the tissue of our society so that it becomes stronger and healthier, we must, in my view, brandish the arms of solidarity against this bourgeois oligarchy allied as it is to the 'macoute' army. That will frighten the bourgeoisie! Yet no one is seeking to destroy them; it's a case rather of overturning the table at which they sit and under which are to be found the poor who refuse to be crushed by such a tiny minority. Why brandish 'the arms of solidarity'? To prevent people from falling into the obvious trap which would be waiting for them if they

were to follow the ill-considered option of taking up firearms. I believe that liberation theology does not invite us in
Haiti to take up weapons to defend ourselves even though
it does allow for such a possibility in other situations. It
condones armed struggle according to the circumstances of
the case. But there's something unique to our situation; we
have a people who have it in them to unleash a second
wave of *dechoukaj* (uprooting) without resorting to arms. As
far as I'm concerned, to take up arms today would be to
face the prospect of immediate failure... We have proof
from what happened last year [1986] that our solidarity
made it possible for us to effect the first wave of *dechoukaj*.
With the same kind of solidarity we'll be able to unleash the
second *dechoukaj* too.

Aristide makes a clear commitment in this paragraph to non-
violence. Yet his language, with its talk of 'class struggle',
'frightening the bourgeoisie', and 'brandishing the arms of
solidarity', creates an atmosphere in which internecine and
unremitting civil conflict is scarcely out of view. And his talk of
'a second *dechoukaj*' even has apocalyptic overtones to it. So his
interviewer pushes him further at this point and asks for an
explanation of this dark and mysterious phrase. Once more,
Aristide's reply is worth quoting in full:

What I'm referring to is a mass movement on the part of
the church where the sons of the people, the daughters of
Haiti, rise up in the name of their Faith and in favour of a
new Haiti free of macoutes and rid of duvalierists. Hand in
hand, they'll start up 'operation *dechoukaj*' all over again
but this time they'll see to it that the big macoutes (whether
in the civil or military branch) no longer enjoy the
protection of the macoute-dominated army. The great
thieves of the people must find no refuge either within
Haiti or beyond our shores. The people's tribunal must be
able to arrest these macoutes, judge them, recoup our
country's money, protect the country's blood. Or, to put it

another way, we who've been under the table (while they've been at the table) must get our proper place around the table. Will this mean that they must be pushed under the table to make way for us? Wouldn't that simply be a crude form of vengeance? I couldn't possibly preach such a doctrine in the name of the gospel. But by a second 'operation *dechoukaj*' I definitely mean a movement that will bring the macoute to justice; he must not escape as he's done up to now; it's my turn to get hands on his wealth rather than see him escape with it. Even so, I'm not abandoning him like an accursed son. Certainly not. I'll bring him back to his place at the table. But only after he's faced his judgment. And all this is not just a matter of wild imagination on my part. This will all come to pass if we commit ourselves to the struggle. The second *dechoukaj*, to my mind, has as its objective this people's tribunal at which the macoutes will be present, not absent, where the country's wealth will be there available for redistribution to our own people rather than sitting in Swiss bank accounts.

Once again, Aristide's commitment to the cause of justice is crystal clear. Yet once again too, in the language with which he clothes his ideas, there is just enough blurred thinking and ambiguous use of metaphor to feed the fears of his enemies. Just what is this 'people's tribunal' which he seems to offer as the key to the whole process of establishing justice in post-Duvalierist Haiti? Is it the summary justice meted out (as so often in the first 'operation *dechoukaj*') on the streets? If not, just how will Haiti's creaking judicial system cope with what would be complicated and highly-charged trials? Can such a thing as a fair trial be envisaged in a Haiti so recently freed from nearly thirty years of dictatorship? And just how much confidence would any macoute feel in Aristide's promise that he might hope for an eventual 'return to the table' after paying his just dues to society? It is very easy to see how Aristide's public discourse can both be analysed for proof of his commitment to non-violence and constitutional solutions to the country's problems and, at the very same time, feed the fears of a powerful group of people who identify this virulent priest as a populist demagogue capable of pulling down the pillars of the national edifice they've built and controlled for generations.

Just a few months after this interview, when the Jean Rabel incident and the Salesian decision to move Aristide to another parish had created a very charged atmosphere across the country, a government minister broadcast a stinging criticism of a speech made by the priest in the north of Haiti. The government minister (the Minister of Information) was Gérard Noël. He was well remembered for his very close relationship with François Duvalier and also with Clément Barbot, one of PapaDoc's most feared henchmen, who'd founded the Tontons Macoutes. There were many people still living who'd been witnesses when Noël had set fire to Jérémie's secondary school in 1957. He was greatly angered by Aristide's actions and he chose this moment to launch into him with a 'report' of a sermon preached in Cap Haitien. According to the minister, Aristide had said that in the country's present situation, it wasn't elections that they were interested in but revolution, total revolution. Noël went on to allege that Aristide had stated that all the towns in the land except Cap Haitien were to be 'mobilized'. Everybody was urged to get hold of an *arme à feu* (gun) to be ready for the armed struggle being actively envisaged.

Aristide was stung by these accusations and penned a letter of rebuttal immediately. *Radio Soleil* gave him air time and newspapers gave him space to defend himself: 'You're lying Mr Minister, as can be clearly proved by the tape recording (and the video recording too) of the event you so wantonly misreport. This defamation of my character is the best a terrorist government that wants to discredit me can come up with. You deserve to be called Minister of Disinformation. Nobody should put much faith in this particular *Père Noël* [Father Christmas—a play on the Minister's name].'

This was the first of a number of attempts to discredit Aristide by misreporting him. The allegations were blatantly false. Yet they took some people in, resonating as they did with deep-seated fears about the crypto-communism that the priest was supposed to be peddling. Even intelligent people found themselves unable to apply their powers of analysis to the facts of the case. They believed outright lies simply because those lies reinforced the image of Aristide they were building in their minds. And once these new lies contributed to a further strengthening of an already distorted image, a kind of vicious circle was created. It became more and more difficult with each successive round of allegation and counter-allegation to distinguish truth from falsehood. Aristide didn't for a moment countenance armed violence or 'revolution' in any Marxist sense. But it is not at all difficult to see how the blurred edges and the ambiguities contained within just about all his public utterances could be construed for propaganda purposes by his opponents. His rhetorical style gave one hostage after another to fortune. The Noël outburst was the first of a number of such incidents, some of which came at critical moments in the political life of the nation and were to contribute mightily to the course of events in the future.

In late 1987 attention turned towards the elections planned for 29 November. The atmosphere was hardly propitious. In August, Louis-Eugène Athis, a candidate for the presidency, was killed in Léogane (about fifteen miles from Port-au-Prince). Although no charges were ever brought, it was widely believed that his murderer was the army chief in Léogane, who did nothing to dispel this suspicion by his flight to the neighbouring Dominican Republic. Not long after the assassination of Athis, an attempt was made on another prominent politician, Bernard Sansaricq. He had dared to accuse Williams Regala, a member of the ruling army clique, of being responsible for one of the worst incidents in the whole of PapaDoc's time in power, a massacre verging on genocide which took place in Jérémie in 1964. Jérémie had been the last major city to be whipped into line by Duvalier. An unusually strong mulatto élite lived there and the Tontons Macoutes had moved in to burn, rape and pillage them into submission. Regala was certainly implicated in all this but clearly didn't appreciate having it all raked up again so long after the event. Sansaricq was obliged to take cover as Regala turned on him with fury. And then, in October 1987, a third incident took place. Yves Volel, an ex-officer in the Haitian army and another candidate for the presidency, was shot dead in broad daylight in the very precincts of the police headquarters in downtown Port-au-Prince.

The Bishops' Conference weighed in heavily on the matter of Volel's murder. They attacked the CNG, the ruling junta, for allowing an atmosphere of fear to develop. They were critical of the number of people associated with the old régime who'd chosen to run for office in the forthcoming election, suggesting that this was a cynical attempt to perpetuate their hold on power. They regretted the number of political parties, each seemingly set up to give an organizational base for the various candidates for presidential office. They regretted the lack of political development present in Haiti and urged everyone to avoid the shedding of blood.

Even while the Bishops were coming out with these lofty statements, however, they were clearly hardening their position against grassroots aspirations. Monsignor Louis Kébreau, about to be appointed auxiliary bishop of Port-au-Prince, offered a prayer in the comfortable Pétionville parish church which said: 'O God, distance us from everything popular...' a clear reference to the *Ti Legliz* and other popular movements.

Throughout this time of preparation for the elections, a clear frontrunner for the presidency was Baptist minister Sylvio Claude. Claude was a veteran of the struggle against the Duvalier régime and, over a period stretching back into the mid 1970s, had been at various times beaten up, thrown into prison, threatened and (finally) exiled. He'd founded the Haitian Christian Democratic Party and was enormously well-liked by Haiti's poorer population. His policies were decidedly 'left-of-centre' and there was real worry on the part of the Americans that he might win the election. Or perhaps Gérard Gourgue might pull it off. Gourgue was little better than Claude from an American point of view. He was a veteran campaigner for human rights and had himself been beaten up and intimidated over the years. But he'd kept up his opposition to Duvalier. Both Claude and Gourgue would have raised the spectre of communism in the eyes of those who suffered apoplexy at the very thought of such a possibility. This was before the fall of the Berlin Wall and the collapse of communism. Cold War polarizations still shaped the prevailing world order and even in humble Haiti, the prospect of a populist winning the November elections was viewed with extremely poor grace by the local superpower. The proximity of Cuba contributed repeatedly to distortions and exaggerations in the way Washington assessed what was happening in Haiti.

The recently endorsed Constitution had a clause which stipulated that no person who'd had direct connections with the Duvalier régime could stand in the November poll. The Electoral Council had to implement this provision and some of its decisions were causing a huge backlash. Wild accusations were flying around. One issue of the right-wing weekly *Le Petit Samedi Soir* ran an article entitled 'Members of the Electoral Council face Prospect of Hard Labour for Life', an extraordinarily virulent attack on those who were risking their lives to see that the elections took place. They were accused of acting against the national interests by excluding certain Duvalierists from standing in the elections. In the eyes of some right-wingers, this was nothing less than high treason, hence the mention of hard labour for life as an appropriate punishment. It was all very fevered and hardly promised a calm electoral exercise.

Meanwhile, Aristide was putting distance between himself and the whole thing. He denounced an article in the *New York Times* whose analysis of the forthcoming Haitian election took the form of a syllogism running something like this:

Elections are necessary to bring order to Haiti's chaos;
The military junta is best placed to bring order out of chaos;
Therefore, it would be best if somehow the election were won by people in sympathy with the army.

Aristide was furious. He saw clearly that this line of thinking was going to threaten any chance of a decent and fair election. He had no doubts whatsoever that the assassinations and campaign of terror that preceded the election were directly attributable to the army. Consequently, he could not even begin to believe that Namphy or his grim co-leader Regala would ever allow the polling to take place in an atmosphere of peace. 'If elections are held with this government still in power,' he warned, 'many many people will perish and disappear and all over Haiti people will die like flies.' And that's just how things turned out.

I saw the events of November 1987 at close quarters. I was there as an observer, part of a team put together under the auspices of the World Council of Churches and the Caribbean Conference of Churches. Cap Haitien was to have been my patch for this task. But the military junta were making things difficult. Roads out of Port-au-Prince were closed and no planes were flying to the provinces. There wasn't even transport for essential election matériel. At the airport on the eve of the poll, still trying to find a way to get to Cap Haitien, I met Bishop François Gayot who'd just flown in from a visit to Rome. A cortège of vehicles was awaiting him and it was clear he intended reaching Cap Haitien by road. Since we know each other quite well, I tried to scrounge a lift, but all available places were taken. In the end it was as much as I could do to get a ride back from the airport into Port-au-Prince. An eerie silence was fast descending on the normally chaotic capital city. There weren't even any taxis or gaudy *taptaps* (local buses). This meant I couldn't get back to the friend's house where I was staying. So I found a place at the Holiday Inn in the very heart of Port-au-Prince, right opposite the presidential palace. A huge contingent of journalists were billeted there, people from all the major newspapers and television networks in Europe and the United States. We all sensed that there was trouble in the air.

At three o'clock in the morning, our sleep was rudely shattered by a huge explosion. A petrol station right alongside the hotel had been set alight. Flames and heavy acrid smoke shot into the air. Bleary-eyed we got out of bed only to find that the electricity supply had been cut off. Not only that, machine-guns were stuttering their unwelcome rhythms, though no one knew whether they were being directed towards us or at some other target. They were too close for comfort, however, and we resorted to getting our clothes on whilst lying on the floor. I for one was scared out of my mind.

We waited for the first light. Then the hardened journalists, veterans of many an international incident, went off in search of something to report. A fire brigade engine went screaming through the deserted city centre and the pack set off in hot pursuit. Polling stations opened on time. But those queuing to vote were soon put to rout. Unmarked cars raced through the city carrying armed gunmen intent on putting an end to the election at any cost. They fired indiscriminately on innocent people standing in line to vote and came back with machetes to finish off their brutal work. At the Bellegarde-Argentine school in Ruelle Vaillant they killed dozens of people including women and children. They also shot at journalists. In the Holiday Inn we saw British reporter Geoff Smith brought back with a bullet in his leg. A young Dominican journalist was killed. Only a heavy tackle by a correspondent from the *Miami Herald* saved me from being on the wrong end of a bullet. And then a truck full of mangled bodies, victims of that murderous morning, drove up and stood in front of the Holiday Inn for a short while; it seemed like a cynical message from the Haitian junta, a message intended to make crystal clear just who was in charge and just how little they cared about world opinion. There was chaos everywhere, to say nothing of utter dejection, and, by nine o'clock, the election was officially abandoned.

In the course of that Sunday morning, a group of us had had to rescue my old friend Alain Rocourt (head of Haiti's Methodist church and treasurer of the Electoral Council) from a siege that had been laid against him. His house had been strafed with machine-gun bullets and attacked with grenades. Miraculously, he and his wife Marlène, and other members of the family, escaped without injury. But he became a wanted man and had to be whisked off into the hills where he was moved from house to house to avoid being picked up. Eventually he and his family were slipped into exile in Miami.

That grim morning in Port-au-Prince, I saw contingents of soldiers strategically placed who could quite easily have guaranteed order and dealt with the desperados who were wreaking death and destruction. But they held their fire. There was no doubt whatsoever in my mind that the army was under orders not to interfere. Truckfuls of soldiers simply enjoyed a ringside view as innocent fellow countrymen and women were mown down in front of them. Geoff Smith did a great deal of investigative journalism in subsequent weeks and months. He got statements from well-placed sources that more than hinted at an American readiness to look the other way while the atrocities took place; or worse, that American money had actually paid for the services of the murderous gunmen.

Aristide, like so many others that day, was holed up in hiding, far from the scene of the action. But he was angry that everything he'd forecast so accurately had come to pass. In conversation with Amy Wilentz, he didn't mince his words:

> The people of Ruelle Vaillant were sent to die a brutal, criminal death. Who is responsible? First and foremost, the butchers who came with their machine-guns and machetes. But the candidates too must accept their share of the blame. Who encouraged these people, these poor, innocent victims, to believe in false prophets, false elections? The candidates, the CEP, the Americans. We have said all along that there is no possibility for free elections under this criminal, Namphy. The Haitian people should not have been led into this trap, this electoral trap from which there was finally no exit but a bloody death.

None of the outcry that followed in the next few days deterred the National Governing Council from pushing forward with its own plans for the country's future. They abolished the Electoral Council and then published an electoral law announcing another round of 'elections'. This was held on 17 January. Very few people voted; in many polling stations, there weren't even ballot papers available. This farcical exercise produced a new president of Haiti, Dr Leslie Manigat. The 59-year-old Manigat had been a junior official in the Ministry of Foreign Affairs as long ago as 1953. He'd been a staunch supporter of François Duvalier too until, after a disagreement between them, he was forced into exile in 1963. He taught in universities in Mexico, Trinidad, Venezuela, France and the United States. He considered himself to be an accomplished politician yet, by the mere act of making himself available for this farcical election, he effectively revealed himself to most observers to be no more than a self-seeking opportunist. He came into power by doing a deal with that part of the army run by Colonel Jean-Claude Paul and thought by this means to be able to keep a control over General Henri Namphy and his right hand man Colonel Prosper Avril who was head of the presidential guard. But this professor of political theory revealed himself an utter novice in the arts of political practice. The moment his attempts to impose his will felt uncomfortable to the army they just kicked him out with impunity. By June, Namphy and Co. were back in charge and this time they were grimly determined to withstand any further pressure to move in the direction of democratic and civilian rule.

For all members of popular organizations and the *Ti Legliz* this was a bad time. Namphy's hit squads roved the streets by day and night disposing of anyone who got in the way. A Canadian priest was ordered out of Haiti for refusing to supply a list of the names of his congregation. Jean-Baptiste Chavannes, a peasant leader from the Central Plateau, was arrested and beaten. Children who'd fled to *Lafanmi Selavi*, the children's care centre founded by Aristide, after the hit squads had burned their houses or opened fire in their neighbourhoods, were arrested and taken to Fort Dimanche for a thrashing. Journalists were hunted down and radical priests spent half their time in hiding. It was a time of great fear.

In March 1988 a Miami grand jury had indicted Colonel Jean-Claude Paul on charges of conspiring to export narcotics to the United States. Certainly, Paul was making fast money somewhere—he was widely suspected of masterminding a flourishing traffic in cocaine—to keep his soldiers in the main downtown barracks, the Casernes Dessalines, in fighting trim.

The US government decided to withhold aid to Haiti until the government agreed to extradite Paul to face trial in Florida. Paul began to worry that Namphy and his second-in-command Avril would betray him in order to get the aid revenues flowing again. This unresolved tension at the heart of the junta made the already uncertain times even more fraught. It was a time for people like Aristide to lie low. He wrote:

> During this time of nightmare, when the light of life and the light of solidarity burned at their lowest intensity, we tried to keep hope alive in the hearts of the people... Hope is always there, even in the darkest times, no matter how heavily the boots of the army tread upon it in their effort to stamp it out. Hope is there like a smouldering fire that cannot be extinguished. The fire is there beneath the earth —like the fire of a charcoal pit—and all it takes is a little air, a little oxygen, a bit of fanning to make it light up and explode and burst through the surface like a refiner's fire... We tried to keep that hope alive in those dark days, to help the people think in useful ways about their future... It was not an easy task.

It was during this time too that the papal nuncio began to display a clear dislike for Aristide. In August another gunman who seemed to have designs on Aristide was discovered. When this would-be assassin had been disarmed by a number of young people at the St John Bosco Church, Aristide took the gun and bullets to the nuncio for verification. He'd done this on previous occasions too, but this time he found he was not welcome. Instead, he had to take the exhibits to a Justice of the Peace. This new note in the relationship between Aristide and the nuncio marked an ominous development in the Roman Catholic Church's policy in Haiti.

On 23 August, Aristide celebrated a special thanksgiving mass to commemorate the anniversary of his deliverance (together with his friends and colleagues) at Freycineau. He preached a sermon on the subject 'Walking in the light of Christ', taking as his biblical text the story of the healing of the man born blind in the ninth chapter of St John's Gospel. He was especially keen to develop the theme of the way people with perfectly good eyesight can often seem to be blind while those who cannot see (in the physical sense) often retain clear-minded powers of comprehension. Then he started to apply this insight. First, in dialogue with his congregation, he itemized those places where people were suffering at that time at the hands of 'blind' authorities who clearly had no understanding at all of just where the will or interests of the people lay. In Grand Goave, Hinche, Papaye, Dichiti and Labadie people were being killed by these unseeing, unenlightened authorities. And it was no good asking God to help. 'The Lord says to us: "Don't ask me this kind of question any more. Ask yourselves the question: When are we going to wrap our faith and our commitment together to build a people's church with a people's power that will boil over and become a revolution?" '

In the course of the sermon, one member of the congregation made the allegation that it was a bishop (Monsignor Colimon of Port-de-Paix) who had called for the Jean Rabel massacre the previous year. And others went on to suggest that a number of the bishops would not have been unhappy if Aristide and his companions had perished at Freycineau. 'But are there no exceptions among the bishops?' Aristide asked. The congregation named Romélus, Poulard and Lafontant. This led Aristide to declare that there were bishops, priests and nuns who 'sat at the table' and also bishops, priests and nuns who remained under the table 'with the people'. Those who sat at the table did so in the company of the army and the bourgeoisie. One day the table would have to be upended to allow it to be re-set in a way that would allow everyone to sit around it. 'If we work to love our enemies,' Aristide declared, 'then how could we come to hate the bishops? We love them.

But we love to tell the truth too. We do not love everything the bishops do. We cannot applaud them unless we like what they do. We cannot lie while we are at prayer.' And then the preacher rose to his climax; 'I have come into the world for a judgment, to make a distinction, to create a division. That is what Jesus said. It was in order to create a real unity that Jesus divided those who accept the truth from those who refuse it. The Pharisees refused the truth; Jesus put them aside. *It is the same evangelical power that causes us to speak the way we speak and act the way we act* [my italics]. The will of Jesus was to gather all of his little ones together—in unity and in truth—not a unity in untruth, but a unity in truth. Then we will be able to worship Jesus who helps us build unity in truth, who helps us construct the church of those who love truth.'

These words give no more than a flavour of Aristide's preaching. The whole discourse would have taken place in the form of an intense conversation between the preacher and his congregation. There would have been lots of humour, clever repartee, interrogation, gasps of surprise and sighs of recognition and sorrow. Aristide's sermons were organic as well as dynamic, breathing organisms pulsating with life. This was hardly the most propitious of times for such vituperative, accusatory, waspish sermons. And the way Aristide claimed the teaching of Jesus as validation for his social and political stances is a clear statement of his understanding that he was engaged in nothing less than a crusade for moral righteousness. Every time he preached in this way, of course, he was putting his life on the line. It was only a matter of time before his enemies would be stung into action again.

By this time (September 1988), Aristide's residence at St John Bosco was being guarded by dogs and alarms. He still undertook the daily journeys across the city to the *Lafanmi Selavi* clinic. But for all the calm exterior, he was aware that things had reached a pitch, that his opponents had become mortal enemies and that he should expect some kind of response from them soon. After all, his was the only public opposition to the régime. It was to him that people turned when the going was tough. He preached sharp sermons at masses to commemorate the life of an assassinated lawyer (Lafontant Joseph), the anniversary of the Jean Rabel massacre, the landing of US marines on Haitian soil in 1915, and (as we saw above) the anniversary of the attempt to kill him at Freycineau. People were beginning to paint messages on their walls *Nou vle Titid*, we want Aristide. All other voices had been silenced; all other political opponents of the régime were in hiding.

On Tuesday 6 September, some men laid siege to Aristide's church, firing guns and throwing rocks. The incident lasted almost four hours. The men left, threatening to return the following Sunday. Rumours came thick and fast. Friends of Aristide in the army warned him that something was afoot. The main morning mass on Sunday 11 September was supposed to be a commemoration of the 1987 Constitution which the junta had suspended after the aborted election in November of that year, but there was keen debate whether to go ahead with it. The young people made the decision for Aristide: the mass was to go ahead if sufficient people turned up. Those coming to the service had all been asked to wear white to show their support of the Constitution. Thus, the matter was left open. But Aristide was very fearful and had even stopped eating.

People started arriving for the service. Some regular worshippers were frightened by a large gang of men on the main road clearly heading for the St John Bosco Church. They were armed with knives, machetes and guns. Some of them were given lifts in lorries belonging to the municipality. The city's mayor, Franck Romain, dedicated Duvalierist and avowed enemy of Aristide, was widely supposed to be the orchestrator of what was about to happen. He was sighted standing by his car just opposite the church, cigar in hand, waiting and watching. Meanwhile the gang were getting ever nearer; the song they were singing said, quite simply: *Jodi-a se jou malè*, today is an accursed day.

In his two books, *In the Parish of the Poor* and *Tout Moun se Moun* (Everybody is Somebody), Aristide sets out the way his mind weighed up the pros and cons of whether to proceed with the service that Sunday morning. He speaks now of the 'Calvary' that he felt called to approach, of the courage of his young people and other members of the *Ti Legliz* who wanted at all costs to proceed. But no amount of gloss added after the event can hide the anguish of mind felt by Aristide before he left the vestry to stand in front of his congregation that day. He had strong presentiments of death. Once he'd entered the church, the doors were locked. And the service began.

Amy Wilentz (in *The Rainy Season*) gives a brilliant, circumstantial picture of what happened next. Just at the time when Aristide was readying himself to preach his sermon, an ugly crowd advanced on the church. They were wearing red armbands. They surrounded the building and, just like the previous Tuesday, began hurling rocks and firing shots. Inside the church people held hands and began to sing hymns. Aristide was appealing to them to keep calm. Attempts by local young people to mount a counterattack against the armed gang were easily repulsed. Meanwhile, some of the intruders began to take a hacksaw to the padlocks holding the main doors. They were, apparently, still singing their chilling little song: *jodi-a se jou malè*.

Aristide later described his feelings; he was sure he was living through his last hours. It is clear he was in a stupor, unsure how to act for the best. But the young people took matters into their own hands. They tore his microphone from him and began hauling him off to his house alongside the church, where the doors had been barricaded against the entry of the thugs and people were tending the wounded. Molotov cocktails were being lobbed and soon any remaining semblance of order disappeared. Some thirty men entered the church and mayhem broke loose. They spiked, hacked, speared, chopped, and fired their bullets on any member of the congregation who crossed their line of vision. They dragged the bodies of the dead into the streets and disposed of numbers of them. Later about twenty dead were counted but, as in so many such cases in Haiti, nobody will ever know the real number. And there were the wounded, almost eighty of them. Amongst these was an

American journalist and a heavily pregnant Haitian woman, slit open by the blade of a machete, who lay groaning on the floor of the church, covered in blood. Those who could ran for their lives. And still the slaughter continued. This phase of the incident lasted over an hour.

Several members of the armed gang now went off in search of petrol. They were soon back and pouring the gasoline over the church building as well as over the cars of people who'd come to church that morning. Everything went up in flames, a grim pyre announcing the triumph of evil over every other human force.

Aristide had been pushed and pulled into a room in his house. A number of his young friends had retreated with him as far as an inner courtyard. They locked and barricaded the gates and prepared to defend this refuge against the enraged and outrageous enemies who were now moving in for the kill.

Members of the Port-au-Prince police force and contingents of troops from the Haitian army had been standing near the church throughout this incident. They'd watched. They'd seen every detail unfold in front of their eyes. They hadn't lifted a finger. But now they moved forward. They ringed the burning church and some of them moved towards the inner courtyard where they helped the struggling gunmen force the gates open. There was no shred of a doubt that the so-called forces of law and order were an integral part of the action that day.

Jean-Baptiste Chavannes, organizer of a long-established peasant movement at Papaye on the Central Plateau, had come to St John Bosco that day for an interview with Aristide, a meeting scheduled to take place after the mass. He'd got caught up in the events and had barely escaped from the church with his life. Now he was alongside the priest and refusing to be separated from him. Army officers ordered a search of the house. They and officials from the Criminal Research branch of the police forced their way into the house and began taunting and harassing Chavannes and Aristide. Father Mésidor, the priest at the head of the Haitian Salesians, had somehow managed to be there too. He'd pleaded with the gunmen that they should withdraw. But all in vain. Now silence was the only course open to them. One younger soldier wanted to kill Aristide and held a gun to his chest for several minutes. Yet there was a strange reluctance to kill him. After several more minutes of uneasy waiting, disappointed that they'd not found the cache of arms that General Namphy had confidently promised them, the whole lot of them left. And Aristide, sitting between two Salesian nuns and with his Salesian superior and his friend Chavannes also on board, was driven away through a large lowering crowd into a distant refuge in the hills.

Wilentz suggests that the papal nuncio had refused to come to the scene when telephoned. He left such matters to the Red Cross, he said. But there are plenty of reports that seem to suggest that he came down from his magnificent mountain retreat at some time during the siege. Indeed, he and Monsignor Wolff Ligondé seem to have installed themselves in the residence of the Salesian sisters where they were able to see just about everything that was happening. It is a startling thought that senior church officials, the city mayor, officers from the army and police were all watching this ghastly event as if it were some kind of entertainment. As Aristide put it later: 'The scene would have been dramatically ordinary if it had not been seen or observed by so many passive witnesses. At a distance of a few dozen yards, the men of the church, headed by the apostolic nuncio, viewed the scene from afar... [No one] intervened to stop the massacre.'

The day after the St John Bosco atrocity, a group of men forced their way into the maternity ward of the State Hospital. They were looking for the pregnant woman who'd been wounded the previous day. They made all the women on the ward lift the sheets covering them; they were clearly wanting to finish off a task they'd begun the previous day. But the wounded woman had been taken to a mission hospital many miles away from Port-au-Prince. It was there that, by a Caesarian operation, her baby was born. It was a girl and they named her Esperancia, Hope, a quality that cannot be killed even by the forces of evil itself.

Later that same day, another group of men (with a woman this time) appeared in the studios of Haiti's television company. They boasted that it was they who'd been at the heart of the previous day's events and that they'd not hesitate to do it all again. Once again, it is Amy Wilentz who captures the mood of this macabre interview. A large young man made it clear he wanted to put an end to Aristide. He went on: 'Any parish that allows Aristide to celebrate a mass, only a bunch of corpses will attend it. It's Father Aristide that makes us do this... He isn't worthy to be in the country... He can hide wherever he wants to but, when he appears, we will kill, we will burn down the church... only corpses will hear him speak.' Then in a grim parody of the wall slogans that were appearing everywhere to show support for Aristide, this young thug declared, '*Nou vle Titid*, we want Aristide.'

The young woman who was in the group appearing on television was then asked how she could possibly condone the attack on the pregnant woman and the innocent child she was carrying. The young woman wasn't abashed. She replied: 'That pregnant woman, her baby, they are not innocent. They were there to hear Aristide. That makes them guilty. Anyone who listens to this Aristide, they deserve what they get. If you were innocent, you'd stay home.'

Franck Romain, Mayor of Port-au-Prince, denied any responsibility for the massacre. But he was in no doubt that Aristide had deserved what he got. In a radio interview he summed up his feelings with a simple text from scripture: '*Qui sème le vent, récolte la tempête*,' he said, 'Whoever sows the wind, reaps the whirlwind.'

The next few days were hectic. Hurricane Gilbert swept Haiti with its own savage destruction the very night of the massacre. But the cyclone also saved many potential victims from further acts of barbarity by driving would-be assassins indoors and making roads impassable. It also gave a shocked population time to draw breath. The events of 11 and 12 September had filled people, even those accustomed to horror, with deep disgust. In the night of 16 and 17 September, some junior officers in the army ousted General Namphy and installed themselves at the head of the military government. Within a few days, however, realizing there was no way they could even begin the task of governing the country, they appealed to Prosper Avril, head of the presidential guard. So the military junta had a new head—another battle-hardened, long-serving Duvalierist.

When the poor people of Port-au-Prince, all those who lived in Cité Soleil and La Saline, came out of their state of shock, they were bristling with anger at all that had happened. They hunted down anyone they could identify as members of the group who'd taken part in the 11 September massacre. In particular they seized Gros Schiller, the man who'd done most of the boastful speaking in the infamous television interview. In front of the burned-out wreck of the St John Bosco Church, the crowd burned Schiller and several others alive. The smell of human flesh roasting in the streets of Port-au-Prince added another grim detail to the narrative of this ugly incident.

Meanwhile, Avril was moving fast to consolidate his hold on power. He sacked large numbers of army officers including the immensely powerful Colonel Jean-Claude Paul. A few weeks later, Paul (now of no further interest to the drug barons who'd previously financed his operation) was poisoned, an ironic end to a cruel life. But a whole raft of people in the army and in civil society were beginning to swear their support for Avril. And he seemed to be making serious efforts to consult a wide swathe of political leaders as he searched for a way forward. With great courtesy, he received a number of such leaders in the presidential palace. Thus Sylvio Claude, Marc Bazin, Serge Gilles, Louis Dejoie, Gérard Gourgue came and went. So too did delegations from KID, CATH (both workers' groupings), and young people from St John Bosco. He even invited René Théodore and Max Bourjolly of the Haitian Communist Party, the first time this had ever happened since the foundation of their party in 1934. Avril was doing his level best to give an impression of transparency and goodwill. But there were those who doubted his intentions. They suspected that this show of tolerance and openness was little more than window-dressing, a bid to win international approval and to re-start the flow of foreign aid.

The church too was moving to get its act tidied up. Father Mésidor, Haitian superior of the Salesians, was fighting a battle to keep Aristide within the Order. But the bishops didn't want him and the nuncio was utterly opposed. The Salesian provincial superior who came from the Dominican Republic had had enough of him. The Vatican itself seems too to have made its feelings known. And so, by early December, Aristide had been expelled from the Salesian order and his licence to preach and serve a parish had been withdrawn. This verdict came down with no right of appeal. Aristide was cast out. The decree for his dismissal declared that 'his attitude has had a negative effect on his colleagues... his selfishness demonstrates a lack of sincerity and of a religious and priestly consciousness... [He is incapable] of a sincere and fruitful dialogue, [but rather shows a preference for] incitement to hatred and violence, a glorifying of class struggle... and the profanation of the liturgy... Father Jean-Bertrand Aristide has always preferred to distance himself from the concrete demands of community, becoming a protagonist in the destabilization of the community of the faithful; and he has done so consistently in a public and incisive manner, so that the organs of the press and various interest groups latch on to him as the 'leader of the popular church' in Haiti...'

The bishops had been able to banish Aristide from Haiti when his radical views became problematical in 1982. He was only recently ordained then and there was no way he could object to whatever measures they chose to impose on him. But when they'd wanted to get rid of him in May 1986 and August 1987, the hierarchy had had less success. On both those occasions, they underestimated the power of the people. But now, in September 1988, the expulsion of Aristide was again on the cards. The bishops had put out a statement declaring that they and the nuncio were as one. And they laid into the popular church, dismissing it as a tool for agitators whose real agenda was to establish a church with no hierarchy, bishops, or Pope. The Port-au-Prince weekly *Haiti en Marche*, in its comment on this unprecedented attack on the *Ti Legliz*, said with stark simplicity, 'The church has just committed suicide.'

The bishops announced that Aristide had been ordered to leave Haiti by 17 October at the latest. But once again this order was frustrated by the mass response of huge numbers of people who took to the streets and brought Port-au-Prince to a halt. *Radio Soleil* announced that Aristide was still in Haiti because, *'il se trouve dans l'impossibilité de partir*, it is physically impossible for him to leave'. And this gesture of popular support led to Aristide staying in Haiti. For all those who'd wanted to get rid of him, they found the situation that now confronted them the worst of all possible worlds. There was Aristide, stripped of his membership of the Salesians, his licence to preach revoked, out and about with nothing to do. It should have surprised no one that he became a loose cannon. Neither an assassin's bullet nor an archbishop's command had been able to dispose of him. So he remained in Haiti with time on his hands and accountable to nobody. This was an explosive combination.

In the immediate aftermath of the St John Bosco massacre, there wasn't much he could get up to, however. He suffered what has come to be known as post-trauma depression. He was haunted by memories of the massacre. He was kept in total isolation for several days after the event, unable to hear any news or receive any visitors. He had nightmares. He cried for hours on end. He needed to be drugged with anti-depressants as he re-lived everything that had happened. He blamed himself for all that suffering, all those deaths. He was on the point of total nervous collapse. And it was while he was in this state that his superiors got him to sign a letter in which he agreed to be transferred from Haiti.

It took several days for Aristide to regain his composure and anything like his old strength. He didn't appear in public until 25 September when a large crowd thronged outside the Salesian residence in Pétionville, about five miles outside Port-au-Prince and a thousand feet above the hot, dusty capital city.

Amy Wilentz has given a graphic description of his appearance on that occasion. 'Aristide was supported on either side by priests,' she writes. 'He walked shakily. His white guayabera hung from his shoulders as though a wire hanger were all that was holding it up. His cheeks were hollow, and his eyes closed. When he raised a hand to salute the crowd, his arm had to be held at the elbow. He had no strength. He stood at the edge of the balcony, holding on to a ledge, and the crowd fell to its knees. "Let the Holy Spirit descend on us," they sang, "we have one mission for Haiti." Tears dropped from his closed eyes.' He was a heartbroken, traumatized, sick man. He was soon whisked away again from view.

Two weeks after the St John Bosco catastrophe, the Haitian bishops finally put out a statement. They condemned the attack without mentioning either the church or Aristide by name. They went on to appeal for a 'disarming of the Tontons Macoutes and the exclusion from government service of all who in any guise contributed actively to the consolidation and perpetuation of the dictatorial system over the past thirty years'. This was a clear signal from the hierarchy that new ways of governing Haiti were desperately needed. But they put out this message at the very time they were taking measures to send Aristide away from Haiti. For the people, these two positions (for democracy and against Aristide) would have seemed mutually contradictory.

On 2 October, three weeks after the massacre, Aristide felt well enough to address the public in a radio message. While his voice was thin and he'd clearly not recovered his full strength, the message was unambiguous and full of the familiar tactics which included naming those offending the criteria of common justice. It was also a carefully nuanced speech, larded with irony. He announced that the most recent message he'd received from Rome had accorded him the right to remain in Haiti. He was always ready, he said, to obey 'the Lord, the Salesian provincial delegate, and the people of God' with all his heart. Since the people and the Salesian delegate were frequently asking for radically different things, this statement makes it difficult to work out how Aristide might resolve such tension. Just how God fitted into it all is also difficult to deduce except that Aristide usually identified God's will with the people's desires. So the poor old Salesian superior could reckon himself outvoted!

Aristide rejoiced at the *coup d'état*, calling it an Easter Sunday after the day of death he'd endured at St John Bosco. He called on serving soldiers to remain loyal to the people and looked forward to a clean-up throughout the country. Then he challenged the new administration of Prosper Avril to achieve a number of objectives within the first month of their tenure of power. This harping on 'the seventeenth of October' was to become very ironical when the bishops came to choose the very same day for his removal from Haiti. But this was how he addressed the Haitian public:

My people:
–Do you believe that before the seventeenth of October, one month to the day after the seventeenth of September, Fort Dimanche cannot be clean?
–Do you believe that before the seventeenth of October, Franck Romain cannot be brought before the people of La Saline to be judged in accordance with the law in a people's court?
–Do you believe that before the seventeenth of October, they don't have time to detach the attachés [armed thugs operating under the protection of the army] who are hidden with their heavy arms; to disarm, arrest, and begin to judge in an extraordinary trial all the criminals who are soaked through with the massacres at Fort Dimanche, Jean Rabel, Danty, Ruelle Vaillant, Labadie, St John Bosco, and the assassination of Louis-Eugène Athis, Yves Volel, Lafontant Joseph, and the rest?
–Do you believe that before the seventeenth of October, they cannot clean up the government-run television and radio stations?

And so he continued to probe and urge the people to hold the new government to account. Then he turned his words directly to the new head of state:

> General-president, it's your turn.
> Many valiant soldiers have taken their turn.
> Many Duvalierist ministers have lost the game.
> It's your turn to play, before a people
> who have no confidence in you.

Then he urged Avril to discharge Duvalierist officers from the ranks of the armed forces, to refuse pressure from the United States to make the army disloyal to the people, to reorganize the various units of the army, and to see to it that justice is offered to the people for all the outrages they have suffered.

Aristide ended this forthright speech with an incantation that verges on the poetical. All the way through his oration, it had been unclear whether this was intended as a sermon or a political speech. That confusion continued right through the last paragraph:

> When we get to [our] distant [destination]
> we will have made a worthy revolution.
> We will have upset the table of privilege so that we too
>   will be
> welcome to sit and eat.
> We have come from far away in order to arrive at a
>   remote destination.
> We want to get there.
> We can get there.
> We will get there,
> in the name of Jesus who has helped us
> come all that great distance to arrive at our rightful
>   destination,
> Amen.

The close juxtapositioning of 'the name of Jesus' and 'a worthy revolution'; the notion of upsetting 'the table of privilege' and claiming 'the help of the Holy Spirit' makes for a heady mix. It is as if the final 'Amen' ought to be spoken with a clenched fist punching the air. This is another example of Aristide's public discourse feeding different expectations, titillating different taste buds. And the only unanswered question relates to how deliberate his choice of words may have been.

And so the eventful year 1988 drew to its close. Slogans painted on walls all over Port-au-Prince expressed the people's increasing confidence in the little priest. *Aristid ou lanmo*, Aristide or Death (an echo of one of the great shouts of the Haitian struggle for independence in the 1790s); *Nons-la pou Wom*, *Titid pou Lasalin*, The nuncio represents Rome, Aristide La Saline; *Aristid kanpe, pale, sikile ak pèp-la*, Aristide, stand up, speak, circulate among the people. But in these last weeks of a fateful year, it was very difficult for Aristide to circulate among the people. He was in deep hiding, moving regularly from one distant hideout to another, sending occasional cassette tapes to radio stations, making his presence felt but without making a public appearance. It was tantalizing for his opponents. But it was also a mode of operation that couldn't last for ever.

Aristide was no longer living in community with his fellow Salesians. He described this as tantamount to a marriage breakup. From time to time he stayed with the *Lafanmi Selavi*, in the home for abandoned children he'd founded a few years earlier. He'd play his guitar and help with the various programmes. But he wasn't secure enough to make this his regular pattern. He encouraged his friends to go on with their commitment to *dechoukaj* (uprooting), urging them to refuse to live under a system of dictatorship. A number of his friends were journalists with one or another of the weekly newspapers that were published amongst the Haitian diaspora in Miami or New York but distributed widely within Haiti, or else in the world of radio. Radio stations kept a running commentary on what was going on across the republic and kept the whole population on its toes through the very difficult months of 1989. But the Catholic hierarchy effectively withdrew from this work when they dismissed the entire staff of their own station,

Radio Soleil, whose work they criticized for being too political.

In November, three popular leaders were dragged into a studio and shown on national television accused of high treason. Jean-Auguste Mesyeux was the executive secretary of CATH (Centre Autonome des Travailleurs Haitiens), a trade union. He'd been accused earlier that same year of causing an explosion during the carnival. With him was Marino Etienne, leader of OP-17 (Organisation Populaire du 17 Septembre), a campaigning organization set up at the time of the *coup d'état* that brought Prosper Avril into power. And the third accused man was Evans Paul, leader of KID (Conféderation Unité Démocratique/*Konfederasyon Inite Demokratik*), another campaigning group. These three were tortured and given a severe beating. It was in a battered state that they were shown on television and accused of plotting against the Avril government. Their bruises and wounds were intended to serve as a warning to others. They were taken straight from the television studio to prison. This incident illustrates the climate of those times.

Once again (as in September 1988), this cynical use of television to put the tactics and determination of the régime on display proved to be counter-productive. It led to a series of general strikes and hunger strikes in solidarity with the three prisoners. There was a countrywide climate of discontent which boded ill for the ruling junta. The government's response was to make widespread arrests and these included leaders of political parties, people like Max Bourjolly (one of the general secretaries of the Haitian Communist Party), Serge Gilles and Hubert de Ronceray (leaders of two other parties). But all this simply gave a degree of unity to those opposing the régime that they'd never had before.

If all this unrest didn't spell out an imminent end for Avril and his cronies, the attitude of Alvin Adams, the newly-arrived American ambassador surely did. On the very day of his arrival on Haitian soil, he reminded the military junta that it had taken power with a firm commitment, 'an irrevocable promise' as he put it, to deliver the country into the hands of a freely elected civilian government. To underline this message he quoted a Créole proverb, *bourik chaje pa kampe*, (the loaded donkey doesn't stop—it has to keep moving or else it collapses). Henceforth, Adams was invariably called 'loaded donkey' (*bourik chaje*) wherever he went in Haiti. His message was bitterly resented by Avril, who refused to receive his letters of credentials for several weeks.

A state of emergency was declared in January 1990 and large numbers of arrests were made. Journalists were killed and there was general chaos. Meanwhile, an Electoral Commission was trying to get the country organized for eventual elections. But it all looked very tentative.

Pressure was now brought to bear on the Haitian junta by 'the international community', with France, Canada, Venezuela and the United States proving particularly outspoken. Within the country, newspapers gradually ceased to publish hard news. *Le Matin* was the one exception. Strangely, no one attempted to stop the circulation of the two weeklies published in the United States. At the end of January, *Haiti Progrès* carried the front page headline 'Restoration of Duvalierist Dictatorship', while *Haiti en Marche* declared 'Return to PapaDoc's barbarity'.

The Catholic bishops, in a radio message, condemned the deportations, arrests, disappearances, media-gagging, and torture that had become daily features of life in Haiti and called on the government to make progress towards free and fair elections.

All this combined pressure forced Avril to make concessions. At the end of January he lifted the siege. Soon afterwards he declared an amnesty for political prisoners and freed Mesyeux, Etienne and Paul. He bought himself a little time by spending some money to liven up the carnival and thereby distracted people's attention for a little while. But his end was nigh. Everybody sensed that. Trade Unions, political parties, the churches, the press, the international community, popular groupings, the Electoral Council were all demanding the resignation of Prosper Avril by the end of February. And a few days later (10 March) he was forced to oblige.

The first three months of 1990 were amongst the most fearsome Haiti had experienced. In March alone there were 83 murders and 120 serious injuries registered with CHADEL, a human rights organization. Amongst the dead were several children. Soldiers in an increasingly disorientated army took to an irresponsible use of their weapons. In one such incident, a little girl was shot dead while standing on the balcony of her own home. Meanwhile, on the other side, those resisting the macoutes and the army began to 'necklace' their opponents—putting tyres around an enemy's neck, filling them with petrol and setting fire to them. This became known as the '*père lebrun*' treatment, a name taken from a local firm that retailed used tyres.

With Avril gone, General Hérard Abraham, the army chief of staff, took charge, promising to give way within 72 hours to a civilian government. Father Antoine Adrien, one of Aristide's most trusted friends, showed some astute political skills during this important period in getting a 20-strong Council of State established and a nominee from the Supreme Court of Appeals to act as provisional head of state. This turned out to be Mme Ertha Pascal Trouillot who was sworn in with great acclamation and joy. General Abraham, true to his word, withdrew his soldiers to their barracks. Aristide made a public statement welcoming the new régime and calling for the disarming of all macoutes and their supporters. There was a perceptible change of atmosphere following the departure of Avril and Trouillot made it crystal clear that her task was to get the country organized for elections in the shortest possible period of time.

The changeover of government brought Aristide out into the open again after several months in hiding. And he began a concerted campaign to force the government to take action against those whose very presence in Haiti constituted a threat to the elections now being spoken of again with great frequency. Aristide began to travel widely and found that his reputation had preceded him. Everywhere, he was received with interest and constantly asked whether he had any presidential ambitions. In April he visited Buenos Aires to attend a conference on the plight of street children. 'The authorities have enough evidence,' he said, 'to charge a number of those who have performed criminal acts. Macoutes must be brought to justice before there can be any elections. We cannot trust the army to guarantee our security during elections; we remember 29 November 1987. Those who have brought so much suffering on our people, and whose presence threatens to do so again, must be brought to book.' On this same occasion, he was asked for his views on the *père lebrun*, necklacing. He replied that the use of such weapons should be seen as a sign of the people's despair in the face of a justice system totally unable to protect them: not a word of criticism for this barbaric punishment.

'Justice before elections' was his theme once more when he addressed 5,000 people in Brooklyn, New York, the following month. It was a point he put even more firmly in June while on a visit to Geneva. In a radio interview for *Haiti Inter* he urged the US ambassador to see that justice was attended to before elections were held. He continued, 'Speak of elections when justice can be seen to have been done, please. The macoutes simply have to be disarmed. If you insist on speaking about elections when the prior question on our agenda is that of justice you become accomplices, you deserve to be treated as criminals because these armed bandits are strutting around in front of your very eyes and spitting out death.'

He went from Switzerland to France where he preached to the Haitian community before giving a press conference. His sermon was full of the old vigour, pointed and personal, focused and splenetic. He denounced what he called 'apostolic nuncios who have the characteristics of members of the mafia, people like Paolo Romeo'. He went on to attack 'cowardly bishops like Monsignor François Gayot and Monsignor François-Wolff Ligondé who are so lacking in courage that they won't shout out even when wolves are devouring their sheep under their very eyes in Haiti'. A number of people in his congregation felt uneasy at the directness of parts of this sermon. But, for all that, he was received warmly by Monsignor Gaillot, then still bishop of Evreux (subsequently sacked by the Pope) and Mme Danielle

Mitterrand, wife of the then French president, as well as a number of leading figures in the world of voluntary organizations. In the press conference which followed the mass, Aristide deplored the obsession of both France and the United States with elections when, by ignoring the question of justice, they were in effect giving licence to the death squads to continue and intensify their work. He was afraid that, were elections to take place in the present context, the only kind of government that was likely to emerge would be one designed by the international community which left all loose ends to be tied up by the macoutes forces just as in the past. He then lashed out at Ertha Pascal Trouillot; her fine white robe was stained with the people's blood, he said. After all, she had the power, Aristide suggested (though few people would have agreed with him), to order the army to take measures against the macoutes. But she'd done nothing at all and was as guilty, therefore, as anyone.

This was certainly a vitriolic outburst. Meanwhile, back in Haiti, the Electoral Council was getting on with its task, establishing centres in all the main regions across the republic. Jimmy Carter visited Haiti too and held meetings with a number of leading groups in the business community, amongst politicians, and with the army. He expressed himself satisfied with the prospects of free and fair elections later that year.

It was during that summer that I first met Jean-Bertrand Aristide. He was visiting London and had asked his hosts for some private time with me. We talked extensively about the various events that he'd lived through in the previous couple of years. We spoke Créole most of the time and he became very animated at several points. He was clearly most worried about the possibility that the same thing would happen if elections were held later that year as had happened in 1987. 'There must not be another Ruelle Vaillant,' he said with passion. Then he outlined a plan he'd been considering and wondered if I would help him implement it. He recognized that the main actors in Haiti's drama could easily get themselves into a stalemate. He wanted to find a way out of that eventuality. Someone from outside was needed. He remembered how powerful the Pope's visit had been in 1983. 'But I don't think I stand much chance of getting the Pope to come back,' he said with a wry grin, 'so I thought of the one person whose personality and influence are on a par with the Pope's. I mean Archbishop Desmond Tutu.' He then went on to ask me, on his behalf, to make approaches to Desmond Tutu to see if he would come to Haiti to help refocus the nation's agenda, putting respect for human rights and the thirst for justice on a par with the planning of elections. I was stupefied with this request but heard myself spluttering some kind of agreement. Only when we stood to embrace did I realize how diminutive a figure he cuts. Somehow, in conversation, he seems bigger!

I did indeed make contact with Desmond Tutu and the archbishop showed interest in Aristide's proposal. He recognized that it would be a very difficult task but promised to explore his diary to find out when he could come. But all these plans were soon overtaken by events—in particular, by the return to Haiti of Roger Lafontant.

4 Taking the reins of power

Macoutism was mean men with dark glasses and Uzis, it was Madame Max [one of its leaders] striding about Fort Dimanche with her sidearms and squeezing dying men's genitals, it was big-bellied Roger Lafontant arrogant in blue and red as he crunched security and justice underfoot, and it was even bigger-bellied Jean-Claude Duvalier allowing him to do it. Above all, Macoutism was the core of the Duvalierist dictatorship. And it was the stunting of lives, the stifling of initiative.

Elizabeth Abbott (*Haiti: the first inside account: The Duvaliers and their legacy*) has got the essence of Macoutism in this one short paragraph. And she's rightly placed Roger Lafontant at the heart of all that it stood for. Lafontant ingratiated himself with François Duvalier as early as 1960. On that occasion he was ready to spy on his fellow medical students at Haiti's State University and supply information direct to the president. Many of those he reported in this way 'disappeared' and were subsequently tortured and killed. Lafontant became a doctor but was always more interested in politics than medicine. In 1972, claiming to have inside knowledge of an imminent *coup d'état*, and benefiting from the absence from Haiti of François Duvalier's widow (who was still the power behind her son's throne), he engineered the removal from office of the Minister of the Interior, Luckner Cambronne. And, of course, he got Jean-Claude Duvalier to appoint him in Cambronne's place.

This didn't last long; Simone Duvalier couldn't stand Lafontant. But it put down a marker for the future.

By the early 1980s, Lafontant had become one of Jean-Claude Duvalier's inner circle, one of his 'superministers'. He was a *noiriste*, a believer in the black man's position in Haiti over against the mulattos. He hated Baby Doc's marriage to lighter-skinned Michèle Bennett, feeling that the president had betrayed his father's revolution by this match. Lafontant was a macoute and curried favour among his fellow macoutes by scattering money and favours among them. He was brutal and couldn't care one iota what people outside Haiti thought of him or his methods. He was responsible for untold numbers of disappearances, tortures and executions. When support for the Duvalier régime began to wither in late 1984, Lafontant's response had been to arrest huge numbers of people and to attempt to intimidate them into submission. A year later, the superminister ordered the killing of a foreign Roman Catholic priest at *Radio Soleil* and then he expelled three others. In the end, it all got too much for Duvalier. Everything Lafontant did seemed to incense the people and bring down their anger on his government. So, in September 1985, he sacked his minister and sent him into exile in Canada. A Haitian newspaper got it spot on when it reported: 'Haitian politics is a cruel mother who devours her own children.'

The return of Lafontant in July 1990 was rightly identified by Aristide as a defining moment in Haiti's struggle for accountable government. He blamed Ertha Pascal Trouillot for allowing the Duvalierist thug to come back. But she doesn't seem to have had much choice. Various officials had issued writs for his arrest or decrees forbidding his entry but his friends in the army and the rest of Haiti's civil society saw to it that these efforts were subverted. He claimed to have come back to visit relatives and friends and that he'd no intention of disturbing the preparations then intensively under way for the elections being planned for 16 December. But no one, least of all Aristide, believed him. Soon, carefully orchestrated demonstrations were being held to support his right to stand in the elections. A number of political parties grouped together for a counter-demonstration demanding that the government arrest him. His very presence was a destabilizing influence and the American ambassador said so openly. Aristide made a public statement accusing the provisional president of 'protecting notorious criminals and allowing people responsible for massacring their fellow citizens to circulate with impunity'. By September, Lafontant was openly campaigning for the election. He distributed thousands of photographs of himself over a caption which read: 'The leader of national reconciliation, the apostle of peace.' He claimed to be the only person capable of uniting the energies of the various interest groups in Haiti in order to save the country from 'an almost irreversible débâcle'.

Then, on 14 October, some 10,000 former Duvalierists from all over Haiti gathered together in Port-au-Prince to form a new political party in readiness for the December election. They called it *l'Union pour la Reconstruction Nationale*, the Union for National Reconstruction, and they appointed Roger Lafontant as its leader. He accepted this honour by making a fulsome public appearance escorted by uniformed soldiers and a bodyguard made up of off-duty members of the presidential guard. In his speech, he declared Article 291 of the Haitian Constitution (the one banning anyone who'd worked closely with the Duvalierist system from standing for public office for a period of ten years) 'null and void'. He was defying those who wanted him marginalized from the political process and openly declaring himself available for election.

It is important to get this picture of Roger Lafontant established before continuing Aristide's story. For the whole of the next year, these two were going to be jostling for power. Lafontant's arrival in Haiti focused Aristide's thoughts; he recognized the real enemy. It was the macoute's candidature that pushed Aristide into standing himself. In January 1991, just three weeks after Aristide's election and four weeks before his inauguration as president, Lafontant attempted a *coup d'état* and succeeded in destabilizing Haiti at a very sensitive moment. Six months later, Aristide gave orders that led to Lafontant's arrest. His trial raised one of the great unanswered questions of Aristide's presidency. Was it a fair trial? And Lafontant's death raised another similar question. He was murdered while in prison at the very moment when the coup that toppled Aristide was going on. Who killed him? And on whose orders? Was Aristide implicated in any way?

The destinies of these two men seem closely linked. In them, two different philosophies struggled for contention. Aristide sensed this from the very moment he heard that Lafontant was back in Haiti. Nothing gave greater impetus to his embracing a political future than the strutting presence on Haitian soil of this archetypal representative of the old order.

Throughout the long hot summer of 1990, Aristide spoke consistently against holding elections later that year. And a note of personal criticism of Ertha Pascal Trouillot was repeated again and again in his speeches. Jimmy Carter, former US president, visited Port-au-Prince in July of that year. Aristide declared that Mme Pascal Trouillot wasn't worthy to speak to Mr Carter in the name of the Haitian people; she protected known criminals. The following month, Aristide joined Bishop Willy Romélus in declaring that Haiti was far too insecure for free and fair elections to take place. And, he added, Mme Pascal Trouillot should resign and be replaced by someone more fitted for the task. In September, Aristide again discounted the provisional president's competence to lead the country into elections. She had to be replaced; she was 'a were-wolf' who was collaborating secretly with 'American imperialism' to destabilize the country and make the holding of democratic elections virtually impossible.

All the time he was sounding this critical note, however, he was offering barely disguised hints that he might himself be prepared to take office. He kept on distinguishing between standing as a politician, the representative of a political party or interest group on the one hand, and being 'ready to heed the wish of the people' on the other. During these summer months, it seems as if any thoughts he might have had of taking office were limited to the possibility of replacing Mme Ertha Pascal

Trouillot as provisional head of state for an interim period. The main objectives he might set himself during the time he held power in this way would be in the field of law and order, the establishing of justice and the *dechoukaj*, shaking out, of macoutism. All his speeches during these months declared the need for justice as an essential prerequisite for democratic elections.

This time of speculation and uncertainty was brought to an abrupt end on 16 October by the announcement that Lafontant intended to stand as a candidate for the presidency. Aristide knew that he must now climb down from his fence. He'd had occasion to consult members of the Haitian diaspora in New York and Miami in recent weeks and they'd left him in no doubt that he must stand. But his repeated and strident calls to abandon the electoral process until security was restored made this a difficult step to envisage. Lafontant's announcement gave him the ideal opportunity to offer himself as the only candidate who could unify the nation. He was fond of quoting an adapted form of an old Haitian proverb, *fouchèt divizyon pa bwè soup eleksyon* (you can't drink your electoral soup with a fork). There were scores of 'political parties' on hand, some of them no more than a dozen strong. They were so disparate that the well-financed Lafontant machine could make mincemeat of them. But if someone could harness their energies, pull the various strands together, then, as one experienced journalist put it, a 'confluence of rivulets and then of rivers could feed the torrent that would sweep away, along with the old régime, all those who hesitated to renounce it once and for all'.

Stopping Lafontant was the first and overriding objective. Aristide didn't pretend that he'd never had thoughts of becoming president. In his autobiography he confesses that he'd had such thoughts. But he'd always pushed them away, thinking of himself as a consciousness-raiser or a spokesperson for the oppressed rather than a politician. And no one knew more clearly than he the Haitian love of office, the status and trappings of office for their own sake and as an end in themselves. Yet he had this conviction, a feeling that was fed to him by all those who'd followed him through thick and thin over the last couple of years, that *Titid ak pèp la se marasa*, Aristide and the people are twins, they belong inseparably together. He felt it in his genes that nobody else could adequately articulate the people's aspirations or ensure their participation in Haiti's political future. And so, after a long conversation with his father-in-God, Antoine Adrien, he decided to stand.

In his account of how he reached this decision he distances himself from any idea that he might be a Messiah figure. 'In our day,' he writes, 'there is no Messiah other than the people.' Miracles have to be worked for rather than waited for, there's no room for resignation or fatalism. And if he's deemed a prophet for spelling out such home truths as these then there are plenty of other prophets around too. He wants to get the people organized and ready to work to shape their own destiny. This he sees as a fitting response to his Lord. 'Unlike those who see Jesus as a divine being,' he writes, 'I discern in him before anything else someone who was fully human. It is out of that human dimension that the divine in him is revealed. He was so human that he was God: I share that theological vision. *That is why I finally agreed to discover and experience the complementarity between the priest and the president* [my italics]. If the people can mobilize so much energy for its priest-candidate, it is because they see in him a human being capable of playing a new political role and advancing toward a country characterized by justice, love and respect.' A close analysis of this paragraph certainly reveals a man who saw himself, at the very least, as an instrument of God's will.

Having decided to stand, he still had to enter the process. The FNCD (*Front National pour le Changement et la Démocratie*, National Front for Change and Democracy) was a coalition of fifteen left-of-centre, non-communist, political parties. The leading voices in its organization were Evans Paul and Victor Benoit. Indeed the latter had been chosen by the Front to stand as their official candidate. But now they revised that decision and offered the FNCD as a platform for Aristide's candidature.

The problems of running without a coherent political base were to return to haunt Aristide during his presidency. But for the moment this offered him the procedural backing he needed.

But he still had to register. The lists were to close at 5pm on 18 October. Lafontant registered his candidature in the morning of that day. Aristide, wanting to avoid a confrontation, held back until the afternoon. But Lafontant decided to hang around the office of the Electoral Council to intimidate his opponent. He was accompanied by a number of heavily armed guards. At 4pm, Aristide telephoned Council officials asking if they could get Lafontant to move. They replied that this was impossible and went on to refuse to push back the registration deadline for Aristide's sake. So, fearing the worst, the little priest set out to deposit his papers. A crowd of soldiers waiting for him proceeded to pick Aristide up and bear him aloft, protecting him from the screaming Lafontant, and landing him directly within the safety of the office of the Electoral Council. Some parts of the army hated Lafontant whose Tontons Macoutes so frequently and consistently undermined their own role. Lafontant was left shouting aloud his determination to deliver the country from 'communists' like Aristide. But round one of this contest had undoubtedly gone to the priest.

Two weeks after this incident, the Electoral Council took the decision to ban Lafontant from standing in the election. They didn't base this conclusion on the hotly contested Article 291 of the Constitution but rather on the somewhat more down-to-earth fact that the would-be candidate's papers were not in order. Two documents (his birth certificate and certificate of *bona fides*) were missing. He was furious at what he considered such a pettifogging pretext for exclusion and threatened to continue to run even if this completely destabilized the electoral process.

Meanwhile, Aristide the candidate was sounding some quite unexpected notes. In a broadcast on *Radio Métropole*, he proclaimed the need for 'forgiveness in the way justice is administered'. He excluded any understanding of justice based on expediency and any possibility of a 'popular tribunal', a people's court. What's more, in his view of the economy, he guaranteed the rights of the private sector and was sure that Haiti could negotiate with the United States with dignity. In an article in *Haiti Progrès*, he promised that, since he'd been allowed to go on living after so many flirtations with death, he wanted to offer the rest of his life to his country. Then he added, 'The day when I betray the people, they will have every right to give me a *père Lebrun*, to necklace me.'

It was about this time that I next met Aristide. He'd just come back from Miami where some 20,000 Haitians had attended a rally in a football stadium. He was on a high; there were clear popular demonstrations of support everywhere he went. A million people had flooded to the local offices of the Electoral Council to register for the poll. It was clear from the outset that his candidature had galvanized an event that had seemed destined to attract little interest. At the time I met him he was in the hands of 'managers', people who were carefully safeguarding his energies and orchestrating his campaign. I arrived at the home of Gladys Lauture, one of his most trusted collaborators. Aristide was due to arrive there at any minute for an important campaign meeting. She didn't know if he'd have time for much more than a greeting. In the event, he told the meeting to carry on without him and we had two hours together in a fascinating *tête-à-tête*. Much of the time was spent talking about some of the events that had happened since we'd last met. On that occasion, just three or four months previously, he'd asked me to invite Desmond Tutu to come to Haiti to help give the country higher profile in the deep crisis it was going through. Now he was the clear favourite in the race for the presidency of the republic. I remember asking him just how he reconciled the role of the priest with that of the politician. By way of response, he told me how, as a priest, he had a vision of the kind of world God wanted his people to live in, a world rather like 'the new Jerusalem' in the Book of Revelation where there is no weeping or suffering and where all the citizens live with dignity and without fear. It is the task of the politician, he continued, to identify the steps, however many, that will get us from where we are now to where our vision beckons us. We went on to talk about the pressures he was living under, the people he was running against, the state of readiness of those organizing the election and many other such things. Then, before I left, I asked him if he'd mind my saying a prayer. I held his hands in mine and asked God to bless him and all the other candidates, and also to hold the Haitian people together in love, respect and honour through the important days ahead. When I'd finished, he took my hands in his and added his prayer. He asked God to bless me and all members of 'the international community' who could do so much to help Haiti make real progress towards its political, economic and social goals. We embraced warmly and parted. It was a very moving occasion.

One theme was beginning to emerge as the campaign intensified, one metaphor began to dominate. This was the word *Lavalas*, avalanche. In Haiti it had little to do with snow, much more to do with the raging waters that flood down the bare mountain slopes and unprotected valleys after a tropical storm. These floods are unstoppable, they destroy everything that stands in their way. In Carl Brouard's poem *Vous*, Haiti's peasant population is pictured as having the potential to be just such an unstoppable force if only they had enough self-awareness. There's little doubt that Aristide's use of the *Lavalas* metaphor draws its inspiration from Brouard. The people could indeed be as unstoppable as the mighty floodwaters and he saw it as his job to raise their consciousness and engage their energies for the great political tasks that belonged to them and them alone. In Aristide's mind, this was the moment when the Haitian peasants stepped out of the shadows where they had been consigned to waste away and onto the pages of history.

He'd already struck this note in a broadcast he'd made two years previously, a short while after the St John Bosco massacre. Much of that speech related specifically to the grim September events that had occasioned it. But there's already a clear delineation of the theme that he was to develop as a candidate (and indeed as president). It opens with an exhortation to the Haitian people:

To my sisters, my brothers,
To all my brothers and sisters in the Good Lord
Who raise their voices together with us,
To the valiant youth of Haiti,
To the peasants—whether Catholic, Protestant, or
    Vodouisant—
To the brave Haitians abroad,
To the courageous Haitians here in Haiti...
Congratulations on your courage.

Alone, we are weak,
Together, we are strong.
All together, we are the flood *lavalas*.

Let the flood descend,
The flood of poor peasants and poor soldiers,
The flood of the poor jobless multitudes (and poor
    soldiers),
Of poor workers (and poor soldiers),
The flood of all our poor friends (and all the poor
    soldiers) and
The church of the poor, which we call the children of
    God!
Let that flood descend!
And then God will descend and put down the mighty and
    send them away,
And He will raise up the lowly and place them on high.

Like the image of Haitian society as a banqueting table around
which the whole Haitian family must sit, so too this picture of
the poor as an unstoppable avalanche is drawn directly from his
preaching days. It is particularly interesting to note the appeal
he makes to the poor soldiers. He was well aware of the ordinary
soldier's plight, how mindlessly he was exploited by his superior
officers who, themselves, were often making huge fortunes from
drug-running and smuggling activities. By linking the lowly
soldier with Haiti's poor, he wanted to appeal to elements within

the armed forces who could make the difference between peace and chaos, democracy and dictatorship. Aristide had never forgotten the way the military had stood by as spectators during the aborted election of November 1987.

This speech provided the great rallying cry of the election campaign. Imagine a litany that runs like this. The diminutive priest, raised up on a distant platform, would intone one word into his microphone. '*Apart*' (On our own), he'd say, and then the crowd, as one, would reply '*nou fèb*' (we're weak). '*Ansanm*' (together), he'd continue, to which '*nou fo*' (we're strong), they'd cry, much louder this time. '*Ansanm ansanm*' (and when we're *all* together), he'd insist, '*nou se lavalas*' (we're an avalanche), they'd hurl back with relish, their voices themselves a veritable avalanche of energized sound. I've heard that litany hundreds of times and every single time I've been aware of the enormous power Aristide possessed in this capacity to unify and articulate the deep feelings of those thousands of poor Haitian people who flocked to hear him and who'd never had a champion before. Far too many of his critics, ultra-suspicious (and not a little jealous) of this gift of his, afraid of the apocalyptic potential of what they dismissed as 'demagoguery', simply prophesied doom and gloom. But Aristide was releasing new energy into Haiti's tired political and societal life. Of course it might all turn out to be froth and these people just an ill-disciplined mob. But, with goodwill and a commitment to harness this raw energy, it could also open a new chapter in Haiti's history. Aristide's critics watched him stir up the feelings of these poor people. Then they'd just wait for all the energy to dissipate and the promises to dissolve. It was easy just to blame him for his lack of political skills and for getting things all wrong. Yet their own lofty cynicism and hand-washing cowardice was arguably a far greater contributing factor to the eventual failure of Aristide's dream. They didn't even begin to understand what was happening around them. Aristide began to call this the participation of the Haitian people in shaping their own future a 'second independence'. The first independence, that of 1804, was always considered a glorious birth but one accomplished without the aid of a midwife. The second might have been no less glorious. But this time the 'midwives' were waiting with buckets of cold water in which to drown the struggling new arrival before it drew its first breath.

Such eventualities were far from the minds of those campaigning for people's votes in November 1990. Aristide was making a huge effort to appeal to all sectors of Haitian society. He had no trouble with the poor. For them he was their champion. 'I've always tried to be the voice of those who have no voice,' he said, 'and now the moment has arrived for me to be the voice of everyone.' Making a walkabout in the *Marché Salomon*, one of the capital city's busiest markets, he was acclaimed by stallholders and small retailers with raised arms, clenched fists and loud cheers. But he made his pitch to members of the police force and the army too. And amongst the lower grades he found real support and spontaneous gestures of sympathy. He even began to make overtures towards the bourgeoisie, the class he'd vilified so often in his sermons. 'Surely,' he argued, 'the business class will be happy when they're no longer hassled by a macoute knocking on their door demanding protection money. Surely they'll be glad when the taxes they pay will go towards the real development of the country. And the army,' he continued, 'who are supposed to be the guarantors of law and order, will be over the moon when they see a Head of State who respects the law. Only someone who respects the law can create a climate of confidence for everyone to work in.' With promises to respect private property and to establish a dignified and honourable negotiating stance with the United States, Aristide was making a huge attempt to shake himself free from the obsessive themes of his vitriolic past and present himself as a statesman who would best represent the whole of his country after the elections. The three key words of his campaign, a 1990 Haitian equivalent of the French Revolution's '*Liberté, Fraternité, Égalité*', were 'Justice, Participation and Transparency.' The first volume of his election manifesto was entitled 'The Chance We've Missed'. The second, which was made up entirely of blank pages, was called 'The

Chance We Have to Take'. What was ultimately to be written in this volume would depend on the collaboration and participation of all Haitians everywhere, he declared.

But the knives were out. Rumours were circulating to the effect that he'd had psychological troubles in the past. This wasn't the first time, nor would it be the last, that such allegations were made against him. It certainly put him on the defensive. 'I've never been admitted to a psychiatric establishment nor been treated for any psychiatric condition in my life,' he riposted. 'Certain people have been so thrown by my decision to run in this election that they're projecting their own pathological frustrations onto someone who enjoys splendid health both as a simple human being and also as a patriot.' He didn't deny the trauma he'd suffered after the St John Bosco massacre. But, as he put it, 'What happened to me then surely showed a sensitivity to other people's suffering, in exactly the same way as Jesus himself wept at the suffering he saw around *him*. Didn't people say he was mad too? It's proof that you're in good health when you can enter into the suffering of other people.'

His was the only campaign that seemed to have any organization or strategy about it. Mass meetings of factory workers, women, young people took place in various parts of Port-au-Prince. He held meetings in Pétionville, Hinche (Central Plateau), Jacmel and Cap Haitien. Tens of thousands gathered to greet him wherever he went. He spoke on various radio stations and also on national television. On the anniversary of the aborted 1987 election, he laid a garland of flowers at the school in Ruelle Vaillant where so many people had been slaughtered. He even made a lightning trip to Venezuela at the invitation of the Venezuelan president, Carlos Andres Perez, who put his personal jet at Aristide's disposal.

In the course of this frenetic activity, his enemies did all they could to disturb his rhythm. On 5 December, in Pétionville, an attempt was made on his life. A bomb intended for him killed five people and left 53 injured, some of them severely. Aristide visited the wounded in hospital. He blamed Lafontant and his supporters for this incident and urged the people to keep calm and not to be discouraged from voting.

Lafontant's candidature had been rejected in early November. But this didn't stop him participating actively in the run-up to the election. He gave countless interviews to (mainly) foreign journalists, constantly portraying himself as 'the apostle of peace'. He likened Aristide to a demon (or else Attila the Hun) and warned of civil war if the priest won the forthcoming election. When Hubert de Ronceray, another right-wing candidate, attempted to bring Lafontant round to a more moderate stance, his intervention was rudely rejected. 'There can be no agreement, alliance or understanding between us,' Lafontant declared. The stage was evidently set for implacable opposition, whatever the outcome of the election.

And so polling day, 16 December 1990, dawned. For the first time in Haiti's history, an election was to take place on the basis of universal adult suffrage. There were 1,618 official observers and journalists present to witness the election. I was one of them, part of a group sent out under the auspices of the World Council of Churches and the Caribbean Conference of Churches. With Monsignor Kelvin Felix, Archbishop of Castries (St Lucia), I was sent to keep an eye on things in Cap Haitien. In 1987 it had been impossible to leave the capital but this time there was no difficulty. Of all things, we were to stay at the residence of one of the people Aristide was known to dislike immensely, Monsignor François Gayot. He'd recently been made Archbishop of Cap Haitien and many people were speaking of him as an eventual Cardinal. He clearly had the ear of Pope John Paul II. The Holy Father had hardly chosen the most auspicious moment to 'promote' Gayot. The rift between the hierarchy and the church at parish level had never been deeper. This new sign of favour for one of the key contributors to the crisis was, to put it mildly, tantamount to gross insensitivity. It meant taking sides. There were to be many other such tactical blunders from the Vatican in the following years. As far as Haiti is concerned, it has not always been easy to understand how the centuries of practice enjoyed by Rome in the field of diplomacy have been put to very much use.

It was an interesting experience being lodged in this particular place while in the company of another Archbishop, especially since, for linguistic rather than theological reasons, Kelvin Felix was somewhat dependent on my lead. Monsignor Gayot's staff were clearly disenchanted with their Archbishop. He seemed to be a traumatized man; I barely recognized the carefree friend whose company and intellectual stimulus I'd so enjoyed just ten years previously when I'd been living in Cap Haitien. By lunchtime on polling day, his household staff had all been out to cast their vote and they came back proudly sporting the indelible ink mark on their thumbs that proved it. But the Archbishop hadn't and was keeping a very low profile indeed. There was talk of threats having been made against his life but, for all that, when we sat at table, the nun who served us didn't spare us a number of sarcastic remarks at the Archbishop's expense and his Vicar General too was openly critical of him. We saw and sensed at close quarters the depth of the chasm that the post-1986 struggles had opened up within the Roman Catholic Church.

When Monsignor Felix and I had toured the polling booths first thing in the morning, we found ugly chaos brewing in many places. The sheer size of the logistical operation was proving too much for the stretched officials. Matériel hadn't arrived in those booths situated in some of the most populous quarters of the city. We had to run to and fro alerting officials, ferrying personnel and matériel, as well as calming excited and impatient crowds waiting under a hot sun for the chance to vote. But in the end, everything got under way. At every polling station the military were deployed in a law-keeping capacity. The young officials could call on the soldiers and direct them to any trouble spots. General Abraham, the army chief of staff, had promised an orderly election and that's just how it turned out. We busied ourselves throughout the day, visiting a couple of dozen polling stations regularly. And everything proceeded in an orderly fashion. This was a remarkable achievement in the circumstances.

Every registered person had to vote on four different ballot papers. First there was the presidential list; then the two chambers of parliament; and, finally, depending on whether the voter lived in a city or in a rural area, there were lists for mayors or local government officials. Each list was colour coded. The presidential list was blue. The others were green, yellow and red. Every candidate's name was followed by details of his party, a photograph and, finally, a logo of some kind. Every effort had been made to help a largely illiterate electorate to vote intelligently. Aristide's logo was a red cockerel rampant, a readily recognizable image in a country where cock-fighting is a national sport. The good humour and patience on display once the voting got under way was most impressive. And the votes were all counted that same evening. They produced a remarkable result.

Some two and a half million people voted. That was well over 90 per cent of those who'd registered and an enormous proportion of the total population eligible to vote. Aristide pulled in 67.5 per cent of the vote, a massive 1.7 million people. The next candidate was Marc Bazin, a former World Bank official and for a long time the candidate preferred by the United States. He got 14.2 per cent of the votes. No one else managed to get to 5 per cent.

So Aristide was elected. I joined the massed crowds in Cap Haitien at the end of a long day and sensed the sheer joy of the people. I'd been present on these same streets in 1974 when Alexandre Lerouge had won a famous victory after daring to oppose the Duvalier candidate in a parliamentary election. Now as then, the euphoria was so tangible you felt you could cut slices of it for general consumption. Aristide made no statement that evening. It took several days to collate the results and make an official declaration. Then the congratulations started rolling in.

Jimmy Carter, who was present on election day, declared the ballot free and fair. Leaders of a number of parties who'd contested the election were generous in their acceptance of the result. The European Community congratulated the Haitian people for their patience and determination. They deserved a brighter tomorrow, said Henri Saby, head of a delegation of European parliamentarians, who was ecstatic and feeling that he'd sensed 'a blast of incredible responsibility in the air'. Accolades came in from the French, German, Venezuelan, Nicaraguan, Taiwanese, Japanese and other governments. And a message came too from the Secretary General of the United Nations. By 28 December, even George Bush had sent his 'warm congratulations' and a promise to help Aristide surmount the huge problems facing his country. 'I commit the full cooperation of my government and my own personal goodwill,' he said.

There's little doubt that the dramatic collapse of communism in the time between the aborted November 1987 election and the 1990 ballot had softened American attitudes. In 1987, when the race had seemed to be between two left-of-centre candidates, Sylvio Claude and Gérard Gourgue, the Americans had taken fright. But now such shibboleths, at least for the moment, could be put back into wraps. A Republican president offered his fulsome congratulations to a Liberation Theologian. Surely the whole wide world should note such a remarkable gesture.

Aristide made a radio broadcast to the nation from his little room in the *Lafanmi Selavi* children's home. He offered the hand of friendship to all Haitians and paid a gracious compliment to the Haitian army. He appealed to the people to bring a halt to all acts of *dechoukaj* (uprooting) and asked those worried about the demands of justice to set up neighbourhood watch committees instead of taking direct action. He ended his speech with one of his great rallying cries: *Titid ak malèrè marassa*, Aristide and the poor are like twins. Then, turning to some of the down-and-out children at his side he said to them quite simply, 'You have a little friend who's just become the president.' His broadcast over, he took to the streets in an open jeep for a triumphal tour around some of the slum quarters of Port-au-Prince.

But not everyone was enraptured by Aristide's electoral victory. Roger Lafontant put out a spiteful statement calling the elections 'scandalous, infamous, insulting'. He promised only a grudging collaboration and even then on the strict condition that the new president called off his vendetta against former Duvalierists like himself. Lafontant's party (the URN) had ominously promised that 'Attila will never enter Rome' and that, with Aristide's victory, 'Haiti would experience a time of cursing and punishment.'

The Roman Catholic Church simply didn't know how to respond. The Justice and Peace Commission of the Bishops' Conference put out a statement on 29 December in which it expressed its total confidence in the result of the election. 'Those who don't know our people,' the statement continued, 'supposed us to be violent, angry, anarchic and committed to street justice. In fact, we've proved ourselves calm, resolved, and well capable of democratic government. These elections signify the will of the majority of Haitians to break with the past with its arbitrary and elitist ways, its structured injustice, corruption and torture. All that is now over.' One of the signatories to this declaration was Monsignor Willy Romélus, Bishop of Jérémie. His fellow bishops were less ready to make such an open commitment, however. The momentous year 1990 ended with no statement at all from the Bishops' Conference, not even a simple word of recognition that the people had spoken and made their choice. Instead, Bishop Pétion-Laroche and Archbishop François Gayot had met Aristide to insist on his resignation from the priesthood before his inauguration to the presidential office. There were repeated misunderstandings between them. Clearly, the bishops had their own agenda and were waiting for some reassurance from Aristide before they gave him their blessing. Meanwhile, the Vatican was awaiting a word from the nuncio in Port-au-Prince before *they* responded. So there wasn't a single word from Rome, not even the duty telegram for a newly-elected head of state which is one of the routine undertakings of the diplomatic service. The spin in which the hierarchy found itself boded ill for the relations of church and State in the immediate future.

And then Archbishop François Ligondé preached a sermon that had roughly the same effect as driving a heavy steamroller over thin ice. The occasion was Haiti's national day, 1 January, and the place was the cathedral in downtown Port-au-Prince. 'Fear is sending a chill down the spines of many fathers and mothers with families,' he said from his pulpit. 'Civil liberties are about to disappear; we are heading for an authoritarian political régime, a police state which will snuff out our liberties, abuse the Constitution and deal out summary justice in the most arbitrary way. Socialist Bolshevism is going to triumph,' he declared. The sermon was sprinkled with quotations from Pope John Paul II and it presented an apocalyptic vision of Haiti. Ligondé predicted that if Haitians thought of nothing but revenge, then 'by the year 2000 we will be eating stones, and in the year 2004 we will celebrate the bi-centenary of national independence in a desert... Fortunately, there's someone watching over us: Holy Mary, the mother of God.'

During the rule of various *de facto* governments which followed the subsequent ousting of Aristide in September 1991, this sermon was to be played again and again on national radio and television as anti-Aristide propaganda. The Archbishop had spoken for all those who'd traditionally held power in Haiti, all who couldn't accept the democratic decision of the people. He evidently spoke without the foreknowledge or prior approval of his fellow bishops. But none of them protested. The nuncio kept his counsel. And Rome was as silent as the grave.

Ligondé was a 'first generation Duvalierist' and had given his support and blessing to a régime that had committed countless offences against the dignity and the rights of the human person. He'd turned a blind eye to atrocities and stood alongside various members of the Duvalier dynasty throughout their years in power. It was his subtlety that had found a way through the labyrinthine difficulties posed by canon law in order to proceed with the marriage of Jean-Claude Duvalier and Michèle Bennett. Ligondé was the very epitome of the 'Constitutional Bishop', cypher to an oppressive dictatorship. And now he withheld his support from a man who'd been endorsed on a massive scale by the Haitian people and—to rub salt into sore wounds—he had the nerve to predict that an

Aristide government would bring oppression and intolerance to the nation. Certainly he could claim the right to speak with authority on such matters after working so closely and for so long with the Duvalierist perpetrators of institutional violence and structural oppression. It is a mystery to outsiders how the Vatican can always find a way to remove someone like the French bishop Gaillot of Évreux from his diocese while they hang on to someone like Ligondé through hell and high water. His New Year's Day sermon was like a torch thrown on petrol.

Five days after the Archbishop's sermon, Roger Lafontant and his accomplices attempted a *coup d'état*. They moved under cover of darkness and gained entry to the national palace. An armoured vehicle brought Ertha Pascal Trouillot, the provisional president, to the palace and she was forced to broadcast a statement announcing her resignation from office. Lafontant then declared himself head of state. But he'd not reckoned with the determined opposition of members of the armed forces. Most of them hated him anyway, but General Abraham, who'd already shown himself committed to the democratic process, refused to allow Lafontant to subvert the result of the recent election. The people, meanwhile, had taken to the streets in their thousands. They brought Port-au-Prince to a complete standstill. And they set out in search of anyone who might be a Lafontant collaborator. They did a great deal of wanton damage. Over a hundred people were killed, many of them burned alive on the streets of Port-au-Prince. A pitched battle was fought outside Lafontant's headquarters. Businesses were attacked and buildings destroyed. The crowd, in their rage, hunted down Tontons Macoutes and also senior church officials. They thought Ligondé was hiding in the old Port-au-Prince Cathedral, an elegant building dating from 1761 and in which Toussaint Louverture had sworn his governor's oath. The mere thought that Ligondé was inside caused them to set fire to this lovely edifice. It burned to the ground. But the archbishop wasn't there. If the crowd had caught him they'd certainly have killed him. Instead they found the papal nuncio and his senior assistant. They gave the latter a severe thrashing and then destroyed the Bishops' Conference Centre and did great damage to the nuncio's house. Ligondé managed eventually to cross the border into the safety of the Dominican Republic.

Aristide was put on the spot by these fast-moving events. In an unguarded moment he seems to have given the impression that he could quite understand why the people might resort to violence in such circumstances. Some reports suggest that he even included the '*père Lebrun*' (necklacing) as a measure that wouldn't have surprised him. Other reports deny that he ever said any such thing. In any case, it is clear that he was speaking under the pressure of events and wanting to express his regret at the absence of any effective system of justice able to protect the people and bring those who broke the Constitution to trial. Soon the president-elect was making statements of a more measured kind. He condemned the sacrilegious acts of the crowd, appealed for calm, pleaded with those still on the rampage to desist from inflicting further damage or loss of life. He insisted that people who wanted to protest should always resort to methods that were non-violent. He was clear and unambiguous in these statements and nothing he said could have been misconstrued. Even though he was adamant that more determined attempts should be made to arrest and restrain the macoutes who were such a constant threat to the peace of the nation, he also went out of his way to show his displeasure at the violence of the mob.

These facts have to be rehearsed in detail because of the interpretation the Vatican (and others) put upon them in subsequent days. There's no doubt that Rome held Aristide personally to blame for the pillaging and for the way the vengeful crowds did so much damage in the aftermath of the *coup d'état*. They were furious at the injuries inflicted upon the Zairean assistant to the nuncio and also the damage to church property. But were they right to lay all this at Aristide's door?

Consider another line of analysis. In mid-December, just three weeks previously, the people had voted massively for an Aristide presidency. And the country was still very much in electoral mode; a second round of parliamentary elections was due on 20 January. Democracy and participation were in the air. And yet one couldn't but note that the hierarchy of the Roman Catholic Church had still not issued a statement confirming the result of the election and approving the people's choice. With woeful timing and extremely bad taste, the Archbishop of Port-au-Prince had preached his grim sermon, showing himself implacably opposed to any prospect of Aristide as president, depicting such a possibility in the most lurid colours. And to cap it all, along came Lafontant with his attempted coup. Surely this combination of implacable opposition and deliberate ill-will offered strong enough grounds for angering any crowd. What interest could Aristide have had in ordering them to take reprisals in the way they did? He was the president-elect. He'd simply have abandoned any pretensions to occupying the moral high ground if he'd urged them to burn and pillage like that. The more likely explanation is that the disenchanted crowds resorted to rampaging violence because they felt something that belonged to them was being stolen or withheld from them yet again.

Monsignor Willy Romélus, Bishop of Jérémie, made an even more pertinent observation. Writing to Pope John Paul II, he suggested that the violence had been deliberately whipped up by Aristide's enemies in order to put him in bad odour with the church. Whatever the facts of the case, the crowds didn't need Aristide to help them decide what they needed to do. And once they'd taken to the streets and done their damage, the church hierarchy, still unable to come to terms with the prospect of Aristide as president, found their undisciplined rage a useful weapon to use against him.

The days following these incidents were packed with action. The second round of elections took place and Aristide could now look at the political makeup of the parliament he'd have to work with. The FNCD, the group that had put his name forward, had won the largest number of seats but failed to win working majorities in either House. In a country that had everything to learn about democracy, this promised to be a stumbling block for effective government.

During the weeks leading up to Aristide's inauguration, fear and uncertainty continued to reign. There were assassinations and demonstrations and rumours of further attempted coups. Roger Lafontant and his cronies were languishing in prison cells, still muttering their dire threats. But none of this dented the positive reactions coming from the international community. Venezuela, Colombia and Mexico promised aid, especially with Haiti's energy needs, and to renew her infrastructure. Jamaica promised to help re-train the police force and army. The United Nations offered technical assistance. Non-governmental organizations were climbing on board a bandwagon that was beginning to acquire real momentum.

Aristide, meanwhile, was meeting Ertha Pascal Trouillot to plan a smooth transfer of power. And he also found time to travel to Venezuela and France. In Paris, the big guns were rolled out for his visit. He had meetings with President Mitterrand, Prime Minister Rocard, the president of the National Assembly, Laurent Fabius, and a clutch of other ministers. Increasingly he began to refer to Haiti's democratic future as her 'second independence'. He also pledged himself to take measures against the drug running operations that had, for some years, found Haiti a very convenient staging post.

It was in early January that I received a telephone call from Aristide's office inviting me to attend the forthcoming inauguration. I'd barely had time to express my pleasure at receiving such a splendid gesture before my interlocutor continued: 'And the president-elect wants to ask you to do him a favour.' This sounded ominous. 'He's very distressed that the hierarchy of the Roman Catholic Church has still not endorsed the election results. It's vital for them to do this and also to support the celebrations on 7 February. The president-elect feels that all the members of the bishops' conference should be present in the cathedral on inauguration day for the Thanksgiving mass planned for that day. He wants you to find a way of interceding with the Vatican to try to bring this about.' I was stunned by this request. But before I could splutter my hesitations (after all what can a Methodist minister in London do to influence the byzantine workings of the Roman Catholic Church?), the president's man had rung off and left me to sort this one out on my own. It proved to be an intriguing challenge.

I got in touch with the apostolic pro-nuncio to the Court of St James (that is, the Pope's ambassador to the United Kingdom), Monsignor Luigi Barbarito. Barbarito is an extraordinary man who'd begun his diplomatic career in Haiti during the 1970s. I'd enjoyed the company of the young Italian priest who'd been the nuncio's secretary at that time. Barbarito had associated himself with my ordination to the Methodist ministry which took place in Port-au-Prince in January 1973. So our relationship went back a long way. I'd already been regally entertained by him in his Wimbledon dwelling and he didn't hesitate to invite me over again to discuss my strange request. We spent a couple of hours in deep conversation. I urged him to use his seniority in the Vatican's diplomatic service to find ways of putting pressure on the Haitian bishops. When we'd finished our elegant lunch and our urbane conversation, he asked me to write up the main lines of our discussion in a short document. This I did. Here is part of that document:

The anxieties I expressed to you verbally, I want now to reiterate in this letter. Haiti will soon have as its elected president Fr Jean-Bertrand Aristide. He is a man of great ability, he certainly focuses the hopes of the Haitian people, but there are many pitfalls and dangers ahead for him. If his mandate is to have any chance whatsoever, it is vital that all bodies and institutions of goodwill find a way to affirm him at this juncture. This will ensure that all such organizations maintain touch with the Haitian people. It will also give such bodies opportunities to advise and discuss policy with the Aristide government as it begins to take on its responsibilities. To become alienated from Aristide at this time is to lose touch with the people and also to lose influence with the future government of the republic.

The church has a problem in this area. Aristide's difficulties with his bishops predate his becoming a candidate in the election. That is well known. Also, the church's view of priests entering politics is clearly understood. For all that, however, Aristide is now *as a matter of fact* the elected president of Haiti and will be inaugurated as such on 7 February.

I believe that the bishops in Haiti who, just three months ago, faced Aristide as a 'problematical priest' now need to be helped to view the realities whereby he is the elected head of state. They need help to do this. This is not just my view, the opinion of a mere Methodist, but also the clearly expressed understanding of my good friend Monsignor Kelvin Felix, Archbishop of Castries (St Lucia).

The church has to face the major difficulty in this area posed by the role, history, and intervention of the Archbishop of Port-au-Prince. One of the clear themes of post-Duvalier Haiti has been its opposition to all who were once in league with the infamous Tontons Macoutes. Monsignor Ligondé, rightly or wrongly, is attributed with being a sympathizer (at best) or a member (at worst) of this body. His role in the last five years has been ambiguous, to say the least. But now it is worse. In his sermon on 1 January (Haiti's national day) he said the following:

> *Est-ce que le pays est en route pour une nouvelle dictature? Beaucoup de petits gens craignent un étouffement des libertés, la violation de la Constitution, des déchoukages et la renaissance d'une police secrète, faisant partie d'un régime autoritaire, gauchiste, et socialo-bolshévique.*

> (Is the country en route for another dictatorship? Many humble people are fearful of their liberties being snuffed out, the Constitution being violated, persecution, and the re-birth of a secret police—all contributing to an authoritarian, left-wing, socialist bolshevik régime.)

This has angered the people (it explains the terrible and most unfortunate actions against the church after the 7 January abortive *coup d'état*). It has also divided the bishops. Monsignor Romélus, bishop of Jérémie (a place you did so much to help), has asked openly why Monsignor Ligondé has expressed his fears of a dictatorship now when he seems to have been happy to support the Duvaliers over 25 years. The whole incident is bad for Haiti. It is shocking and damaging to the church.

In all this, I place my hopes in a Roman Catholic Church that, with its centuries of experience and its consummate diplomatic skills, will find a way to respond to the present crisis with pragmatism and understanding. My dear friend, Monsignor François Gayot, seems at the moment to have been traumatized by the situation. His reputation is not so good right now. If the Archbishop of Port-au-Prince could, in some way, be marginalized, and if the universal church could come to Gayot's help with wise counsel and solidarity, he could still be a worthy leader for the Body of Christ at this critical juncture. He has a brilliant mind, a deep knowledge of the Haitian realities, and could become a fine figurehead for the church in its relationship with the State.

I blush now at my naivety in writing some of this. After all, what Roman Catholic Archbishop needs a character reference from a Methodist minister? But I don't shrink from the main thrust of my argument. Monsignor Barbarito's reply was short but generous:

I am deeply grateful to you for writing to me at length about the situation in Haiti and I have taken very seriously all that you say. I am well able to appreciate your concern and anxiety which indeed I share and the position of the church is particularly problematical. The contents of your letter have been made known to the Holy See and the information you have provided will prove, without doubt, to be of inestimable help.

Armed with these assurances, I prepared to go to Port-au-Prince for Aristide's inauguration.

A few days before the great day, the bishops met and, at last, issued a statement endorsing the election results. They'd failed in their efforts to get Aristide to resign from the priesthood and, at the eleventh hour, realized that they must either get on board the moving bus or else be left on the street. By committing themselves to stand with the people in their search for justice and accountable government the bishops had at least given themselves a chance of playing some part in the construction of the new Haiti. There was a lot more they needed to do; but the public affirmation of Aristide's legitimacy was an important first step. All the bishops (with the not unexpected exception of Ligondé) signed the statement. The stage was now set for 7 February.

The day dawned and Port-au-Prince was as clean and bright as most people could ever remember. Bands of citizens had formed themselves into co-operatives to sweep the gutters and clean the sidewalks of the capital's streets, in the suburbs and the slums, in the markets and the public squares. Miles and miles of kerbstones had been painted red and blue, the national colours, and bunting hung from trees and telegraph poles. Artists had been hard at work too. On newly whitewashed walls, pictures of Aristide and scenes of Haitian life had appeared as if by magic, most of them sporting a proverb, a slogan, or some free advice to the new administration. One painted bedsheet carried a picture of a flapping cockerel keeping a bloodied guinea hen (symbol of the Duvalier family) at bay. Its inscription read: *Pèp vayan se pèp oganizé, lit pèp la fek koumansé* (A watchful people is an organized people; the people's struggle has only just begun). The whole frontage of a small school carried the slogan *San Titid pa gen lekol* (No Aristide no school), a touching expression of faith in the new president. But it was also a comment, of course, on the fact that the political disturbances of the previous five years had disrupted the country's educational system so dreadfully. *Men anpil chay pa lou. Ansanm nap rebati ayiti* (Many hands make light work. Together we'll rebuild Haiti) declared a huge poster which showed a stirringly patriotic scene where one peasant was bearing the Haitian flag and another an enormous drum. The other people in the picture, about a dozen of them, were clearly ready for a great celebration and the time of their lives. But another piece of instant advice, this time on a hospital wall, went far beyond the simple exhortation that Haitians should merely work together; it established the only basis on which such collaboration could happen—an end to the mutual recrimination that had always torn the country apart. *Li lè pou'ou sispan di zafè kabrit pa zafè mouton an'n di pito problèm yon aysyen se problèm tout aysyen* (It's time to stop saying that what matters to goats has nothing to do with sheep and say instead that one Haitian's problem is the problem of every Haitian). And some street artists didn't hesitate to write their 'shopping lists' of requirements for the new government. The wall of the school where I'd once been deputy headmaster carried quite a programme. It read:

Lit kont kraze zo
Lit kont dominasyon
Lit kont eksplwatasyon
Lit pou tè
Lit pou konstwi kilti natif natal
Lit pou libète

(Struggle against assassinations, domination and exploitation. Struggle for land, the building of a genuinely local culture and liberty).

There were thousands of examples of this instant art and ready advice spread across the length and breadth of Port-au-Prince that day. One of the key words that had been used by Aristide in his election campaign was 'participation'; it seemed now as if the whole population had taken him at his word and were offering their five pennyworth before he'd even been sworn in.

The city offered a fitting backdrop for a day filled with simple pageantry and rich symbolism. The proceedings began in the parliament building in downtown Port-au-Prince close by the seashore. There Aristide swore his oath of allegiance and received his sash of honour. Ertha Pascal Trouillot, as outgoing president, might have been expected to drape the red and blue band around her successor's shoulders. Instead, 'Madame Sara', a peasant woman from the country, did the honours in a ceremony that was simple and brief. Now the president and his entourage drove slowly through the streets of Port-au-Prince's commercial sector towards the city's cathedral for a Thanksgiving mass and *Te Deum*.

The extraordinary thing about the imposing service was that it proceeded in Créole rather than in French (or Latin!). The very first hymn set the tone for everything that followed. It was straight out of the textbook of Liberation Theology. It didn't mince its words or clothe everyday pre-occupations in the swaddling bands of mystification or blandness. What could be simpler than this?

1. Our brothers are without work, our sisters have no food, our children live in misery:

Come down Holy Spirit, we have a mission for the earth.

2. Our brothers can't read, our sisters weep bitter tears, our children have no schools to go to:

Come down Holy Spirit, we have a mission for the earth.

3. Our brothers have no land, our sisters are humiliated, our children are reduced to begging for charity:

Come down Holy Spirit, we have a mission for the earth.

The sermon was preached by the president of the Haitian Conference of Bishops, Monsignor Léonard Pétion Laroche, and it was full of the language of reconciliation. He congratulated the people for the wisdom of their choice, their courage and determination in opting for Aristide as president. 'This morning,' he said, 'Haiti is in party mood. A people filled with enthusiasm is celebrating a great occasion—the existence in Haiti of a State established on the foundation of law, something so long waited and yearned for... The whole church wants to be part of all this and, like a mother, dear president, with warmth and affection, welcomes you and prays for you now... As for you, Excellency, the nation, in mandating you to oversee the '*res publica*', the republic, is confiding to you a responsibility of the first order. When Moses was charged by God to lead his people towards the promised land, he cried out, 'But who am I?' And God replied, 'I shall be with you!' Today, Excellency, you have been given a similar mission.'

This was very moving but nothing he said was more powerful than the kiss of peace, that moment in the liturgy when everyone is invited to make a gesture of love to their neighbours before moving forward to take Communion. All the bishops (except, of course, Ligondé and Colimon) were there and it was very moving to see each of them approach the new president and embrace him publicly and warmly. The television close-ups were even more touching; this either represented a new beginning for the church (as well as the nation), or else it was pure charade and hypocrisy. Bishop Willy Romélus was clear in *his* view of what it all represented. Writing to the Pope, he put it this way: 'For the Haitian people who so warmly applauded this meeting in the Lord's temple, this [thanksgiving] mass demonstrated the reconciliation of the church hierarchy with Father Aristide. A page in our history seemed to have been turned over.'

Gathered in the chancel were the great and the good. Danielle Mitterrand and Jimmy Carter were there; so too were leaders from Jamaica, Belize, Venezuela, the United Nations and the Organization of American States. I was sitting in the nave and, about half way through the service, the doors of the cathedral were opened and the vast crowd assembled in the streets outside began to move in. At one stage the atmosphere became very volatile, even threatening, and a number of guests (including myself) began to look for ways to leave—Marc Bazin, who was runner-up to Aristide in the presidential election, left at the same time as I did. It was difficult since the crowd had invaded all available space and looked on those leaving the 'coronation' of their hero with utter disdain. But there was no incident and the service proceeded normally. After the mass came the *Te Deum* and, before the final hymn, a special prayer for the Head of State. It asked God to bless 'Father Jean-Bertrand Aristide who is our new head, so that he may be able to work on this earth for the liberation of the Haitian people which is your will. Help him to act with full respect for the Constitution so that the State can enjoy order and stability.' It is interesting to note that Aristide's continuing priestly status is acknowledged in the way he's described in this prayer.

Later that afternoon, the palace grounds were opened up for the last event of the day. The great white house which had housed successive Haitian presidents since it was built during the American Occupation (its predecessor had been blown up along with the then Head of State in 1912) was festooned with red and blue and its façade dominated by a specially constructed balustrade. A huge crowd had gathered. Aristide had refused to sit on any throne-like seat; he'd certainly not wanted to sit on chairs that the dictators who preceded him had used. Instead he'd had a simple chair made by some of the children at the *Lafanmi Selavi* home which he'd founded and where he'd lived and worked since being expelled from the Salesian order. He sat demurely as the ceremony proceeded in front of him. The national anthem was sung by a group of 'Madames Sara', peasant women from distant parts of rural Haiti. Their untrained voices conveyed an earthy sense of Haitian realities. Some fulsome speeches were made in elegant French by those who contributed to the early part of the programme. But everyone was waiting for Aristide. And then at last it was time for him to speak.

His diminutive figure approached the microphone. No one even knew what language he'd use. His first word was 'Cric!' and, as if it had been scripted and rehearsed, the vast crowd responded with one voice 'Crac!' I've never experienced anything like it. Last thing at night in farflung rural Haitian communities, people often gather round a dying fire to have a social moment before they retire to bed. There's no electricity and the fire offers both warmth and light. Stories are told, proverbs and jokes exchanged, and great fun is had by one and all. Convention has it that the oldest person present begins this time of social intercourse by clicking his middle finger and thumb and saying 'Cric!' to which everyone else present, snapping their fingers in like manner, responds 'Crac!' With this brief exchange of formalities the fun and story-telling begin. By using this same little formula at the very beginning of his first presidential utterance, he was tuning in to the folk culture and the deepest sense of national identity that holds all Haitian people together. The spontaneity and vivacity of that exchange was as illustrative as anything can be of the symbiotic relationship that exists between Aristide and his people. It is that which makes him strong. And it is that which also makes him potentially dangerous in the eyes of those who function in other ways.

In his speech, Aristide promised that not a drop of blood would flow during his presidency. He refused the official salary of £5,000 per month because he considered it excessive. He announced various aid packages and was particularly anxious to speak of those amounts that didn't come from the United States of America. He wanted to convey the impression that Haiti had other friends too and wasn't just dependent on American generosity. But none of these details had the same effect as the very last part of his speech. Turning to members of the armed forces, he praised 'the marriage of the army and the people' and announced pay rises for junior ranks. Then he revealed details of a major shake-up in the high command and, in particular, the early retirement of six generals and one colonel. He promoted the man who'd overseen the safe-conduct of the elections to Chief of Staff. That man was none other than Raoul Cédras who became one of the principal actors in the coup that would oust Aristide from office just seven months later.

A twenty-one gun salute brought the day's proceedings to an

end. But those firing the guns ran out of powder after a mere nineteen shots had been fired. The crowd, who'd become very excited by this unprecedented opportunity to participate in such splendid events and also with the still barely digested information about sacked generals and the like, had been counting each canon burst with increasing rowdiness. They were getting into a noisy and joyous rhythm by the time the guns had got to nineteen. When there was no twentieth, the multitude broke into a baying chant which they continued for several minutes: *Manke dè, manke dè*, they intoned persistently, Two missing, two missing. I don't know how crowds identify the messages they rally round, how thousands and thousands of people fix upon words which they then utter in unison. I can't even begin to understand how such a thing happens. Aristide does. And that's his power.

I returned to London with unforgettable memories of this defining moment in Haiti's history. I wrote to the papal nuncio, Mgr Barbarito, of my satisfaction with what I'd seen, especially from the church hierarchy:

> It was so magnificent. The Haitian bishops put out a statement that was conciliatory and affirming of President Aristide. It was generous and charitable. And it came from *all* the bishops (except, of course, Ligondé). Then, at the mass, each bishop warmly embraced the new President before leaving the cathedral. I was so happy to see it all and can now believe there is new hope for Haiti and for the church. I cannot believe that all this happened without your benign influence. I suspect you have put some considerable effort into making these things happen. I am most grateful. Let us continue to pray for Haiti, the bishops, and the church in the days that lie ahead.

Aristide was only thirty-seven when he became president. His childhood in Port Salut seemed distant now. So too did his schooldays at St John Bosco in Port-au-Prince and at the seminary in Cap Haitien. His studies in Santo Domingo,

Jerusalem, Rome and Montreal were all part of a distant past. Much nearer were those sermons in La Saline, his skirmishes with death at Freycineau and St John Bosco. He could look back with joy at the Haitian people's march onto the stage of history through their participation in the general election. But from time to time, he must also have contemplated with great sadness all the senseless and cruel deaths that had been part of the price paid for this new turning point in Haiti's history. They were many—amongst them, the peasants of Jean Rabel, the worshippers at the 11 September mass, the people in the election crowd at Pétionville, the countless (and so often nameless) dead in Cité Soleil, the Central Plateau, the Artibonite Valley, the northern plain and the Grand Anse. The only question that mattered now, of course, was how Aristide's arrival in office might make a difference to those who'd survived.

5 Seven brave months

Once the excitement of 7 February was over there were some very practical and hard-headed decisions facing His Excellency President Jean-Bertrand Aristide. He had to appoint a government. And the most delicate office to fill was that of prime minister. Many people expected Monique Brisson, a human rights lawyer and personal friend of the president, to be appointed. But, to the surprise of most people, Aristide chose René Préval. He came from an urban, middle-class background. His family were landowners in the fertile Artibonite valley and his father was minister of agriculture in the 1950s but the family was forced into exile during François Duvalier's 1963 purges. Préval went on to study agriculture in Belgium after which he went to live in New York for about five years where he worked in a French-language bookstore. He returned to Haiti in 1975 and worked for two years at the National Mineral Resources Institute followed by a year's further study in Italy. He opened a bakery in Port-au-Prince in 1983 and, as a pro-ecology gesture, used sugar cane to fuel its ovens. He took an interest in *Lafanmi Selavi* and Aristide and he became very close friends. He had been at the priest's side during the massacre at the St John Bosco Church in September 1988. Now he was to be both prime minister and also Minister of Defence and the Interior. With Aristide, he set about choosing ministers for the different departments of his government.

Clearly a decision was taken that the government would be drawn entirely from within the ranks of the FNCD, the coalition that had sponsored Aristide in the election. This raised a howl of protest from a wide cross-section of people who'd thought the new president would appoint a broadly-based government of national unity, especially since the FNCD didn't enjoy an absolute majority in either chamber of the parliament. They had 27 of the 83 seats in the House of Deputies and 13 of the 27 in the Senate. Marc Bazin's ANDP party (Bazin had been runner-up to Aristide in December) could claim 17 and 6 seats in the two chambers respectively. Several other parties had smaller numbers of seats and it was clear that the legislative arm of this brand new democracy was going to have great difficulty finding ways of getting its work done. When the left-of-centre PANPRA party of Serge Gilles withdrew its support from the ANDP because it preferred to combine its strength with that of the FNCD in the hope of forming a strong socialist bloc in parliament, the FNCD leader chose to spurn this approach even though it was difficult to see where else he might get the votes he'd need to conduct parliamentary business with anything like efficiency. And Aristide didn't help matters very much when he gave the presidency of each chamber to a member of the FNCD.

The most widespread criticism of Aristide's first government was that it represented a 'cabinet of friends'. The president, far from denying this accusation, agreed with it wholeheartedly but added by way of rejoinder that he was sure that 'no minister in my cabinet is capable of pillaging the national treasury'. One or two of his ministers (Leslie Voltaire at Education and Daniel Henrys at Health, for example) were people of undoubted experience and stature. Henrys had the added point of interest that he was the one member of PANPRA, the Social Democratic party led by Serge Gilles, to break the FNCD stranglehold on power. But the rest were unknown and untried. They were people whom, above all, he felt he could trust and their number included some ex-priests. There was a marked absence of technocrats. The average age of his first cabinet was less than 50 and there were three women heading departments of state.

With the inauguration over, Aristide began to engage in

'gesture' politics. This is far from being a critical description of his actions; on the contrary, it could well be that he should have limited himself far more to the symbolic actions at which he so excelled. On his first full day in office, for example, he went to the Fort Dimanche prison to plant a tree in memory of the countless people who'd died within its walls. This was a simple ceremony but it had the effect of helping people recognize and 'deal with' an important part of the country's oppressive past.

In a series of 'prophetic acts', he opened up the presidential palace to different sectors of the population. Members of the Haitian diaspora in the United States were welcomed home in this way. It was clear that he'd be counting on the enormous presence of Haitians abroad in the search for allies for his political struggles over the months ahead. And he'd also be appealing to them for money, especially for help with funding the literacy programme so dear to his heart and which he was anxious to get launched as a matter of priority. He knew too that the only way he could keep a strong negotiating position with the IMF and the World Bank was to show that Haiti and Haitians could be counted on to raise money themselves for some of the developmental work waiting to be done.

But members of the diaspora were by no means the only people to pay the new president a visit. The palace doors were also opened to receive the poor and the beggars of Port-au-Prince. And, in quick succession, there were receptions for soldiers, church leaders, the Electoral Council, women, non-sighted people, journalists and others. And when, in the distant Artibonite valley, some peasant farmers got involved in a bitter dispute with the military, the president invited a delegation from each party to meet him in the palace in an attempt to resolve their differences. He wanted to enlist the energies of as many sectors of the population as possible and sought to achieve this by opening up his official residence and using his meetings there to reinforce his frequently repeated exhortations for national unity.

He issued a decree ensuring that all government pronouncements would be made in future in Créole as well as

French. After all, it was Créole-speaking people who, for the most part, had voted him into power. Elevating their language was just one more step in enfranchizing them. And he saw to it that their religion wasn't marginalized either. He invited voodoo priests along with Catholics and Protestants to a prayer breakfast at the palace. He also honoured the bi-centenary of Bois Caïman, the August 1791 ceremony on a plantation in the north of Haiti when the voodoo spirits were invoked and the struggle of the slaves against their French colonial masters began. In all these ways, Aristide showed he had flair for the symbolic dimension of his new office.

He was less sure-footed in other areas. Anxious to ensure that Duvalierists who'd committed crimes against the people would be brought to justice, he banned over 200 people from leaving the country. One of these was Ertha Pascal Trouillot, his predecessor, who, in the president's view, needed to answer certain questions concerning her part in Roger Lafontant's failed coup the previous January. She was put in prison for 24 hours before being released into house arrest. This evoked widespread criticism from many people within Haiti and a number of foreign governments too, including a stinging rebuke from one of Aristide's staunchest supporters, the Venezuelan president Carlos Andres Perez. Trouillot's restrictions were soon lifted and she was later allowed to leave Haiti. No charges were ever brought against her.

The Haitian people now had elected representatives to look after their interests in the various branches of government. But these people had almost no experience of government, nor did the country have any kind of workable political infrastructure to help shape and focus their energies. One of the most pressing needs facing the new administration, therefore, was the rationalization of government departments as part of a drive for greater efficiency in this direction. There were 42,000 people on the government payroll when Aristide came to power. But these figures needed careful scrutiny. On the whole, there were a few senior officials who were paid handsome salaries and large numbers of others whose take-home pay was derisory. What is more, there was a thriving traffic in 'zombie cheques', salaries being paid to non-existent or even dead people. This was a practice that enabled some public employees to accumulate a number of monthly payments. Aristide called it a *véritable gabégie*, a right old mess. Soon, there were the inevitable sackings; hundreds of Town Hall staff went in February, 400 port employees were dismissed in April, 350 at the Ministry of Health in July and so on. The Haitian government was being prodded towards this action by the International Monetary Fund who made it a pre-condition for the flowing of aid. By August some 8,000 jobs had gone. For a while whole ministries (Social Affairs, Health and Agriculture, for example) had to be closed down and all their employees dismissed before being reconstructed from scratch in an attempt to create something like efficiency and a capacity for action. Unfortunately, these tended to be the very departments whose programmes needed to be implemented immediately so that people could see that their new government was getting on with things. The organizational chaos in the institutions of government was a major contributing factor to the slow progress which outsiders soon began to notice and criticize.

The ruthless dismissal of public service employees created a great deal of lasting resentment and stored up trouble for the future. I visited Haiti in October 1993, two years after the *coup d'état* which ousted Aristide. Things were at their lowest point; the Governors' Island accord which should have brought the president back to Haiti had been subverted by the activities of a number of gun-waving drunken thugs who'd managed to get the *USS Harlan Country*, bringing technical experts and logistical supplies, turned away from the Port-au-Prince harbour. The day after this rebuff, I went out with two other journalists to try to meet the high command of these armed men. We were able to talk our way into their headquarters in the Café Normandie, a dank and dreary building in the city centre, just a block away from the presidential palace and the military headquarters. These men were activists associated with the neo-fascist group known as FRAPH.

Although it was only mid-morning, rum was flowing freely and a couple of dozen red-eyed and loud-mouthed men waved their automatic weapons with an abandon that wasn't good for my nerves. They were shouting loudly to make themselves heard against the blaring noise of heavily amplified music. I asked them to tell me what they thought of Aristide. The very name evoked a Pavlovian response. They bristled with violent anger as they told me just how much they hated him. And one of their most deeply felt criticisms was the way he'd dismissed government employees during his short period in power. There are so few jobs in Haiti. Those in work cherish their employment greatly and considerable patronage is applied to create opportunities for favoured people. Those who get this kind of work are not in the least interested in questions of efficiency or capacity or even justice. In flushing this system out, Aristide had pulled down a house of cards and destroyed a corrupt order built on nepotism and racketeering. The people talking to me, some of whom had clearly lost out in the sackings, wanted to tear him apart limb from limb. Fired up with alcohol, they didn't spare me any details in their account of just how they'd inflict the slowest and most painful death possible on him if he ever showed his face in Haiti again.

Prime Minister Préval was soon facing the parliament with an outline of his government's programme. He promised a major overhaul of the health system, an investigation into recent political crimes, the decentralization of power away from Port-au-Prince towards the provinces, a continuing fight against corruption, and a strengthening of ties with other countries (especially Caribbean countries). He promised that his government would respect private property and protect foreign and local investment. But over and above all these items, he set the need for a thorough reform of agriculture. 'Our stomachs should never depend on those outside our country,' he said. And he called on people of goodwill, employers and workers alike, to co-operate with the government to achieve these ends. For Aristide, this whole programme could be summed up quite simply as a battle against illiteracy, malnutrition and deforestation. Préval got the list down to two items by August: an increase in productivity and a radical agrarian reform.

In his autobiography, Aristide spelled out some of the policies and approaches he believed necessary to achieve these objectives. He was clear that there had to be a redistribution of wealth and that this needed to be attained through fiscal policy. But this was not socialist ranting based on the politics of envy. Such language might have justified that conclusion in other places. But Aristide was simply wanting the law of the land applied. There was widespread tax evasion, especially on the part of those who should have been paying the most. Smuggling and a thriving alternative economy based on contraband was also robbing the national exchequer of a great deal of money. So the president was above all interested in shifting wealth from the illegitimate sector to the mainstream of Haiti's accountable economic life. And he was desperately keen on achieving this in a way that respected local realities. 'It was better to proceed slowly,' he wrote, 'at our own rhythm, with the insights of those who were in touch with the popular consciousness, than to follow recipes from foreign models provided to us by specialists.'

Aristide repeated this appeal for a pace of progress consistent with local capacity and culture again and again. He kept on reminding his audiences that he could only at best hope to lead the Haitian people *'de la misère à la pauvreté'*, from [sheer] misery to [dignified] poverty. There were no economic miracles on offer. Of course, the World Bank and the IMF soon began to apply pressure for greater urgency and were offering their pre-packaged adjustment programmes that took very little account of the realities of Haitian culture. Even someone as astute as Greg Chamberlain, a shrewd journalist who has become a specialist on Haitian affairs over the last twenty-five years, was soon weighing into Aristide for his lack of progress. Within a month of the inauguration, Chamberlain was reminding a conference in Paris that Haiti now had a president who was a kind of demi-god, a saviour figure who'd even compared himself with Christ. Would he content himself,

Chamberlain wondered, with mystical utterances, charismatic and populist gestures, or would he use his undoubted gifts to change attitudes and move the country on? 'The people are waiting, demanding a great deal,' he added.

No one can doubt Haiti's need for speed and a sense of urgency. But equally, no one should remain ignorant of the dangers of aid-driven programmes formed by people with little knowledge and less interest in the countries whose needs they address. I'll never forget a meeting I had—just after the ousting of Jean-Claude Duvalier—with an Argentinian, Marcelo Elysettche, who, after ten years co-ordinating World Bank and IMF aid to Haiti, was taking a sabbatical in London. He told me of a meeting that had recently taken place in Washington, a 'cry meeting' he called it, where senior executives from the different programmes met for forty-eight hours to share their Haitian experiences. The meeting was off the record and people were free (indeed they were encouraged) to be as open and frank as necessary, taking no heed of the usual need to dress up their work in the terminology of 'success'. It had been a horrendous meeting. No one could report anything of substance. All spoke of millions of dollars going down the drain. The whole aid programme had been mounted by external bodies who knew almost nothing about Haiti. The overriding objectives had been to underpin the Duvalierist government in its need for prestige projects, fat pay cheques for its favourite sons, and a no-questions-asked freedom to divert funds into their own bank accounts. Since Fidel Castro was still supreme in neighbouring Cuba, and since his every Marxist move sent shivers of paranoid fear down the spines of Cold War besotted American governments, this uncritical approach to 'aid' for Haiti could always be justified on political grounds.

A very similar picture was painted (in an article in *The Caribbean*, March 1991) by Kathie Klarrelch. 'Haiti is a country,' she wrote, 'which has received one of the largest volumes of international assistance in the world without any noticeable improvement... Those projects that have survived have been seriously impeded by weak institutional structures and corrupt handling of public funds.' She concluded with the declaration that Haiti now needed a highly creative approach to problem-solving, drawing on the undoubted recent successes of grass-roots organizing. Aristide would certainly have given his amen to that.

Haiti's experience of aid had left a bad taste in the mouth. The kind of aid Haitians had tended to receive had little to do with building infrastructure, developing self-reliance, offering basic human rights or investing in long-term stability. It was all opportunist, short-term, political; a bankrolling of supposedly friendly (even if unscrupulous) governments. Is it any wonder that Aristide, knowing all this in the very marrow of his bones, should have had mixed feelings about receiving aid? Or that he preferred a slower rate of progress with programmes that respected Haiti's poor and engaged *their* energies in the task of meeting their crying needs?

For all that, promises of aid started pouring in. When Aristide took the reins of power there was a serious electricity shortage in Port-au-Prince. The World Bank and the French government were quick off the mark with $9 million for the purchase of new generators from Canada. There was a delay in providing these because of the Gulf War—whose demands, of course, overrode the needs of a tinpot little country like Haiti. From France, Taiwan, Canada, Venezuela, Japan and the European Community came promises amounting to tens of millions of dollars. Grain worth $150 million over four years was promised to Haiti in March under the terms of the Lomé agreement on cooperation between Europe and the world's poor countries.

Aristide was not very enthusiastic about this kind of aid. The scale of Haiti's food needs may have dictated this agreement but the president knew that flooding the market with surplus grain from the developed world would only demotivate local farmers whose own crops could never compete with these imported handouts. Even worse, since much of the food aid was wheat (which isn't grown in Haiti), there would be the highly questionable consequence of changing local tastes in favour of crops which could never be cultivated on Haitian soil.

The United States waited six weeks before making the first announcement on its own proposals for aid to Haiti. Ambassador Alvin Adams, in a radio interview, spoke of a total of $82 million for the current fiscal year. And, for the first time since the aborted election of November 1987, part of that aid would go direct to the new government as a mark of respect for its legitimacy. But, for all these fine words, it took a long time for any American money to find its way to Port-au-Prince. By April there was nothing and Aristide was driven to plead with the wealthy Haitian bourgeoisie to lend his government some money so that public service employees could be paid. In May, the president was appealing to the Haitian diaspora around the world for financial commitments that would enable his government to proceed with essential and urgent programmes.

Throughout this time there was great political uncertainty. Two former Duvalierists were arrested on 26 March for conspiring to overthrow the government. On 23 April, Prime Minister Préval announced that another plot had been uncovered, part of a sustained campaign to destabilize the government and undermine the constitution by inciting people to loot and kill, to attack people's property and stir up disturbances. The army, he said, was on full alert. And indeed there were a number of outbreaks of violence on the streets. In one of these, in the northern city of Cap Haitien, food depots were raided by a crowd protesting at the cost of essential foodstuffs and, in the uproar that followed, a man was killed. There was an ugly mood abroad.

In mid-May, the Secretary General of the United Nations, Javier Pérez de Cuellar, made a general appeal to member states 'to send aid urgently to the new, democratically-elected Haitian government... The situation in Haiti is not only serious,' the Secretary-General added, 'but it seems to be getting worse all the time through a combination of economic and social factors that Haiti has no means of controlling and even less chance of overcoming on its own... Haiti isn't wanting billions of dollars, only a tiny fraction of that, to push forward some essential programmes. The Haitian government is hoping that agreed bilateral and multilateral packages can be forthcoming so that its economy can start moving forward.' This is truly an astonishing speech. It makes it abundantly clear that the international community knew full well just how difficult things were in Haiti. And it also reveals how slowly the wheels of cooperation were turning, how empty so many of the fine promises were. The month of May was on the point of passing into history with little other than fine words for the Haitian government to chew on.

It was 31 May before the American government signed an accord with its Haitian counterpart for a $12 million payment from the total aid budget of $82 million promised for the year 1991–92. It was two months since Ambassador Adams had announced this package, and four months since Aristide's inauguration. And the $12 million announced now was granted for very specific purposes. Under the general title 'economic stabilization', the money was intended to repay debts to foreign countries contracted either by the current government or its predecessors. It was not money that could be spent on government programmes in education, agriculture, or primary health care. Yet these were the overriding needs at this time. Just a little help with these 'front-of-house' spending programmes would have given huge encouragement to a government seeking desperately to give its people some evidence of getting on with things. All they had to show were promises. Lots and lots of promises.

These reached their apogee in July. At a meeting of industrial nations in Paris, a Haitian delegation, seeking to lose its status as the only LAC (Less Advanced Country) in the Americas, put forward an application for $250 million to finance a number of development projects. Renaud Bernardin, leader of the four-man delegation, declared: 'If people are to believe in democracy, it isn't enough just to have a vote. Democracy only means anything at all if it translates itself into the terms of everyday life.' To everyone's surprise, a group of nations comprising the United States, France, Germany, Canada and the European Community came up with promises that actually exceeded the amount asked for by a full $100 million, an amount that might even rise to $420 million if certain conditions were met. This money would go towards a reduction of the national debt, reforms of public sector institutions, and some ninety-four social and economic projects. It was all very startling and the rather emotional vote of thanks given by the Haitian delegation was received with a heartfelt round of applause from the audience. This warm and human touch from what would normally be such a matter-of-fact gathering was somewhat modified by an acid-dry codicil that stated in flat and deliberate prose: *'Les déboursements ne seront effectués qu'après élaboration par Haiti d'études techniques'*, no money would be forthcoming until detailed studies had been made. A reasonable stipulation, no doubt. But it inevitably meant further delay.

The performance of the international community in offering such slow support for this fledgling democracy taking its first frail steps in a brave new world leaves so much to be desired. It recalled some of Haiti's first experiences as a new nation in 1804. The slave-owning nations with colonies in the region had been terrified at the news of Haiti's slave rebellion. They had feared that the defeat of Napoleon's army and the creation of the first black republic in the world might destabilize their own colonies, so no government had taken any steps to recognize or support the new régime in Port-au-Prince. France had opened up trading relationships only after an already impoverished Haiti agreed to pay a huge indemnity against French losses in its former colony. The Haitian government was still faithfully repaying this debt in 1915 when the American marines landed. One of the first acts of the occupying power was to pay off Haiti's debts in Paris with a huge loan launched on Wall Street, making the Caribbean republic an American vassal state at a single stroke.

Denmark was the next European nation to recognize Haiti, followed by Britain in 1827 when its own anti-slavery legislation was safely passed. The Vatican waited until 1860 and the United States until 1862 before putting their relationship with Haiti on a formal basis. For the Americans, only the Civil War and the leadership of Abraham Lincoln could lead them to recognize a nation led by blacks. They held fast to this racist position despite the fact that a contingent of Haitian blacks had fought alongside the Americans in their own wars of independence against the British, and even though the Haitian government had helped an embarrassed US administration in the 1820s by receiving thousands of American blacks as part of a mass colonization movement. Perhaps the most disappointing experience of all, however, was the treatment accorded to the Haitians by Simon Bolivar. Bolivar had received encouragement and supplies in 1816 from the then president of Haiti, Alexandre Pétion. This had helped him in his efforts to free Colombia and Venezuela from the Spanish yoke. But at the Congress of Panama in 1825, an event which gathered the heads of state of all the newly independent nations in the Americas, Bolivar colluded with American intransigence in a way that led to the exclusion of the Haitian president from the assembly. John Quincy Adams, the American president, refused to sit at a negotiating table with Jean-Pierre Boyer, the Haitian head of state. But Bolivar's own reported views are as vile as any. He underlined how important it was for the ruling classes of the newly independent states to keep together to safeguard the continent from the fear of 'this tremendous monster which has devoured the island of Santo Domingo and the numerical preponderance of its indigenous inhabitants'.

So Haiti had a long experience of being kept at arm's length by the international community and of being allowed to fight its own battles and find its own way in the world. Even so, it would have made such a difference to Aristide's government if there had been a more concerted, committed, and immediate response to the opportunity afforded by the successful election of December 1990. As it was, the fact that Aristide, for all the lavish promises he'd received, could show almost no material progress at the end of his first six months in power gave ammunition to those who were blaming him for inefficiency, an inability to deliver, and lack of know-how.

Chaos in the institutions of his own government and

procrastination on the part of the international community in sending aid were two serious problems for Aristide to contend with. But that was by no means all.

As early as mid-March ominous noises began to emanate from the neighbouring Dominican Republic. President Joaquin Balaguer declared that his government was not yet ready to deal with the new Haitian administration. 'The political scene in Haiti is not yet stable enough,' he said, 'to be able to dialogue in an atmosphere of tranquillity and order or to lay the ground rules for the development of normal relations between our two countries.' This statement about Haiti's lack of stability was clearly intended to contribute to the very problem it identified. Within a week, General Rafael Bello Andino, secretary to the blind President Balaguer and widely considered to be the strong man in his administration, issued a warning about the 'delicate' situation in Haiti and alleged that a number of Dominican citizens had been arrested in Port-au-Prince and forcibly repatriated. This led a former president to call for the immediate expulsion of the half million Haitians living in the Dominican Republic, arguing that it was a matter of life or death for his country. The presence of these Haitians, he declared, was 'a cultural menace and a time bomb which might one day prove catastrophic for all Dominicans'.

These anti-Haitian views were hardly new. There had been a long history of animosity between the two republics stretching back to the beginning of the nineteenth century. For over twenty years (1822–44) a Haitian government had ruled the whole island. It is no exaggeration to suggest that the bitter resentment caused by that episode continues to rankle in the Dominican mind. Through the 1850s the armies of both republics were in a constant state of alert as threats of invasion were uttered by both sides. The fires of mutual hatred were fanned to their greatest intensity in a border incident in 1937 which saw thousands of Haitians slaughtered. That incident continues to fester in the collective Haitian memory.

For all that, however, the two countries have always been very dependent upon each other. Every year, thousands of Haitians have crossed the border to cut the sugar cane in the harvesting season. Numbers of them have settled in the neighbouring republic and never returned. Thousands of children have been born there. An agreement between the governments of Balaguer and Jean-Claude Duvalier in 1978 gave the Dominicans an assured supply of cheap labour (15,000 day labourers for up to one month during the season) for which the Haitian dictator was given a little blood money (US$1,225,000 in cash). The treatment of these migrant workers has been scandalous, with widely recognized flagrant abuses of human rights. The US-based Lawyers' Committee for Human Rights reported how children, some as young as eight, were lured across the border from Haiti, sold by racketeers to plantations and forced to work up to sixteen hours a day, seven days a week, cutting cane for about 20p per day. Armed guards patrolled the overcrowded work camps which had no electricity or water. The plight of these workers has been brilliantly chronicled in Maurice Lemoine's barely fictionalized novel *Bitter Sugar*. That a Haitian government could have been complicit in such an arrangement and party to such abuses is one of the greatest acts of treachery in the whole of the country's turbulent history.

Dominican feelings about their neighbours contain an undoubtedly racist element. Many, including Balaguer, like to talk of racial purity. The Dominican leadership was mostly white and the population of the country mostly mulatto. Such racial prejudice was now clearly in evidence in these latest declarations about the need to rid the country of large numbers of its Haitian population. But before long, the matter moved beyond mere rhetoric and Aristide, sensing trouble, indicated a readiness to meet his opposite number. He was well aware that the Dominican Republic was the place of refuge for a number of Duvalierist exiles who were well placed to influence the Dominican government and to exploit any destabilization in Haiti. So Aristide sought to pour oil on troubled waters. The last thing he needed was a running battle with his neighbours; he had plenty to preoccupy him at home. So he said he was ready and willing to meet Balaguer, that any differences should be addressed in a sensible and friendly manner. Meanwhile, his foreign minister was denying rumours of bad feeling, avowing that the relationship between the two governments was in good shape.

But this façade of sweetness and light was torn apart in mid-June by an announcement from the Dominican Minister of Labour. He decreed that all Haitian workers under the age of fifteen who were engaged to cut cane, even if accompanied by their parents, and all who were over sixty, were to be repatriated. Soon, there was news of 800 Haitian workers, mostly young, being thrown into prison. This was done with no expression of regret by a government that even made moves to seek the aid of the United Nations and the International Red Cross to achieve its ends. 'Our country can no longer tolerate the massive numbers who come,' a government spokesman said, 'we need help to get them to return to their own country.'

The Haitian Foreign Minister, Marie-Denise Fabien Jean-Louis, was at the border to receive the first contingent of expelled workers, a group of twenty-nine children. But others followed in a quickening succession. The Haitian government protested, calling these arbitrary acts inadmissible and contrary to accepted practice. It called for official discussions between the two governments so that the interests and rights of those being expelled could be safeguarded. The Haitian press was far more outspoken, calling the expulsions 'shameful' and 'humiliating', and even going to the point of calling them 'racist measures'. Balaguer rejected all these protests as 'absolutely inacceptable'.

Soon the trickle of expelled workers grew into a steady stream: 270 crossed the border in mid-June, 800 a week later, 90 in mid-July. The total had reached 3,000 by the end of July and 8,000 a month later. In addition to those being forced to leave, as many as 20,000 others were thought to have crossed the border of their own accord for fear of possible expulsion. The situation was causing great anxiety to the Haitian authorities who feared the confusion would give macoute elements an opportunity to stir up unrest. Leaders of the different political parties denounced the Dominican government. There were any number of suggestions about what needed to be done—that reprisals be taken against Dominican citizens living in Haiti, that a tent village be established to house the returnees, that a fund be created to help them, and (a suggestion by Marc Bazin) that a special commission be set up to define Haitian nationality. This last proposal was intended to prevent the Dominican Republic using the crisis to offload its own undesirables by pretending they were Haitians. Aristide's response was cautious. He set up a special crisis committee to monitor developments and co-ordinate information about what was happening.

Roman Catholic bishops in Santo Domingo added their voices to those protesting against the expulsions. The whole policy was based on 'false nationalism', they declared and they went on to suggest that the crisis was a deliberately stage-managed affair on the part of Balaguer who wanted to detract attention from the fact that he was about to sign a stringent IMF loan package which was bound to be unpopular. Haitian bishops joined their Dominican colleagues in denouncing the expatriations and calling on their own government to act intelligently in the search for a speedy resolution to the crisis. But all the calls for calm could not prevent demonstrations taking place on the streets of Port-au-Prince, and loud criticisms of the Haitian government's slow and moderate responses began to be heard.

A delegation from the Organization of American States (OAS) arrived at the end of July to attempt to mediate a settlement of the dispute. Sharp disagreements with the Dominican expulsion policy had been voiced in the United Nations as well as in OAS and CARICOM (Caribbean Economic Communities) forums. A UN spokesperson talked of the 'serious economic problems' which the return of these workers would cause within Haiti. Such voices were being raised on Haiti's behalf just a matter of weeks after the UN Secretary General had appealed to the international community to help the Haitian government with its financial needs. The delay in directing aid to Haiti, together with the serious destabilization caused by the

Dominican crisis, were two heavy storms which any third-world country would have had difficulty in riding out. For a nation whose experiment with democracy was so utterly brand new to have to undergo such tempests was nigh on catastrophic. When judgments are formed about who was responsible for making a military takeover possible just seven months after the euphoria of 7 February, it will not suffice to identify internal causes alone. The collapse of Haitian democracy occurred under the very noses of those who'd had the dimensions of the country's needs spelled out for them in the clearest terms but had been able to offer nothing more than fulsome words and empty promises.

The OAS peacemaking initiative got under way. Meanwhile, the expulsions continued throughout the first weeks of August. The death of five children at the hands of the Dominican military stimulated yet further and even more vigorous denunciations. One human rights group in Europe accused the Dominican Republic of 'inhuman behaviour, slavery, and racism in its anti-Haitian policies'. Under all this pressure (and with its IMF agreement safely signed and tucked away), the Dominican Republic finally agreed, on 19 August, to suspend its expulsion policy for one month. This would allow the International Labour Office to set up appropriate mechanisms to regulate the movement of workers across the border. This took the steam out of the crisis and, in the event, Aristide's ouster brought this unsavoury incident to an end before the ILO's findings could be completed. The whole affair undoubtedly made life far more difficult than it need have been for Aristide and his government.

At the end of September, Aristide addressed the General Assembly of the United Nations. He formulated his speech in the form of 'ten commandments' for democracy. He devoted a key passage to the Dominican crisis. This is what he said on that occasion:

It is not that we should weep at what is happening in the Dominican Republic, it is a matter rather of defending human rights in the name of the Haitian people. Haiti and the Dominican Republic are two wings of one and the same bird, two nations that share the beautiful island of Hispaniola... that is why we must always continue to work with the Dominican people as brothers and sisters... It is regrettable when human rights are trampled underfoot as is now the case... and that the question of colour enters the picture.

Arrested and expelled to Haitian territory, these people ordinarily have neither roof, nor family, nor employment. Already, conservative estimates set the number of repatriates at more than fifty thousand. In the hope that the international bodies concerned will help us to ensure that the fundamental rights of the persons are respected... we proclaim with pride and dignity that:

> *Never again*
> *Never again*
> *will our Haitian sisters and brothers*
> *be sold*
> *to convert their blood into bitter sugar.*

To my Dominican sisters and brothers whom I love so much, I say: let us go forward together to build this peaceful world.

When due account is taken of the formal setting for these words, the passion and the depth of Aristide's feelings are barely disguised. The whole of this incident shook him to the core. It also made Haiti a much more volatile place to govern.

A properly functioning democracy assumes the effective working of three different arms of government. It pre-supposes a focused executive to formulate policies and to put them into practice. But those policies have to be agreed by a legislative body which must vet them and modify them according to their understanding of what is best and most workable for the country as a whole. They must certainly prevent an over-powerful executive from steamrollering its programmes into action without due regard for financial, cultural, or other considerations. And a healthy judiciary is the third arm; it must hold every citizen and institution to the law of the land and the requirements of the constitution. The seven brave months of legitimate rule experienced by Haiti in 1991 showed just how ill-equipped the country was in all three of these sectors. Most of the analysis of Aristide's first period of government has tended to weigh up his own personal performance and that of his government. Any shortcomings in the executive, however, were as nothing compared with the total chaos that reigned in the other two arms of Haiti's nascent democracy.

The parliament was a disaster. It was not helped by the existence of so many political parties. In the Chamber of Deputies there were twelve parties represented and the Senate counted eight. It is probably a euphemism to speak of 'parties' at all. The largest were coalitions of various interest groups while the smallest were little more than a few people who'd got together and given themselves an imposing title. Just one example will tell the whole tale. The PNT (Parti National du Travail, National Work Party) won three seats in the Chamber of Deputies and one in the Senate. This little party (there were several others just like it represented in the parliament) was itself a combination of four mini-parties with grand acronyms: PNUD, PPH, PPNH and PRN. It was all very confusing. Since no one party commanded an absolute majority in either Chamber, and further, since Aristide's decision to impose an FNCD president on the deputies and senators alike was so resented, it was clear that this parliamentary body would not quickly understand its functions in the outworking of democracy. The mere business of getting a majority of votes around any particular issue proved difficult again and again. It was always so much easier for the parliament to block the executive's suggestions than to contribute to a purposive and effective legislative programme. By mid-August, the parliament had voted on a mere three of the 100 laws submitted by the government. In all this, of course, it didn't help very much that Aristide had never really been part of the FNCD; that body had put him forward as a candidate but there was never a close relationship between them. Consequently, the FNCD (which was by far the largest group in both Chambers) found itself on the opposite side of government proposals quite as often as other, smaller parties.

One of the first things the new parliament did actually agree on (a unanimous vote in both Chambers) was to bring into force an article in the Constitution that accorded special powers to the president 'to implement urgent reforms in the apparatus of the State'. These special powers, defined as 'any reform judged necessary', were to last six months. It is interesting that, during the whole of that period, Aristide was accused again and again by the parliament of acting 'unconstitutionally' when, in fact, all he was doing was to use the special powers they'd granted him. These powers were accorded on 1 March. Yet less than two weeks later, the Senate rejected unanimously his nomination of five new appeal court judges. Similarly, they blocked his nomination of a number of diplomats including ambassadors to Canada, France and the United States. The parliament got so worried about the special powers they'd granted the president that they set up a committee to review the arrangement. But they never rescinded those powers and the six months accorded for their implementation ran their full course until the end of August.

After the *coup d'état* that removed Aristide from power, a concerted effort was made by his opponents to give some kind of legitimacy to the ousting. In a special number of the journal *L'Union* published in November 1991 (six weeks after the coup) a long list of complaints was published alleging that Aristide had acted repeatedly in breach of the Constitution. Of the seventy-nine instances listed, sixty-four occurred during the very period of the president's special powers. Yet this fact is never once mentioned in this long (and pettifogging) indictment. Aristide is accused of stepping outside the bounds of the Constitution in order, for example, to add his 'unlawful' signature to a loan agreement, to issue a decree separating the rural police from the army, to proceed with the installation of new judges, to accept an aid package from Germany, to pay an unannounced visit to the parliament, and to make an appeal to the army to do everything it could to safeguard human lives in its search for a gang plotting a coup. The whole document is pathetic in its attempt to establish a 'constitutional' case to justify the violent overthrow of legitimate rule. That it could set out this case without once mentioning the special powers openly conceded to the president by both houses of the parliament is surely a sign of desperation on the part of those who conspired to terminate Haiti's short experiment with democracy in this way.

Clearly the context within which Aristide was working to establish Haiti's first experience of democratic government was fraught with difficulty. Barely functioning government institutions and an ill-disposed and inexperienced parliament offered a poor prospect for rapid progress on the domestic front. Put alongside this a judicial system that had withered and rotted on Duvalier's bough and it is clear that Aristide had almost no political infrastructure to work with within Haiti. Meanwhile over the border, the huffing and puffing in Santo Domingo was also an unpleasant fact of life for the new government, and the arrival of thousands of expelled Haitian workers from the neighbouring republic was an undoubtedly destabilizing factor. And all the while, the slow delivery of aid from the international community added its own turn of the screw. All these negative factors were harbingers of a less-than-propitious future and you didn't have to be an expert in politics to sense the fragility of the situation.

An incident which heaped its own combustible material onto a bonfire waiting to ignite was the trial of Roger Lafontant. Since his arrest in January, he and a number of his accomplices had been languishing in the city's penitentiary. Despite all the rhetoric of justice that had characterized Aristide's months in power, no known Duvalierists had been brought to court for their offences against the people. It became more and more evident, therefore, that Lafontant, the 'bird in the hand', was likely to be offered up on behalf of all those others 'in the bush'. At a time when Aristide was feeling under the greatest pressure, with nothing seeming to go right at all, he ordered that Lafontant be brought to trial. He hoped this would buy him some time and give people something else to focus on for a while. But it proved to be a very difficult trial to organize, and it brought its own problems too.

The trial was planned for 29 July, the date which, in Duvalier's time, had been set aside as a special day in honour of the Tontons Macoutes. A few days before that date, on the fourth anniversary of the Jean Rabel massacre, Aristide went on national television and made a very strong speech in which he condemned all those who'd shown opposition to the forthcoming trial. Those who continued in this path, the president hinted, would themselves run the risk of being arrested. Nothing would stop the course of justice which would be done and seen to be done 'according to the will of the people'. He went on to explain this phrase in terms of the huge majority who'd voted for him in the general election the previous December. To some it sounded ominous and laden with a populist notion of justice that had little to do with the courts. But he went on to correct this image. 'It is the law that must prevail,' he proclaimed. 'As God is my witness, we'll sweep the whole country with the broom of justice.' Then, turning his attention to a judge who'd recently freed a known macoute arrested for alleged complicity in a plot to overthrow the government, Aristide lashed out at the cowardice of those judges and government legal officers who—too many of them— had bathed in the waters of corruption.

It proved almost impossible to find a judge ready to take Lafontant's trial at all. And it was even harder to find people ready to serve on the jury. Warnings were issued both to those who were eligible to serve and also to doctors who might issue them certificates of exoneration about the penalties for such tactics of evasion. But that didn't make things any easier. Another ominous development was the formation of neighbourhood vigilante committees who set themselves the task of ensuring that there were no escapes from prison before the trial could take place.

The day of the trial was marked by disturbances and an attempted mutiny at the Navy headquarters. A number of officers were arrested and accused of planning a *coup d'état*. Businesses closed for fear that violence would erupt on the streets. A large and noisy crowd gathered around the courthouse carrying banners with anti-Lafontant slogans such as: 'A guilty verdict for Lafontant equals justice for 80,000 victims.' Others were carrying tyres clearly destined to become 'necklaces' if that should prove to be necessary. There was an ugly atmosphere.

The trial proved to be a marathon. It opened at 10am on 29 July and ran throughout the day and the whole of the following night, ending at 7am on 30 July, a twenty-one hour continuous stint. The crowd followed every detail on radio and television which carried the proceedings live. Lafontant was charged, along with twenty-one others, of organizing a *coup d'état* and seeking to prevent the accession to power of Jean-Bertrand Aristide. In the absence of any ready volunteers from the ranks of Haiti's experienced attorneys, five young trainee lawyers had been chosen by the Minister of Justice to conduct the defence. But their services were spurned by Lafontant who also chose to keep silent rather than give evidence in what he considered a rigged trial. This didn't stop him interrupting people giving evidence, however, or accusing the authorities of abusing his rights.

The jury took two hours to reach their verdict before finding Lafontant and seventeen of his co-defendants guilty of the charges brought against them. This was greeted by wild applause from all those who packed the courtroom. The judge then passed sentence, the maximum allowed by the Constitution, of hard labour for life. He gave the prisoners leave to appeal.

The trial evoked a mixture of responses. Government supporters rejoiced at what they called 'the burial of the macoute system', and the 'funeral of Duvalierism'. But independent observers agreed that the proceedings could have been carried out under far better conditions. Jean-Jacques Honorat, director of CHADEL (a human rights organization), described the proceedings as a 'judicial farce' and called for a new trial. This call was echoed by a number of other political figures in Port-au-Prince. There could be no doubt that this was a show trial, a device deemed necessary by Aristide as he sought to keep faith with his public and prove to them that he was as good as his word in bringing Duvalierist criminals to book. That public showed the strength of its feelings within earshot of the courtroom and its physical presence was an intimidating factor for those conducting the trial. Any less severe verdict would certainly have incensed the crowd and driven them to vent their anger in other directions. Aristide admitted as much in a speech he gave a few days later to a gathering of schoolchildren. He spoke of his opposition to necklacing before saying: 'When those in charge of [Lafontant's] trial referred to a possible sentence of fifteen years, the crowd outside got angry and some bounced tyres on the pavement, but when life sentences were announced the people put their matches and petrol away. Necklacing will disappear gradually as corruption is eliminated.' This was hardly a ringing condemnation either of necklacing or of street justice.

In the light of all these factors which, between them, made Aristide's task so difficult and dispiriting, it is extraordinary that some real progress was being registered in a number of directions. In a speech to the parliament in early September, Prime Minister Préval announced an eleven per cent increase in total State receipts and a 3 per cent fall in expenditure. Inflation had gone down from 22 per cent to 12 per cent. Money owed to the exchequer had fallen to $13 million and Préval was confident that that figure would be entirely wiped out within a month. Two government monopolies were, for the first time in a number of years, yielding a profit for the treasury. The cement factory was showing a profit of $300,000 per month and the figure for the flour factory was $100,000. All this was a remarkable achievement. Even Aristide's main political rival Marc Bazin, who had some real criticisms of the government's record, admitted its successes. 'The government has done some splendid things,' he said, drawing attention particularly to 'their cooperation with the army, the struggle against smuggling and insecurity, the increased efficiency in fiscal policy, the provision of electricity and the dismissal of those in government service who have shown themselves disloyal to the ideals of democracy'.

In two other areas Aristide's government could show good progress. The first was his record in cracking down on drug trafficking. Another political leader, reflecting on this matter some years later, put it very succinctly.

The lack of will [to deal with drug dealing] in Haiti reflects a similar tendency to be found in the international community at large. Under Aristide, whose opinions on most things I don't even begin to share, there was a real desire to combat this evil. That was one of the main reasons which led to his downfall at the hands of the military. Today [this was 1994], the junta wants to remain in power at all costs in order to go on taking its cut. Throughout these three years of military rule, and in the time preceding Aristide too, not one drug trafficker was ever picked up. Yet more than 200 were arrested in the short time of Jean-Bertrand Aristide's fleeting presidency.

This is a fine testimony from a political opponent who paid this compliment under the cloak of anonymity.

The other sign of progress came in the field of human rights. Figures gathered from various sources showed the following pattern:

Prosper Avril

June 1989–February 1990

89 deaths and 636 other violations

Ertha Pascal Trouillot

March 1990–January 1991

241 deaths and 349 other violations

Jean-Bertrand Aristide

February 1991–June 1991

26 deaths and 94 other violations

189

Very soon after Aristide's removal from power, his critics were expressing concern at his human rights record. This was part of the general discrediting of Aristide that soon began to take place. But it is very important to maintain a sense of perspective. Independent commentators, writing near the time of the coup, were all speaking of 'a very significant improvement' over the record of his predecessors in the field of human rights.

In this maelstrom of events and pressures, achievements and dangers, it is difficult to catch a glimpse of Aristide the man. He rushes from one crisis to another, often interfering where it might have been better to leave matters to others, making speeches and appealing to the international community. I was in Haiti several times in these months but found it impossible to pin the president down. I had to watch from the edge of the crowd and listen to the opinions and advice of fellow-bystanders. I've been able to find just one personal account of Aristide during this time. It is part of a feature article written by Bella Stumbo in the magazine section of the *Los Angeles Times* in April 1991. Stumbo interviewed Marjorie Michel, daughter of Smarck Michel who was Minister of Commerce and Industry in Aristide's government at that time (he was replaced a couple of months later). There had been many rumours about the president's friendship with a woman, a relationship that had raised eyebrows and set tongues wagging. After all, Aristide was still a Roman Catholic priest. Marjorie Michel was soon ready to be identified as the woman in question. She was twenty-seven and a Brussels-educated psychologist. Her testimony is worth quoting extensively:

> ...He's a very secret person, you'll never know exactly what's on his mind. And the man is ridiculous. For a psychologist, he has no idea how to take care of himself. He doesn't eat, he doesn't sleep... This is why I'm first lady. I run into his office, and I say, "Please, I think now we should go eat." When he stays [at her father's house], I go into his

room and I turn off the light and I say, "OK, now it's time to sleep."

She became his friend, she says, right after the Salesians expelled him, an event that didn't simply anger him—'He was crushed. He felt so alone. He was so used to living in groups, with other priests. But, suddenly, he was left so alone. He told me, "Now I'm sitting here in this room alone, with no family, except the poor people."'

During the inaugural she sat in the family box. She shows up at most of Aristide's press conferences. Just recently, a New York Haitian newspaper announced her engagement to the new president. She laughs, enjoying the gossip, but says pointedly, 'We are social friends. Political friends. With Aristide, if you don't fit into his priorities, you're out. And my priorities are also the poor people. I don't have a superiority complex. I want people to be *like* me. So Aristide and I, we fit.'

Politics besets the friendship. 'He worries that we are not born into the same class. He tells me that. He has no problems with me, or any other social class. But when people see him with me, they see the bourgeoisie. It's a very big problem for him. And if he has to sacrifice me for the people, he will. For example, if we have to have a civil war, the people's feelings are first. If I get killed, he accepts it. If 20,000 are going to die, it's fine for the movement. It is all that matters to him.'

She agrees with Aristide's critics, that he's surrounded himself with yes-men: 'All these people, Gladys [Lauture], René [Préval], [Antoine] Adrien, William [Smarth], even my father, they will never push him very hard,' she says, exasperated. 'They fight behind the scenes, but in front of him, they're peaceful. They protect him. They say, "Oh, no, we will not tell him this or that now, because he's so tired." They are always pampering him, protecting him. I tell them to stop it. I am the first lady because I am the only one who will tell him the truth. I don't swallow anything from him. I tell him when he's so full of it!'

She is also looking ahead to the end of Aristide's five-year term. 'I keep telling him, it is very important that he takes someone near to him now, to teach. Because in five years more, Haiti will need another Aristide. If Aristide died today, there is absolutely no one who can replace him. The people don't just like him, he is their *God*. I want Haitians to be their own god. He's human! Over my dead body will he be king."

BELLA STUMBO, 'FROM HORROR TO HOPE: A REPORT FROM HAITI, THE NEWEST DEMOCRACY IN THE AMERICAS', LOS ANGELES TIMES MAGAZINE, 21 APRIL 1991.

This appears to be a genuine personal picture of Aristide during these months. The swirling of events around him is mirrored in his own chaotic and unstructured lifestyle. The sycophancy of his closest advisors tells its own story. Friends they may have been. Whether they were exactly what Haiti (or Aristide) most needed at such a critical juncture is another question. And, from this account, the symbiotic relationship between Aristide and the people is clearly a reality that's rooted deep within his being. It is not just a matter of rhetoric, or a cold desire to gain power by manipulating their emotions. Aristide and the people belong together; he is their mouthpiece and the embodiment of all their hope. It is a powerful picture. But it is shot through with strong presentiments of failure and tragedy.

By the month of August, a number of policy matters were beginning to meet opposition that felt increasingly dangerous. Aristide's known dream of launching a nation-wide literacy campaign to follow up the Roman Catholic Church's aborted *Misyon Alfa* had caused him to impose such a campaign as a matter of priority on a Ministry of Education which already had huge demands on its extremely limited resources. This hijacking of already established programmes, for that's exactly what it was, was deeply resented by a number of people.

Bitter opposition was stirred up in another (and far more ominous) quarter by the president's announcement that he intended to set up a government outlet for the sale of certain kinds of cloth. This would enable poor parents to be spared the exorbitant prices of the market when they needed to provide school uniforms for their children for the start of the new school year. This plan directly challenged the business activities of some powerful merchants who had cornered the school uniform market. The business sector had already been greatly displeased by the declaration of Aristide's Finance Minister that the Haitian gourde would soon be completely detached from the American dollar. This would end an arrangement that had tied the two currencies together since 1919. The gourde had already been partially deregulated before Aristide's time. But the prospect of a freely floating gourde didn't please Haiti's business class. Marc Bazin, former World Bank official and Haitian Finance Minister, probably spoke for them all when he attacked the government for its inability to defend the gourde despite having made fulsome promises to do so. He put this down to Aristide's mad chase for foreign aid (this was July), something he had always said he would never do, and foresaw that this action would represent 'an immediate disincentive to investment, a speeding up of the flight of capital, and increased unemployment'.

But nothing galvanized the opposition of the business class more than Aristide's persistently repeated intention to increase the minimum daily wage of manual workers. The president had convened a meeting of employers in early April to urge them to view an improvement in their workers' standard of living as being more a question of the natural rights of those workers than an act of charity on their own part. A few weeks later, Aristide put a figure on his proposed rise. He suggested it should go up from 15 to 25 gourdes (US$3.57) per day, a rise of 67 per cent. This proposal was a little lower than the 28.5 gourdes being demanded by the unions but considerably higher than the 18.75 being offered by employers.

Aristide tried to pacify the anticipated displeasure of employers with one of his little speeches that seemed more like a conjuring trick than a carefully weighted political utterance. He called for the forging of an alliance between capital and the revolutionary masses (he was speaking on 1 May, Labour Day, which partly accounts for his choice of words). He distinguished between the 'anti-national oligarchy', rich people who turned their back on the country's needs, on the one hand, and the 'patriotic bourgeoisie' on the other, those who saw this as a time of great opportunity for everyone. He assured the rich that he had no plans to dispossess them. 'Yesterday it was fear,' he said, 'today it's peace. Your dollar lives in peace. May the peace of the dollar always be with you, may the fear of peace ever remain far from you.' But these quasi-liturgical cadences wouldn't keep the bourgeois élite at bay for much longer. I was in Haiti at the time of this speech and I had ample opportunity to speak with leading businessmen who were furious at what they perceived to be Aristide's intention to undermine their profits by boosting their wage bills.

It was announced in July that Haiti had lost 8,000 jobs in the industrial sector over the preceding nine months. This had led to a fall in exports to the United States of 9 per cent. This gloomy performance was put down to a diminishing of the competitiveness which Haiti's cheap labour had always offered. Rising production costs (the threat of higher wages) were blamed for the marked cutback in this sector of the Haitian economy. It is ironic that, even while Haiti waited for the international community's promised aid packages to arrive, there was a serious disengagement of foreign finance taking place. And all this was happening before the question of a minimum wage was settled. Even the suspicion of the possibility of rising labour costs was enough to send American capitalists running for cover.

When the parliament eventually confirmed Aristide's measure raising the minimum wage (from 15 to 26 gourdes per day, US$3.70), a storm erupted amongst Haiti's employers. It would do untold damage to commerce, industry and agriculture, they protested; it would discourage investment. Indeed, this piece of legislation was 'bad economics and an act of pure anti-nationalism', they concluded. Only a few months earlier, 'anti-national' had been Aristide's word for the rich who refused to invest in Haiti's future. Now his enemies returned him the compliment. He ignored their criticisms and the law stood. It was due to come into effect on 1 October but, in the event, it never saw the light of day. Aristide was deposed from office the previous day.

He was fast accumulating a number of powerful enemies. As well as all those who'd lost their jobs in the public sector, there were now thousands who'd been dismissed in the industrial sector. Many of these held Aristide personally responsible. What's more, and this was far more significant, the business class were furious with him. They were ready to be shot of him. But even this list of opponents wasn't all. It just went on getting longer.

On 13 August, outside the parliament buildings, there were violent demonstrations by a crowd of Aristide supporters. The ostensible reason for the disturbance was a move on the part of some parliamentarians, including members of the FNCD, to force the resignation of Prime Minister René Préval. The demonstrators were determined to protest loudly against this proposal but they were also angry with US Vice President Dan Quayle who'd addressed the parliament a few days earlier and reminded them of their constitutional duty to put restraints on the powers of government. The crowd's wrath boiled over. Used tyres and cans of petrol, which by now were more and more widely seen on the streets at times of tension, were very much in evidence that day. The demonstrators threatened the deputies with necklacing if they voted against the government. They even attempted to lynch one member of parliament, who was only saved from such an end by police armed with tear gas. The president of the chamber became very alarmed and ruled that conditions were too dangerous for the proceedings to continue. He suspended the session.

The mood was ugly for several days. Soon the presidents of both houses of the parliament resigned. Ernst Pedro Casséus, FNCD leader in the House of Deputies, gave way to Dully Brutus of PANPRA (a member of the ANDP coalition favoured by the US in the 1990 elections). A week later, Eudrice Raymond (also of FNCD) gave up the presidency of the Senate in favour of Déjean Bélizaire of the ANDP. So anti-Aristide forces had won significant concessions in both chambers. In addition, there were defections from the FNCD and accusations were flying about the real reasons for this. Brutus and Bélizaire were to play a key role as 'negotiators' after the coup, as was Senator Thomas Eddy Dupiton, a key defector from the FNCD. The parliament had always been ineffective but now, as a response to the volatility of these times, it found itself moving towards implacable opposition to Aristide and his government.

Opposition was also mounting in the army. General Abraham, who'd overseen the transition from the old order to the new, resigned from his position as commander-in-chief of the armed forces in early July. He was replaced by another general, 42-year-old Raoul Cédras, who had been made Chief of Staff at Aristide's inauguration and who had overseen the successful elections the previous December. Abraham's departure led to a wide-ranging shake-up in the top levels of command. In particular, it brought forward one man who had old scores to settle with Aristide. Lieutenant Colonel Michel François, who became head of the Port-au-Prince police, came from that part of the army that had formerly been under the command of the now dead Colonel Jean-Claude Paul. Paul and his associates had profited enormously from the smuggling and drug running activities organized with Colombian cartels. They were greatly affected by Aristide's crackdown on these sublunary rackets and, therefore, had their own reasons for wanting to mobilize opposition to his presidency. Cédras had had a fairly decent track record and had had no direct involvement in these matters. Soon, however, he would have to decide which side he was on.

All these strands of opposition, though numerically very small, represented huge interests. Aristide was in a no-win situation by the beginning of September. If he remained silent people grew anxious and restive. Yet, when he spoke, his rhetoric sometimes inflamed their passions. Just one example will illustrate this. In a speech he made on *Radio Soleil* on 12 September, he spoke directly about the way he saw justice being administered:

The executive power will keep a close watch, without interfering in the judicial system. This does not mean we are shirking our responsibility; we are simply respecting the rules of democracy as required by the Constitution, rules which have their limitations because of the possibility of corruption within the judicial system. Matters cannot always be handled the way we the people would like them to be. You have given me authority which I pass on to you. This power entitles you to organize to defend your rights wherever, however and whenever possible.

This is highly inflammable stuff. But, for all that, there can be no doubt that Aristide was conscious of the grave shortcomings (even the non-operability) of the judicial system and its utter lack of capacity to contribute to the development of a democratic future for Haiti. This, together with a constipated legislature, meant a total absence of those effective infrastructural bodies so necessary for the functioning of anything resembling accountable government. It was this lack of maturity in the parliament, the judiciary, the business class and the military which, quite as much as any personal defects in the president, contributed to the mounting pressures which ultimately drove Aristide onto the defensive. Finding himself in a corner, he appealed to that one sector of Haitian life where he knew he could count on loyal support, the people. The populist and the demagogue in Aristide, a sleeping monster for the most part, was stirred into life by the ill-will and incompetence of other sectors of Haitian society and by their refusal to acquire the discipline necessary for the new social and political opportunities to be grasped. Infelicitous utterances and dangerous rhetoric were drawn out of Aristide by the despair he felt at a situation moving ineluctably beyond his control. None of that, of course, makes his rhetoric any less dangerous or irresponsible.

The president left Haiti in late September for a visit to New York. On 25 September he addressed the General Assembly of the United Nations where he spelled out what he called 'the ten commandments of democracy', a speech widely applauded even by his political opponents in Haiti. Democracy, he declared, was all about freedom and the respect of human rights. The rights to eat and work were among the most fundamental of all. And no democracy worth the name could rest content while the vast majority of its citizens were held down in poverty, ignorance and idleness. The greatest resource any country had was its people. And he ended with one of his rallying calls:

> *It is better to perish with the people*
> *Than to succeed without the people.*
> *With the people*
> *We know no defeat, so,*
> *Victory is ours!*

A hypothesis that was soon to be put to the test.

He made a triumphal return to Haiti a couple of days later. But for all that, he sensed that there was trouble in the air. He made a widely quoted speech at the Port-au-Prince international airport which, like so many others he'd made over the years, was studded with ambiguity. This is a translation of part of that speech, words which were used by the army and his opponents to justify subsequent events.

> Your tool is in your hand. Your instrument is in your hand. Your Constitution is in your hand. Don't neglect to give him what he deserves...
>
> Your equipment is in your hand. Your trowel is in your hand. Your pencil is in your hand. Your Constitution is in your hand. Don't neglect to give him what he deserves...
>
> Throughout the four corners of the country, we are watching, we are praying, we are watching, we are praying, when we catch one of them, don't neglect to give him what he deserves.
>
> What a beautiful tool! What a beautiful instrument! What a beautiful appliance! It's beautiful, it's beautiful, it's

pretty, it looks sharp! It's fashionable, it smells good and wherever you go you want to smell it...'

At the beginning of this quotation, the tool being referred to is undoubtedly the Constitution. What is less clear is whether that remains the case a few sentences later. His enemies were convinced that by then he was referring to the *Père Lebrun*, the notorious necklace of burning rubber, which he was increasingly counting on for the maintenance of his hold on power. He himself has consistently and repeatedly denied this.

In a press conference the following day, Aristide declared that he no longer feared a Duvalierist threat to his government; 'democracy has won an irreversible victory,' he said, 'and its roots are getting stronger and stronger'. In less than forty-eight hours any remaining evidence that democracy was working in Haiti was torn to shreds.

It was the Port-au-Prince police chief Joseph-Michel François who masterminded the coup that took place in the night of Sunday 29 September. He was the son of an officer in François Duvalier's presidential guard and had close links with the death squads that operated during Henri Namphy's time in power. Aristide had tried to secure his resignation just weeks previously but Cédras had resisted this. Now he was out to get the president. His first move was to overcome the tank and heavy weapons depot at Frères situated about four miles from the city centre. This was accomplished after a short exchange of fire and the death of a few soldiers. François now ordered heavily armed contingents of soldiers to move against the densely populated bidonvilles of the capital. He'd not forgotten the way the poor people from places like Cité Soleil, St Martin, La Saline, Carrefour and Lamentin had moved en masse to prevent Roger Lafontant's attempted coup a few months earlier.

Lafontant himself, still in prison, was soon made aware of what was happening. He and François had enjoyed a reasonably good relationship. As ex-head of the Tontons Macoutes and former Minister of the Interior, Lafontant had often offended and even humiliated large sections of the army.

Certainly General Raoul Cédras would have considered him an opponent. But for all that, he'd worked well with the police as well as that part of the army run by Colonel Jean-Claude Paul. So when Lafontant heard the first news of the impending coup (and that François was its chief organizer) he must have begun to hope not only for his freedom but even for a share in power. But such hopes had hardly had time to form when a gunman marched into his cell and fired a salvo of shots into him at point-blank range.

To this day, a mystery hangs over this strange and gruesome event. The military junta, even then sweeping into power, were not slow to blame Aristide. But there was a strong case for suggesting that it was the army itself that ordered his death. They had as much reason as Aristide for doing so. And yet both these hypotheses are flawed. Aristide was in no position to order Lafontant's death. At that particular time he was under great duress and preoccupied only with his own survival. As for the section of the army which had launched the coup, they had no ostensible reason for getting rid of Lafontant. They'd worked closely together in drug-running and smuggling not so long previously and might well have had ideas of resuming these activities when they'd seized power.

Nicolas Jallot and Laurent Lesage, in their recent book *Haiti: Dix ans d'histoire secrète* make a third suggestion. They hint at the involvement of French secret service agents under orders to eliminate a man who might prove embarrassing to French interests in the event of a successful coup. This seems far-fetched but the very fact that it can be offered at all indicates the uncertainty that shrouds the whole affair, which remains cloaked in mystery to this day.

This was the last tragic act in a drama that had linked the destinies of Jean-Bertrand Aristide and Roger Lafontant so closely together. The parish priest had often denounced the Tontons Macoutes in his sermons at St John Bosco. It was Lafontant's own declared intention to stand as a candidate for the presidential office that goaded Aristide into running. Aristide's stunning success at the polls was matched by

Lafontant's abortive *coup d'état*. He was arrested and his judicial trial took place while Aristide's presidency was itself under trial from the pressure of events. Now, almost to the minute, in the very same midnight hour, a presidency was killed and a prisoner assassinated. The parallelism in this tale of two destinies is uncanny.

The soldiers sent to keep control of the populous slum areas of Port-au-Prince did so with ruthless efficiency. People were killed without mercy, up to 750 of them in Cité Soleil alone. Men, women and children were gunned down in their beds or on the streets. Trucks full of corpses and the seriously injured (no distinction was made between them) headed for the burying fields of Titanyen where they dumped their loads with little ceremony before heading back for the capital for more. Despite the carnage, people were soon scurrying to and fro in the city's popular quarters raising barricades in an attempt to mount some kind of resistance to the heavy firing of the soldiers. But it was an unequal battle from the outset. In his book *The Uses of Haiti*, Paul Farmer presents the account of an eyewitness, a young doctor who'd worked for Aristide's government. She headed for the palace with her brother-in-law to protest at what was happening. 'When I drew near to the park in front of the palace,' she recalled, 'it was pure chaos. There were large numbers of protesters but the soldiers were just firing on them. I couldn't believe it, I saw them shoot people lying injured on the ground. Some of the demonstrators had climbed onto the base of a statue and they were just picked off by marksmen one by one. I threw myself to the ground and heard my brother-in-law calling me to run for my life. But those who were running were the ones being killed. I didn't know human beings could treat each other like this.'

As well as sending soldiers to subdue the slum-dwellers of Port-au-Prince, Michel François moved in against Aristide himself. His soldiers surrounded the president's private home and shots were fired. He intended to capture Aristide and deal with him personally. But by now, army chief Raoul Cédras had been put in the picture by the American Embassy. Cédras was given instructions by ambassador Alvin Adams that the life of the president must at all costs be saved. The army commander-in-chief had his own personal agenda too. He needed to act fast to gain the upper hand over François if he were to emerge from this affair with his authority intact.

The French ambassador, Jean-Raphaël Dufour, who'd also by now heard of what was going on, turned up at Aristide's house just as he was being bound and arrested. Dufour insisted on accompanying the president and they arrived before Cédras together. Neither knew of the American order to keep Aristide alive. It all looked very grim. Aristide was totally overwhelmed by what was happening and when Cédras smiled at him and announced that, to all intents and purposes, it was *he* who was now president, he just broke down.

'What shall I do with the priest?' Cédras, as if he were Pontius Pilate, asked his soldiers with evident glee. '*Tué-l*, Kill him,' they replied. At this point Aristide became incontinent, his body functions collapsing under a virulent attack of rampant fear. Two years after the event, a senior army officer was talking to me about Aristide's time in power. He recalled this small detail of the president's arrest with evident pleasure. He still savoured the memory of Aristide's humiliation. 'He just stood there wet with urine and smelling of shit,' the officer said smacking his lips with relish.

Aristide never forgot that moment of total degradation. He had no idea that the coup had been mounted by François and taken over by Cédras, nor that Cédras had orders to keep him alive. To his mind everything could be laid at the door of Cédras and this affected his attitude to the army chief throughout the following three years in the wilderness. But for now, escape from this madness was all that mattered. A plane was put at Aristide's disposal by Venezuelan president Carlos Andrés Perez.

In the early hours of Monday 30 September, with mindless killing still taking place on the streets of Haiti's major cities, Aristide departed into a sad exile. The dream was shattered.

6 The army's reign of terror

The sun rose on another day and gave warmth and light to a Haiti waking up to its new night of the soul, one that was to be longer and darker than any she'd ever known. Aristide flew to Caracas where he'd have time and space to get himself together again. Behind him, he left a suffering people who'd find themselves with virtually no opportunity to recover their nerve or rediscover their will. Their champion had gone and the country was at the mercy of mindless thugs whose only plan was to keep power, and to do so at any cost.

For five days and five nights there was mayhem across the length and breadth of the land. Police chief Michel François was determined to terrorize the poor into total submission. The angel of death passed through many neighbourhoods but the gunmen who invaded the Cité Soleil bidonville near the city centre and the Lamentin area of Carrefour (on the southern edge of the capital) seemed to have a special message to impart. They shot anyone they could, including old people and children. They left a few corpses in full view as a grim reminder of what others could expect. They ransacked people's homes looking for evidence of support for Aristide or any other incriminating material. The night raids were particularly terrifying, the people's screams and the noise of bullets rending the air in eerie and discordant counterpoint. The soldiers set fire to people's homes and there was utter chaos everywhere as people fled or hid or else, with a courage that mocked at reason, threw stones or shouted slogans in vain gestures of resistance. In the country areas, the armed forces hunted down members of popular organizations, destroying their records and offices, beating and arresting their leaders pitilessly. One of Haiti's best-known singers, Manno Charlemagne, and one of its richest merchants, Antoine Izméry (both Aristide supporters), were tortured and imprisoned. Radio stations were shut, journalists intimidated, the press muzzled. Soldiers who refused to co-operate were locked up in the national penitentiary. There was widespread looting and pillaging.

The army took over the national radio and television station and used the air waves to justify the coup to a reeling nation and to issue an appeal for calm. At first, their calls seemed to fall on deaf ears. Barricades appeared in the streets; across the provinces police stations and military outposts were set on fire. Demonstrations formed in the streets, anti-coup propaganda was painted on walls and pro-Aristide slogans were chanted at passing soldiers. But these brave efforts to keep up a spirit of resistance were short-lived. They simply incited the oppressors to increase their level of intimidation. A radio journalist was arrested and disappeared. His mutilated body was found two days later missing a tongue and an ear, his teeth smashed to pieces. People reported seeing mass graves, there were hundreds of bodies at the Port-au-Prince hospital, and dogs could be seen devouring human torsos on a road leading from the capital. Within three weeks of the coup, the Platform of Haitian Human Rights Organizations was reporting that the dead numbered at least 1,000 with as many more injured. Tens of thousands began to flee the capital city for the countryside. Chaos reigned on all hands.

This picture of a suffering people is the unremitting backdrop to all the events and developments to be reported in this chapter. It forms the constant and daily experience of the Haitian people across the whole republic. The number of those who died in the three years of *de facto* government is generally thought to have exceeded 4,000, but the true number will never be known. The casualties came from every sector of Haiti's national life with peasant activists and journalists paying a particularly heavy price.

From a very early moment the army moved against the press. Radio stations were shut, reporters silenced. A book, *La Presse sous la Mitraille*, The Press under Fire, catalogues the deaths, sackings, beatings and intimidation inflicted on the fourth estate in the days and months following the coup. It was all part of a concerted effort to control the flow of information and to keep people in the dark. Michel Favard, director of *Radio Nationale*, was arrested while the coup was still taking place. Within twenty-four hours, five other stations were closed. A very brave reporter, Jacques Gary Siméon, was seized at his home after he'd been forced to watch soldiers rape his wife. His severely mutilated body was found several days later in a ditch. Montlouis Llérissé met a similar end after being interrogated and beaten by the police investigating some work he'd done for one of Aristide's ministers. His body, riddled with bullets, was found at Titanyen, the notorious dumping ground for the bodies of dissidents, fifteen miles north of the capital. In addition to the violence perpetrated against people, the authorities sabotaged station after station destroying equipment and buildings alike. It was a very concerted campaign, executed with the clear intention of preventing the free flow of information and analysis.

Similar pressure was brought to bear on newspapers. The one and only Créole-language paper, the weekly *Libète*, was shut down. Those selling *Haiti en marche* and *Haiti progrès*, (weeklies produced in New York) were intimidated with threats and beatings. Yet all this served merely to drive journalists underground. A welter of samidzat publications began appearing. Some, *Bulletin résistance et Démocratie* and *Kawoutchou* in particular, managed to reach Haiti-watchers in countries all over the world. And *Radio Enriquillo*, set up by Roman Catholic priests just over the border within the Dominican Republic, offered a Créole-language service directed towards Haiti for many months. This annoyed the Haitian bishops, the *de facto* authorities and the government of the Dominican Republic alike. An order was given to those running the station that they should cease broadcasting news in this way. The journalists accepted the order but felt they could get around it if they *sang* their news bulletins instead of speaking them. This continued for several weeks, a kind of Gregorian chant, intoned by imaginative people being musical with the *actualités*. The inevitable came, of course, and, in July 1992, the station was finally closed down.

One particularly brutal crime, that which led to the death of Jean-Sony Philogène, must serve to illustrate the suffering of many nameless victims and also to indicate the exact nature of the wanton violence that reigned in Haiti throughout this time. One evening in December 1992, the 20-year-old Jean-Sony was out with some friends. With no warning and for no apparent reason, they were all arrested by a group of heavily armed men in civilian clothing and taken to Titanyen where, they must have known, there was only one thing waiting them. All seven were shot with automatic weapons and left for dead. But Jean-Sony was only wounded. He pretended to be dead, however, and waited for the assassins to depart. Then, somehow, he managed to drag himself to the side of the road and attract the attention of a motorist who drove him to the Canapé Vert hospital in Port-au-Prince where he received surgical attention to remove a bullet which had lodged in his left leg. This, and the other four bullets which had passed into his body, had done no serious damage and the operation was judged a success. Jean-Sony was taken back to his room where his grandmother was waiting anxiously to look after him.

In mid-afternoon of that same day, a group of uniformed soldiers came to the hospital asking for him. The nurse at the desk told them she knew of no such person and the soldiers left. Later that evening at about 10pm, a group of five men in civilian dress entered the hospital. Two of them went directly to Jean-Sony's room where they found the young man with his grandmother. They shot him at point-blank range and he died immediately. It was a senseless murder, one of hundreds that left families in grief and the country in despair. Yet no one ever knew why Jean-Sony Philogène and his friends had been arrested in the first place. Nor was any sorrow expressed by those in authority. And, of course, no action was taken subsequently to bring the murderers to book.

Jean-Sony Philogène and the thousands like him who died in these *de facto* years failed to make even a ripple on the pond of international concern. Only the the boat people managed to do that, those who risked everything to leave the oppression and the misery of Haiti by taking to the seas in rickety ships in a desperate search for refuge. Within weeks of the coup, a trickle of such asylum-seekers swelled to a flood. In many places along the northern coastline and in the south too, in particular near Léogane, ramshackle boats were being hastily constructed for a mass exodus. The demand was incredible and whole families readied themselves for flight. They had to cope not only with the wiles of ruthless entrepreneurs who charged them huge amounts for their journey, nor even with the unpredictable mood swings of the open seas, but also with rising alarm in the international community and an increasingly draconian implementation of US law to stop them.

An agreement had been signed in 1981 by the governments of Jean-Claude Duvalier and Ronald Reagan which allowed US coastguards to intercept Haitian 'flag vessels' found in international waters heading for the American coastline and to turn them back to Haiti. US officials were obliged by that agreement to screen Haitians for claims of persecution and, if judged appropriate, to allow them the right to press their case in the American courts. In the period from the instigation of this agreement in 1981 till the September 1991 coup, some 22,716 Haitians had been repatriated in this way. A mere 28 were allowed into the United States after screening to pursue asylum claims. These figures were made to seem very modest in the immediate aftermath of the coup. In the first five months of *de facto* government in Haiti, more than 16,000 boat people were picked up on the high seas by American coastguard vessels (there were to be around 40,000 all told in the whole period). All of these were screened by officials of the Immigration and Naturalization Service according to the procedures established in the 1981 agreement. Over 6,000 people were deemed to merit further consideration as possible political refugees. These were taken to a camp on the American army base in Cuba at Guantanamo Bay for processing. Clearly a system that was accustomed to dealing with about two thousand cases per year was going to be hard pressed by the numbers fleeing Haiti in these months.

The practice of holding Haitian refugees in this manner was soon being questioned in the American courts. One judge issued an injunction preventing the repatriation of Haitians on the grounds that, in light of what was happening in Haiti, a large number were likely to be political refugees. In his references to those who had been singled out for further consideration, he didn't mince his words. It was 'unconscionable', he said, 'that the screened-in plaintiffs are isolated from the world and treated in a manner worse than the treatment that would be afforded to a criminal defendant. Their access to the outside world, whether by telephone, mail, or otherwise has been completely restricted. They are confined to a camp surrounded by razor wire and are not free to leave, even if they have the financial capability to do so, to any country but Haiti, from which they flee for fear of political persecution, torture, and even death.'

The parameters for the discussion of this thorny question changed dramatically in May 1992 when President George Bush issued the 'Kennebunkport Order' under which all Haitian boats making for the United States would be intercepted by US coastguard vessels and their passengers returned directly to Port-au-Prince *with no prior screening* for asylum-seekers. Any Haitian wishing to seek refuge in the United States would have to do so via an In-Country Processing system. It was, of course, madness to repatriate boat people in this way. Many of them were clearly fleeing for their lives. No one monitored their progress once they were back on Haitian soil even though there was a clear case for supposing that some of them were very likely to be persecuted for their well-known views as Aristide supporters. What's more, there was a widespread feeling that this way of dealing with Haitian refugees was in direct violation of international law relating to such matters. And the In-Country Processing procedures simply invited people to register their grievances under the very noses of those of whom they were in fear. This order was a unilateral abrogation of the 1981 agreement and it led to widespread criticisms from many quarters. It was tested in the American courts and this led eventually to a ruling by the Supreme Court in June 1993 which stated that the forced repatriation of Haitian boats was neither against American law nor international law because all incidents took place out of the country and in international waters. Needless to say this was a judgment that was hotly contested by human rights groups around the world. And the Democratic Party's challenger for the presidency that year, Bill Clinton, was one of its most vociferous critics. He promised that, if elected, one of his first foreign policy actions would be to cancel the Kennebunkport Order.

The minuets and polkas being danced by lawyers and politicians with such attention to the detail of precedent and expediency, were taking place against a background of immense suffering by poor people. Whether they were political or economic refugees, they were treated like vermin by so many of those who discussed their case or dealt with them physically on the high seas. On 15 November 538 were turned back to Haiti. Another 1,000 were repatriated the day after the Supreme Court overruled the injunction of a lower court banning such acts. Soon all those being taken to Guantanamo Bay were being tested as a matter of course for AIDS. And some of the hundreds who tested positive were kept in the camp for up to two years. One of these people wrote a graphic description of the conditions that framed his daily living:

We were in a space cordoned off with barbed wire. Wherever they put you, you were meant to stay right there; there was no place to move. The latrines were brimming over. There was never any cool water to drink, to wet our lips. There was only water in a cistern, boiling in the hot sun. When you drank it, it gave you diarrhoea... Rats crawled over us at night... When we saw all these things, we thought, it's not possible, it can't go on like this. We're humans, just like everyone else.

THE TESTIMONY OF YOLANDE JEAN ABOUT EVENTS AT GUANTANAMO BAY, FROM *THE USES OF HAITI*, BY PAUL FARMER.

Humans or not, they were allowed to linger and fester in this godforsaken place. I once visited some of those who'd actually made it to Florida and were being held in the Krome detention centre outside Miami. The discrimination I found being practised there was palpable. Detainees from every other national group had their cases processed in a very short time, a matter of days or, at most, weeks. Haitians, however, could often be kept in custody for up to two years. They were herded around the camp in their bright orange uniforms, men, women and children penned like animals into different parts of a corral. I've always wondered how a humane and civilized government could *automatically* assume that a Cuban escaping across the sea to Florida would always have political reasons for doing so while a Haitian making his way across the identical waters would, again automatically, be presumed to be doing so for economic (rather than political) reasons. I suppose that such a distinction could have been justified prior to September 1991. It was definitely no longer the case after the coup which ousted Aristide, yet the same bland assumptions continued to be made. And hundreds died ugly deaths at sea, or slow deaths through starvation or dehydration. Many, of course, were just sent back to Haiti. No one will ever know how many of these were maltreated by the very people they'd been fleeing; another inglorious aspect of this whole tawdry tale.

The first six months after the coup saw hundreds of thousands of internal displacements apart from those who took to the seas. Many crossed the frontier to the Dominican Republic and yet more left the cities to find refuge in the hills and plains of the Haitian countryside. Meanwhile, soldier/politicians in Port-au-Prince announced to the world that it was they who, having seized power from an arrogant megalomaniac, were now the best bet for the future of democracy in Haiti. It all felt and sounded like something from *Through the Looking Glass*.

Aristide seemed a very distant figure in the months following the coup. For three months he made Caracas his base and resorted to shuttle diplomacy in an effort to secure the commitment of the outside world to the finding of a speedy solution for the Haitian crisis. He moved at bewildering speed. Within three days of his humiliating exit, he was in New York addressing the Security Council of the United Nations. He was sure that the Cédras régime would not last more than a few days. At first he seemed to favour the swift intervention of a UN military force; or perhaps he remembered the promises made by the Organization of American States just three months earlier at their Santiago summit. There, they'd given solemn undertakings to come to the assistance of any one of their number if and when the military seized power against the freely expressed views of their people. Little of that determination was in view now. The UN Security Council refused even to pass a formal resolution condemning the coup. Its non-aligned members were fearful of expressing a view that might be tantamount to interfering in the internal affairs of a sovereign state. So Aristide, after a short meeting with President Bush, went back empty-handed to Caracas.

Two weeks later he travelled to Europe, visiting Switzerland, Belgium and France, meeting (amongst other political leaders) President Mitterrand. I was able to corner him and have a few minutes' conversation during his visit to Geneva. He looked exhausted. When I remembered how long it had taken him to get over the St John Bosco massacre in 1988, I found it remarkable that he was cutting such a public figure at all so soon after the trauma he'd undergone just four weeks previously. Yet he seemed very withdrawn and made poor contact with the press who'd come in great numbers to interview him. He told me he didn't think Cédras could last long, was sure it was the money from drug-running that had been a major reason for the coup, and was equally sure that he'd soon be back in Port-au-Prince. With a little joke we'd once shared and a couple of Créole proverbs I tried to get him to laugh and relax. But my efforts didn't achieve the desired result. He was a mere shadow of his usual self.

Soon he was visiting leaders of the English Caribbean at a meeting they were holding in Dominica. He was back in Paris a week later. By now, he'd developed a clearer view of how the international community could help restore legitimate government to Haiti. He accused Cédras of 'crimes against humanity' and demanded that he be arrested and brought to trial. He was worried about proposals to impose an embargo on Haiti, envisaging enormous difficulties in keeping it watertight. He was fully prepared to consider establishing a broadly-based government of national unity, but only on the condition that the *de facto* leaders could have no part in such arrangements.

A visit to Bolivia (for a meeting of the Socialist International) was followed by yet another to Paris, this time for a summit of Francophone countries. Then he attended an OAS summit in Colombia before paying a visit to Canada where Prime Minister Brian Mulroney was becoming highly active in a plan to bring the crisis to an end. This led Aristide to announce that he confidently expected to be back in Haiti by Christmas. But it was not to be. His punishing schedule, interspersed with regular visits to the United States, made Caracas less and less suitable as a base for his operations. He began to sense that his return to Haiti might take longer than he'd hoped. So, in early 1992, he moved to Washington.

The international community were quick to voice their condemnation of the coup. There were many unequivocal statements of support for Aristide, none more so than that made by US Secretary of State James Baker: 'This junta is illegal,' he declared, 'it will be treated as a pariah, without friends, without support, and without a future. This coup must not and will not succeed. It is imperative that we agree for the sake of Haitian democracy and the cause of democracy throughout the hemisphere, to act collectively to defend the legitimate government of President Aristide.' Nothing could be clearer than that and it received a rapturous round of applause from the delegations of the thirty-three member nations of the OAS who'd heard it. President Bush added his own endorsement a couple of days later. 'We want to see President Aristide returned to power,' he said at the conclusion of a meeting between the two men at the White House.

The determination 'to act collectively' amounted to a speedy visit to Port-au-Prince by the Secretary General of the Organization of American States, Joao Baena Soares, accompanied by a handful of foreign ministers from member states. They failed dismally to extract any concessions from Cédras, however, and were even treated to a display of outrageous physical violence directed at Evans Paul, the Port-au-Prince mayor, who was beaten senseless under their very eyes at the international airport where he'd come to meet them. The OAS delegation left with its tail between its legs, afraid for its own security, and seeming to have no options other than the imposition of a trade embargo. This was duly endorsed in early November. It was to be one of the most controversial aspects of the whole of this unsavoury chapter in Haiti's history. The leader of the Haitian Senate, Déjean Bélizaire, called it 'an act of genocide against the Haitian people'.

It was the OAS, not Aristide, that resorted to a trade embargo. It was the best way they could think of for implementing the Santiago declarations they'd made in July. But it was a poor instrument right from the start. President Bush signed the order putting the embargo into operation on 5 November. Within the same calendar month, a tanker registered in Liberia was discharging 90,000 barrels of oil at the Shell company's off-loading point in Port-au-Prince. In January another tanker, this time from Colombia, discharged 149,000 barrels, a shipment that had been registered for the Bahamas. Three tankers arrived in March. And so on and so forth. These huge ships seemed able to break the OAS embargo with impunity. The same American coastguard vessels which never missed a single one of the tiny Haitian boats attempting to carry their pathetic human cargoes into the supposed utopia that began on a Florida beach seemed to suffer a major failure of their instruments every time another huge oil tanker sleuthed its way towards the Shell sluice. And the amount of oil offloaded was always just enough to tide the country over. Supplies never ran out.

Time was being bought by these regular arrivals and this allowed a great deal of huffing and puffing to go on. By the turn of the year, with the *coup d'état* now three months old, it became the received line to talk up the humanitarian consequences of the embargo. There was talk of famine and disease spreading across Haiti on a huge scale. The US government announced a $15 million emergency aid programme to be directed through the Red Cross at half a million of Haiti's poor with pregnant women and children receiving priority. This fact should be held together, however, with the announcement made just one month later that Washington was going to soften the embargo in a way that would allow the assembly factories in Port-au-Prince to continue to operate. This meant keeping jobs open for 40,000 people. According to James Baker, losing them would deal a severe blow to Haiti's prospects for democracy. He might have added: nor would it have been beneficial for those American entrepreneurs who were reaping huge profits from cheap Haitian labour.

And why stop there? He could have gone on to say that it was the *way* the embargo was being applied rather than the *fact* of an embargo which was contributing to a truly disastrous state of affairs in Haiti. The rich found no difficulty in getting round the embargo either by smuggling their goods into Haiti over the porous border with the Dominican Republic or in other ways. But the artificial trading conditions which were created by the embargo allowed the rich to hike the prices of their goods in accordance with the dictates of a supply-starved market. This meant that the poor and middle classes suffered while the rich made huge amounts of money from the skewed market. The Haitian government, certain overseas institutions, and church leaders in Haiti, began to orchestrate an appeal to the international community to raise the embargo in the name of the poor people who were suffering so dreadfully.

Yet again, the poor were being used by the rich and the intelligentsia to justify a return to the status quo. Nobody consulted the poor. They were clearheadedly determined that they'd suffer any and every deprivation rather than lose their right to have their champion Aristide back in Haiti at the head of a legal and constitutional government. Those who wasted their time arguing the hardships being suffered by the poor should have been directing their righteous indignation against the *de facto* authorities in Port-au-Prince whose barbarism and cynicism were almost indescribable. The 'right-thinking class' were attacking the wrong target. Aristide had for weeks criticized the embargo and the effect it was having in encouraging smuggling and effectively undoing a number of the trading reforms he'd instigated while in government. But by February 1992, with costly feeding programmes being organized and paid for by Washington and the factories of American businessmen being kept open, he made an impassioned plea for a considerable tightening of the embargo. If you were going to have one, he argued, then you should do all you can to maintain it. It should be tightened to the point where the *de facto* authorities screamed their submission. A weakened embargo threatened to prolong the crisis for many, many months and that was bound to be far worse for the poor and the factory owners alike. For daring to offer such a rational analysis, Aristide was vilified at home and abroad for being unfeeling and intransigent.

Long before Aristide had come out in favour of strengthening the embargo, the Americans had begun to revise their commitment to him as a part of an eventual solution to the Haitian crisis. A document surfaced in Port-au-Prince in October 1991 which was widely considered to have been written by a consultant to the US embassy. It rehearsed a case for delaying Aristide's return to Haiti by several months. On his return, it argued, he should either be set up as a mere figurehead president or else, if allegations about the abuse of human rights during his time in office were upheld, he should be impeached. His supporters in the *Lavalas* movement should be excluded from any government formed after his return. OAS countries could be shown to be increasingly aware that Aristide was 'a very bad guy'. It should be possible to keep negotiations going and to string out the time of Aristide's absence. Meanwhile, he could be vilified and even 'compared to the Ayatollah'. If he did eventually return, it should be to a situation where the prime minister should be the real power in the land and the government should be one of 'reconciliation'.

The State Department denied the validity of this document but its details are remarkable in the light of what happened subsequently. And it is known to have been widely used for the briefing of various Haitian officials who took part in discussions with OAS and UN officials as part of the search for a 'solution' to the crisis. Whatever its status, the document shows the emergence of a negative and personalized (almost a demonic) picture of Aristide. There was lots more of that to come. And, as his stance on the embargo became more and more determined, he was increasingly portrayed as uncompromising and intransigent by a political class who seemed to prefer criticizing the deposed president to pointing the finger at Haiti's *de facto* leaders and their stubborn refusal to budge one inch in their singleminded intention of clinging to power at all costs.

In the immediate aftermath of the coup, General Raoul Cédras and his army chiefs had had sole charge of Haiti's affairs. But their stated aim was always to return power to a civilian government. The big problem was to find someone ready to accept such a poisoned chalice in the name of the constitution, but such matters are rarely difficult to arrange in Haiti. No one had forgotten how in January 1988, just six weeks after the cynical and violent abortion of a general election, Leslie Manigat, one of Haiti's most respected and experienced political theorists, allowed himself to be 'elected' into the presidential office. It was either the act of a political naif or else unadorned and blatant opportunism, power for power's sake.

Now, in October 1991, two other matadors stepped into the bullring to show off their skills. Joseph Nérette, an ancient judge and a nonentity, was sworn into the presidential office. He proved to be a mere cypher. In contrast to this, the prime minister's portfolio was accepted by someone of standing, a heavyweight, well known to many beyond Haiti's shores. This was Jean-Jacques Honorat, who for many years had headed an organization (CHADEL) which monitored human rights in Haiti. His work had for some considerable time been funded by the National Endowment for Democracy and the Agency for International Development, organizations that were styled 'US government democratization programs'. Beside these sources of support, a number of non-governmental organizations from around the world, amongst them Christian Aid and Amnesty International, had backed CHADEL too. Now they all found themselves with egg on their faces and began to withdraw support as fast as was decent.

Honorat, who'd been in close cahoots with the international community and was as well placed as anyone to appreciate its strengths and weaknesses, now abandoned his friendliness to his erstwhile international supporters. Since Aristide's election, the impartiality of information provided by CHADEL had begun to be suspect. Its reports became biased, 'ferreting out every little bit of information' against Aristide that could be found. It was widely acknowledged that these reports had become less valuable yet the US government continued to give 'firm backing for military training, radio spots, and other forms of civic education'. For all that, a number of those who'd financed Honorat's work now began to be highly critical of him. His response was to turn on his erstwhile supporters with venom. He 'vigorously and pugnaciously attacked anyone who questioned' his right to join the government. It all became as unedifying a tale as any in this murky saga.

Honorat was sworn in for three months. In the event he stayed for nine. From the time he took office, he mocked the declared intention of the international community to impose an embargo on Haitian trade. He didn't think they'd have the nerve to do it. When they did, he expressed his surprise at their action and alleged that it was tantamount to a declaration of war on Haiti. A few weeks into his prime ministership, he and the army chief Cédras gave some early Christmas presents. Cédras told the world that he'd promoted himself to the grade of Lieutenant General, clearly as a mark of the esteem he thought he'd earned for the splendid way he'd conducted the *coup d'état*. Honorat struck a more altruistic note. He reinstated 10,000 people to jobs in the public sector, thus undoing at a stroke one of the most painful clearing-up operations undertaken by Aristide. He also named seven appeal court judges, apparently in the hope of packing the judiciary with judges of his own persuasion. He ordered the French ambassador Dufour, who was proving to be a thorn in his flesh, to leave without delay. He repeatedly mouthed the language of democracy, declaring his readiness to consider forming a broadly-based government of national unity, but he refused to offer any olive branch to those seeking Aristide's return as the constitutional head of state. He warned that any such move would lead to civil war. Aristide, in his view, was arrogant and intransigent. There could be no part for him in Haiti's future.

Honorat and his collaborators refused to admit that any human rights abuses had taken place in Haiti after the coup. The stupidity of someone who could make a statement so at odds with everybody's daily experience was truly breathtaking. Meanwhile, CHADEL kept the US embassy supplied with heavily slanted and jaundiced accounts of abuses that had taken place in Aristide's time in office. This 'intelligence' was used by gullible (or else ill-intentioned) American politicians and others in their attempts to discredit Aristide. It is still almost impossible to believe that a view of Aristide was being formed by reasonable people in the United States on the basis of evidence supplied by the president's foremost critic, the very man who'd benefited most from his ousting.

It was December before Honorat was prepared to concede that the armed forces had been responsible for the death of civilians. But the army's aggression, he argued, should be seen as a response to the destabilizing opposition of priests and so-called popular movements who were, in his view, nothing other than terrorists. By January his self-delusion had reached its apogee. He argued that his government (and the military) had never laid a hand on anyone, that everything was now back to normal and that the arrival of an oil tanker in the port, a potent symbol of his government's ability to defy the OAS embargo, was proof positive of the smooth running of the state. The man's capacity for self-deception is well summed up in a speech he made to his parliament when announcing a cabinet re-shuffle: 'Foreigners,' said this man whose work in the field of human rights had been built in close collaboration with foreigners, 'foreigners get as agitated as devils in a holy-water stoup in their endeavours to get the marines and Latin American "neo-whites" to come and spit on our native land... No white man has any love for Haitian blacks. Whites never slap an embargo on other whites. We can expect nothing from the OAS.' He'd obviously never heard of sanctions levelled against the white régimes in Southern Rhodesia or the boycotting of South African goods. He must have been pleasantly surprised at the embargo later imposed by NATO on the Bosnian Serbs but astonished at how people living in Latin American countries might have felt about his rather racist description of them as 'neo-whites'.

It became a popular sport during Aristide's years in exile to question his mental state. Honorat's condition, despite showing what some might describe as hysteria and paranoia, seems always to have escaped similar examination. The prime minister ended his address to the parliament by thanking the legislators for urging him to take the reins of government in such times. He intended to prevent Haitians from tearing each other apart and from falling into a bloody civil war. When he eventually laid down office in the summer of 1992, he was able to describe his momentous time in power as 'the least troubled eight months in Haiti's history'. Amazing.

Towards the end of Honorat's time in office, serious discussions took place in Washington in an attempt to find a formal basis for a solution to the Haitian problem. These negotiations were brokered by the US government and brought Aristide together with a group commissioned by the Haitian parliament. The protocol agreed in February 1992 as a result of these talks recognized Aristide as Haiti's legitimate president, though it failed to give a precise date for his return. A government of national consensus would be established with the leader of Haiti's Communist Party (!), René Théodore, as prime minister. Once this government was in place, the embargo would be lifted. It would be a task of the new government to negotiate a date for Aristide's return and to begin the work of reconstructing Haiti's democratic institutions. A general amnesty would be proclaimed *which would not include those who had broken the civil law* (my emphasis). The army would be 'professionalized' and separated from the police. All legislation put on the statute book since the *coup d'état* would be confirmed, including the extension of Cédras' position as head of the army for a further three years. A 'civil mission' would be sent by the OAS to oversee the return to constitutional rule. All parties put their signatures to this accord. It should be noted that for Aristide this demanded some very significant concessions. The most significant of all, surely, was his readiness to leave a date for his return undecided. It must have been a bit like offering a blank cheque and illustrated a great deal of trust and flexibility on his part.

Almost immediately, Aristide went on American television and, in response to some keen questioning, made it clear how he would attempt to sideline Cédras once he (Aristide) returned to Haiti. He would seek to get the courts to agree that the army chief had offended against the civil law and that, therefore, he was not covered by the proffered amnesty. It was this line of argument that brought virulent criticism down on Aristide's head. He was accused of reneging on an agreement before the ink of his signature had properly dried. It was clear to many that the deposed president was allowing his personal animosity for Cédras to distort the spirit of the accord. Others, on the other hand, saw that Aristide's remarks were little more than an attempt to save some face. After all, he risked never being allowed to return to Haiti if he became too outspoken on this or any other matter; his destiny on this rested with others. In any case, all he'd threatened to do was test his feelings in the courts. It would be the judiciary rather than he who would have the last word on what might happen to Cédras.

In the following days, support for the Washington protocol came from the Haitian Chamber of Commerce, several political parties, the Association of Haitian Industries and both houses of the Haitian parliament. But *de facto* President Nérette declared that the accord would lead to an interference by outsiders in Haiti's internal affairs. This was followed by a deposition by a number of Haitian lawyers, including the very right-wing Mireille Durocher Bertin, who argued that the Washington agreement was unconstitutional and, therefore, it would be illegal to ratify it. This view was supported by the Haitian Supreme Court, led by an 81-year-old retired judge brought out of wraps for the occasion. This led to a flurry of diplomatic activity with leaders of the OAS, the UN, and the US government urging the ratification of the accord. Both houses of the Haitian parliament were now convened in plenary session for a final decision. A number of its members were armed and there was considerable disruption. Angry civilians pressed in on all sides and there was an ugly atmosphere. Pro-coup members then withdrew, leaving the assembly without a quorum, so no decision could be taken and the whole agreement fell. To cap this sequence of events, Honorat's government now called for a 'national conference' to define other ways forward. This brought Cédras onto national television to support the proposal, arguing that it would represent a decisive moment for Haiti. He urged Haitians not to be too impatient, assuring them that 'democracy will not go backwards under our leadership. But we must be careful about falling to those who are either too far to the left or too far to the right.'

The failure of the Washington accord led to a tightening of sanctions and a more furious search for a solution within Haiti. This led to tri-partite talks taking place in May 1992 between the army, the parliament and the government at the Villa d'Accueil. A protocol was hammered out but it proved to be very divisive. It promised the retirement of Nérette from the presidency but gave no indication of any eventual successor. It recommended the setting up of a government of 'consensus and public salvation' made up of people of proven experience in the realm of public administration. This government would seek to satisfy the proper hopes of the Haitian people, the international community and those sectors of national life that had overthrown Aristide. It would also seek an end to Haiti's diplomatic isolation and get the embargo lifted.

This declaration was bound to fail to commend itself because of its total lack of precision. Most importantly, it offered nothing to those who saw Aristide's return as essential to any meaningful solution of the crisis. The Villa d'Accueil agreement was widely criticized both within Haiti and beyond its shores. Yet it now became the only basis on which the Haitian *de facto* authorities were prepared to negotiate. The auguries were not good.

Poor Aristide must have felt like a spectator at his own funeral. He scuttled hither and yon, meeting important people all over the place. Even so, he had to suffer the frustration of hearing a public discourse which affirmed his legitimacy and made commitments to his return while at the same time put up with endless prevarication and a total lack of action. It had all the elements of farce. All he could do was hope someone would hang on to his one-liners and hear his repeated calls for something to be done. In November he made a speech in Paris in which he noted the way President Gorbachov of Russia had been restored to his post after an ousting that had lasted a mere three days. He called for similar determined action in his case and urged that 'the invisible hands' which always seemed capable of pulling rabbits from a hat in such circumstances should work their magic now. He was to go on making this plea again and again in the coming months.

A warning note crept into his New Year message to the Haitian people at the beginning of 1992. He reminded the more privileged people of Haiti that they would have to accept the fact that the majority previously excluded from national life had now had ten years to get used to the fact of being participants in their country's life and history. You couldn't put the genie back in the bottle. To refuse to see or accept that would be tantamount to pressing the auto-destruct button. No external power could help Haiti if Haitians were not prepared to help themselves, he added.

He made it clear that Haiti could hope for nothing while Cédras and his collaborators remained at the helm. At one stage the search was on for an interim prime minister acceptable to both sides who would help to plan Aristide's return according to the terms of the Washington accord. 'Even if God the Father were prime minister,' Aristide declared, 'if Cédras were at his side, democracy would have no chance. Neither history, the OAS, myself, nor 95 per cent of the Haitian people, nor the international community could accept the luxury of becoming the accomplices of such a criminal.' This same note of hatred for Cédras was sounded again and again. With people in the international community beginning to voice their conviction that some of those responsible for ethnic cleansing and other war crimes in the Balkans should be prosecuted, Aristide became more and more pointed in suggesting something similar for Cédras and his closest collaborators.

To the general council of the OAS, he repeated his intention of having Cédras arrested and pleaded passionately with his audience: 'All these months after the coup we see the same weapons in the same hands. The people's blood is flowing with a sickening inevitability under this repression... What shame! What sadness!' But the OAS went on its ineffective way, convincing itself that the regular visits of high-powered delegations and a leaky embargo would one day bring the army chiefs to their senses. It all smacked of *mañana*.

In his Easter message to the nation, broadcast on *Radio Enriquillo* (operating in the Dominican Republic despite the protestations of the Balaguer government) he made an appeal to members of the armed forces. 'Find ways of demonstrating on the streets,' he urged his listeners, 'so that the whole country can come to boiling point in its search for justice, freedom and love. And why don't those of you who carry arms but who can't say what you think join the demonstrations? I know that the Haitian army is itself suffering even as it makes the people suffer. Come on, you soldiers, open your eyes, understand what's going on. I want Easter to be a time when we all come to our senses. Let there be an avalanche of demonstrations in the streets.' His words seemed to fall on deaf ears.

So too did his appeal to officers in the army to effect a second *coup d'état*. He would grant an amnesty, he said, to anyone ready to undertake such a deed. If someone didn't make a move, he went on, then Haiti could go up in flames just as Los Angeles had done that same week after racial incidents there. All these warnings and all this advice were reaching the Haitian people from places like West Palm Beach, Bogotá and Paris. It was all so distant. Throughout all this time he seemed like a little man on the edge of a boisterous crowd trying to get noticed but generally being ignored.

Meanwhile, back in Haiti the Honorat era came to an end and a new prime minister was announced who was expected to operate within the spirit of the Villa d'Accueil accord. Once more Haiti-watchers held their breath. Such critical moments in recent years had seen quite a queue of turkeys signing up for an early Christmas. And we were not to be disappointed this time either. For that's exactly what happened again. On this occasion, it was none other than Marc Bazin who, in June 1992, committed political suicide and agreed to wear the stolen robes of office. He'd come a poor second to Aristide in the December 1990 election. He'd always enjoyed the support of the American government and his experience as a World Bank official and minister of finance in Jean-Claude Duvalier's government certainly gave him a number of skills appropriate for the role of prime minister. But to accept it at this precise time was sheer folly. And since Nérette was effectively sidelined by the Villa d'Accueil accord, Bazin became president and prime minister at the same time. A penetrating pen-portrait of this ambitious man had been written by Kenneth Freed for the *Los Angeles Times* a few weeks earlier. It is worth quoting at some length. Freed is discussing the Haitian drama, 'where all the heroes are doomed to acts of betrayal because of the tragic failures of their own souls'. He continued:

Marc Bazin is an apt example and object lesson. He is the U.S. Embassy's favorite Haitian politician. A middle-aged man of some wealth, Bazin seems on the surface an ideal Western, democratic politician. An internationally recognized economist and former senior official of the World Bank, Bazin moved comfortably in the orbit of U.S. ambassadors, foreign investors and journalists with his perfect command of English and French. He has a bit more problem at home, since he does not speak the local language, Créole [at all well].

Although a finance minister under the inept and brutal Jean-Claude Duvalier, he became the bright hope of American officials here, who convinced themselves that because of his educational and social background, his moderate pro-American rhetoric and his general demeanor, he was the country's best bet for democratic reform. Bazin made several tries for the presidency in the various doomed elections of the 1980s, finally running a bad second to Aristide when an honest vote finally took place.

Bazin pledged not to back any anti-Aristide coup. But when the army moved, he hesitated only briefly before speaking out in support. Of Aristide he said: 'He is no democrat, he is an autocrat... who sees himself as a combination of [Fidel] Castro and [the Ayatollah] Khomeini. I was against the coup in principle but... I think the army has developed a social base of its own and more people are now willing to support them... The army leaders,' he continued, 'are a new breed, better prepared to do good; the army will do more good than Aristide for the people.'

KENNETH FREED, *LOS ANGELES TIMES*, 15 JANUARY 1992.

For Greg Chamberlain, veteran Haiti-watcher and committed journalist, this was the case of a man thirsty for power, overweeningly ambitious, ready to shut his eyes to the political realities in the context of which he was to exercise power. Aristide, meanwhile, denounced Bazin as a 'consenting hostage' in the hands, and at the mercy, of the military and with no legitimacy whatsoever.

I'd sat near Bazin at the cathedral service which marked Aristide's inauguration in February 1991. He and I left the service before it finished and had to force our way through a pressing crowd at the main cathedral doors. I saw the hostility on the faces of the poor people gathered there; and I heard Bazin voice his contempt for them too. He was one of those people who could have given great impetus to the Aristide experiment but who rather contributed to its demise by his high-mindedness and disdain. In this, he was typical of many others of his class.

Bazin's acknowledged expertise lay in the realm of economics. Yet within weeks he was announcing a programme to create 17,000 jobs in the public sector. Honorat had already boosted the State payroll beyond the grossly inflated 42,000 which Aristide had had to deal with. Now Bazin was proposing a further expansion. It just didn't make economic sense for a bankrupt public treasury to be going in such a direction. Was Bazin opting for simple populism rather than sound economics? If so, he'd be guilty of the very thing he'd always accused Aristide of. It was no wonder that the Haitian gourde plummeted to its lowest ever level against the American dollar. After Bazin had been in office for just six months its value plunged from 14 US cents to 10, half its value in the days when it was tied to the US dollar. Yet this was the man who'd always argued for sound money, tight fiscal policy, and a lean public sector.

In August 1992, just two months after assuming power, he admitted he was '*bouleversé*', overwhelmed, by evidence of repression and atrocity that had come to his attention. He was discovering what most people had known all along, that the decent army types he'd come to appreciate so much with their broadening social base were actually responsible for deaths, beatings, intimidation and terror on a large scale. He admitted this in a speech to the parliament and promised 'to make a firm and public declaration of principle' on the matter. What on earth that meant is anybody's guess since no such declaration was immediately forthcoming. It certainly reveals the inadequacy (and the naivety) of the man.

As for the parliament itself, Bazin effectively neutered its legitimacy by announcing elections for a number of seats to fill vacancies in both houses. He went ahead with these despite widespread opposition within and beyond Haiti. The election was boycotted by the pro-Aristide FNCD. Consequently, the new senators and deputies were almost all supporters of the PANPRA/MIDH coalition which backed Bazin. It meant that he could now count on getting parliamentary support for his government's measures. But the problem of an unconstitutional legislature continued to be a thorn in the flesh long after Bazin's fall from grace. No one knew who could properly initiate discussion or endorse any of the proposals emerging in the search for a solution to the crisis.

Eventually, Bazin ran out of steam. When the army started to crack down seriously on the university sector, the PANPRA party of Serges Gilles pulled out of its coalition with Bazin's MIDH. This was the beginning of the end for the prime minister. He'd been unable to persuade Aristide or his supporters to negotiate with him. To be more precise, Aristide agreed to see Bazin but only as a Haitian citizen, not as head of government. So there was a diplomatic deadlock and virtually none of the action promised by the Villa d'Accueil accord had been achieved. When the United Nations began to formulate a plan to introduce a team of civilian observers to Haiti for the purpose of monitoring human rights abuses, at first Bazin agreed to co-operate but then he prevaricated and finally refused to allow the team to come. He'd clearly lost control and, in June 1993, he resigned after exactly one year in office.

One of the memorable things about Bazin's investiture had

been the absence of just about the entire diplomatic corps. The international community refused to confer any sign that could be interpreted as recognition for this new phase of *de facto* government. The event was not quite blackballed, however, for there was one representative of a sovereign state very much present. This was Monsignor Baldisseri, the papal pro-nuncio. The Vatican, having withdrawn its ambassador after the crowd violence which followed the Lafontant coup attempt in January 1991, was content to be without official representation in Haiti throughout Aristide's seven months in office. But now, to a universal chorus of displeasure, the Holy See sent its new ambassador in a way (and at a time) when it was almost impossible to prevent the impression forming in people's minds that this was an act of recognition of the *de facto* governments of Honorat and Bazin. Certainly that's how it was used by the Haitian authorities. Naturally, the Vatican gave its own explanation. It drew a distinction between the Holy See's relationship to a state and that with a government. By presenting its credentials during these *de facto* times, the Vatican was wanting to demonstrate its pastoral concern for the Haitian people rather than its recognition of a particular government. It was the pastoral rather than the diplomatic role which was being emphasized, a nuance that was inevitable (so the argument ran) when a State is also a church.

The explanation may just about hold water at the level of logic. But it was perceived quite differently. It was widely held to confer legitimacy on a government that had no right to claim it. For the Vatican, with its consummate diplomatic skills and unrivalled experience in such matters, to make such an elemental mistake simply added to the impression that the Roman Catholic Church wanted by every means at its disposal to keep its distance from Aristide.

As late as November 1991, two months after the coup that ousted the priest-president, the Haitian bishops had still not denounced those who had perpetrated the anti-constitutional deed. Then the Pope called for prayers for the Haitian people and the bishops offered to organize a chain of prayer for peace and reconciliation. The Haitian Conference of Religious Orders, meanwhile, had gone well beyond the language of faded piety and, within days of Aristide's ousting, had denounced the coup in fierce terms, calling it treachery and betrayal. 'In the name of our respect for life, in the name of the dignity of God's children, we say and we repeat: "No, and again No. This will not be allowed to happen."' Similarly, the Caribbean Bishops' Conference was forthright in its condemnation. It expressed deep admiration for Aristide's readiness to make the needs of the poor the foundation of his political programme and called on the international community to condemn the Haitian military and to work for the restoration of constitutional government. The Haitian bishops, however, were far more circumspect. Only Willy Romélus spoke out: 'Those responsible for this massacre are criminals who are murdering a defenceless people,' he said. His colleagues and the Pope, meanwhile, went on promising a few prayers.

As the military reinforced its hold on power, so they began to turn on recalcitrant priests and members of religious orders. They arrested, tortured, and beat up a number of them. The climate of fear within the church led some two hundred priests and members of religious orders from Haiti and the Dominican Republic to write an open letter to the Pope. It offered His Holiness a detailed account of the people's suffering and criticized the comfort being offered to the régime by the presence of the nuncio. It drew the Pope's attention to the persecution of priests and also to a systematic campaign of intimidation being conducted against the Bishop of Jérémie. It accused the hierarchy of purging the seminary of trainee priests who showed sympathy for Aristide and it blamed the Catholic *Radio Soleil* for putting out disinformation, especially about the ousted president. It urged the Pope, who would shortly be visiting the island for the commemoration of the 500th anniversary of Christopher Columbus's voyage of discovery to speak out for justice in Haiti, to urge the restoration of democratic rule, and especially to demand the return of Aristide.

There is no record of how the Pope received this missive. There is a clear record, however, of the public stance he took on Haiti when he visited Santo Domingo in October 1992 for the 500th anniversary events. He invited Haitians to remain united to their bishops. Then he continued: 'I pray to the Lord to support the action of all those who, *remaining within Haiti* [my italics], seek to renounce the logic of violence and to establish a climate of toleration and peace.' His overriding concern was the unity of the church and the exclusion of those outside Haiti (in other words, Aristide) from any future resettlement. There wasn't one word of condemnation of the coup, nor criticism of the widespread killings, displacements, and persecution that had followed it. Aristide added his word to these exchanges by wondering 'how the Pope would have reacted if the army had seized power in Poland and had gone on to kill 2,000 people as had been the case in Haiti'.

The Pope left the Dominican Republic to return to Rome. A few days later, the exiled Archbishop of Port-au-Prince left the same haven to return to Haiti. The return of the Duvalierist prelate was savagely criticized in a radio interview for the BBC in London by Father Hugo Triest, a Belgian priest who'd worked in Haiti for twenty-six years. He went on to point out how *Radio Soleil*, which he'd directed for a number of years, had been ordered by the bishops to change its call sign from 'the voice of the people of God', to 'the voice of the bishops' conference'. Its new director had refused to broadcast the speech Aristide made on the night of the coup. And he'd sent letters to right-wing groups in the United States saying that Aristide would have been a worse dictator than Duvalier. This was deliberate disinformation and yet the bishops were allowing it to go out. But then, added Triest, the bishops had never, as a body, actually condemned the coup. So what could anyone expect?

Radio Vatican put out a virulent attack on Aristide in late February 1993, accusing him of inspiring a reign of terror in Haiti. A whole month passed before an apology was given by a station director who admitted that there had been far worse human rights abuses since the military takeover than there had ever been during his time in office. But the apology was both late and limp. Clearly the Vatican was hardening its position towards Aristide. This was certainly evident from a nasty piece in the May issue of *Catholic World Report*. Entitled 'Democracy? Or Aristide?' it made a number of wide-ranging and unfounded allegations about Aristide's probity, his character, his fitness for office and his love of violence. It ended by suggesting that the president was living lavishly in Washington and spending $1 million per month to support his administration while his fellow-countrymen were starving under the effects of a wicked embargo.

This mean-minded and scurrilous piece of 'journalism' represented the lowest depths to which Aristide's opponents within the church sank in their efforts to undermine confidence in him. I wrote a detailed analysis of the piece at the time and urged people with any responsibility to keep their eye on the question of constitutionality (the real issue) rather than be deflected into assessments of a complicated situation based purely on psychology and personality. I defended Aristide against the particular criticisms put forward in this piece but went on to argue thus: 'Let's analyse the personality of Jean-Bertrand Aristide if we must. But let's also look at Marc Bazin, Raoul Cédras, Michel François, Wolff Ligondé, François Gayot, René Théodore and others who have all played their part too in this drama. And let's also remember the truly national spirit of hope and unity that surrounded the coming-to-power of President Aristide in February 1991. Raymond Alcide Joseph's immoral and self-serving article [in *Catholic World Report*] does the Haitian people a very great disservice. I deplore it with all my heart.' I might have added that I deplored equally those in the highest reaches of the Roman Catholic Church who were fanning the flames of these malevolent sentiments throughout these turbulent times.

This chapter began with an indication of the scale of suffering endured by the Haitian people in these months of dashed hopes and shattered dreams. Murder, arson, persecution, arrest, flight, torture and contempt made mockery of any understanding of justice or dignity that might have taken shape in their minds after the December 1990 elections. And now, in February 1993, after so much wickedness, Nature seemed to conspire with the perpetrators of Haiti's ills. A passenger/cargo boat, the *Neptune*, which plied the waters between Jérémie and Port-au-Prince ferrying poor provincial tradespeople to their most lucrative market, sank with the loss of 1,743 lives. It was a ghastly tragedy. But the moral depths to which Haiti had sunk were no more clearly in evidence than when pro-coup elements administered a severe beating to Bishop Willy Romélus as he left the Port-au-Prince Cathedral after preaching at the funeral mass of the victims of this disaster. He was attacked in full view of foreign journalists and diplomats. He bore the sufferings of his people that day in a truly Christ-like way. It was only the latest in a series of attacks he had suffered. But the Vatican, which had been so furious when its nuncio had been attacked by 'pro-Aristide mobs' in January 1991, seemed strangely dumb now in the face of this atrocity.

A more rounded picture of Aristide than some of those lurid portraitures his opponents had been putting out, appeared from an interview given to Howard French for the *New York Times* in April 1993. French found Aristide relaxed and self-assured. Aristide received the journalist in the 'small, carpeted apartment' in Georgetown, Washington D.C. in which he was staying. Faxes kept on arriving during the interview, but the interviewer was impressed by the simplicity of Aristide's lifestyle. He spoke of his admiration for the South African leader Nelson Mandela and King Juan Carlos of Spain who, he said, had helped navigate their countries through difficult times of transition. 'What we have to do and what they did,' he declared, 'was to have the technical ability to make every single citizen feel comfortable... In our situation too, the president must be the president of every single citizen.' He rejected revenge and retaliation and spoke clearly of the obligation of poor people to seek justice through the courts rather than on the streets. Yet a system of justice that could adequately deal with the people's needs would take years to build. Aristide said he was now seeking to put his focus on the future rather than the past and called on rich and poor to pull together to build a better Haiti. He identified political stability and tolerance as key elements in this act of reconstruction. He would accept an amnesty for those who'd supported the coup, even the rich whose money had financed it. But there would have to be a sweeping overhaul of the military and the creation of a separated police force. He was also prepared to look for a prime minister who did not necessarily come from among his friends. He would choose someone after taking the advice of the business sector.

In this interview, Aristide revealed a readiness to be pragmatic and to make concessions. It is clear he'd learned a great deal from his experience of exile. With Bill Clinton now heading the US administration and the United Nations taking responsibility for the Haitian crisis from the Organization of American States, he began to hope for a speedy resolution to a problem that had already lasted far too long. Little could he have guessed, eighteen months after the coup which ousted him, just how much more time it was going to take before he'd be back in Haiti to complete the task he'd begun in February 1991.

7 Dealings with America

In November 1992 a new player entered the scene. This was Bill Clinton whose electoral victory over George Bush was received ecstatically in the streets of Port-au-Prince. Clinton had, after all, made an unambiguous promise to reverse his predecessor's policy of automatic repatriation for the Haitian boat people. He reiterated this pledge in a speech at Little Rock, Arkansas, a week after his election. 'There's a proper distinction to be made between political and economic refugees,' he said, 'and I believe we must give these people a chance.' For the Haitian people, the conviction grew that Clinton's arrival in power would herald the beginning of the end of the bad times they'd all been living through.

The American press, however, seized his words and used them to paint a truly apocalyptic picture of what was likely to happen if the new president should ever be foolish enough to follow through on his promise. Media gurus envisaged countless thousands of poor Haitians putting to sea in the hope of benefiting from the new era of accommodation ushered in by Clinton. And if the OAS and the UN were ever to tighten further the trade embargo with Haiti, the numbers of people taking to the waters could become truly astronomical. These reports, published in an atmosphere of increasing hysteria, began to limit Clinton's room for manoeuvre long before he got into the White House. The American public was being informed by its press that Haiti would present their new president with his first foreign policy crisis.

'President Clinton wants me to get back to Haiti,' Aristide

announced to reporters after the first meeting of the two men in November 1992. But the few weeks that followed saw unparalleled efforts to persuade Haitians not to contemplate taking to their boats. Pressure was put on the *de facto* leaders in Port-au-Prince to make concessions in the search for a solution to the crisis. Clinton announced that he'd had second thoughts about rescinding the Kennebunkport Order and that the policy of repatriation would 'for the moment' continue unabated. He apologized for this U-turn and explained that he'd changed his mind in order to save Haitian lives: 400 people had drowned when the vastly overcrowded boat they were travelling in sank off the shores of Cuba in late December. He was afraid that many others would meet a similar end. But his change of stance was never so simple as that. It was clearly aimed at getting some kind of control on what he feared would be a disastrous flood of unwanted escapees. In the weeks prior to his inauguration a highly intensive repatriation programme was undertaken by the outgoing Bush administration. This clearly had the approval (and cooperation) of Clinton's transitional team. What's more, the new president succeeded in getting Aristide to add his voice to the appeal for restraint. The Haitian president, in a radio broadcast, urged his people not to take to the waters, to stay where they were. This represented, in the circumstances, a genuine mark of trust and respect on Aristide's part for the new American president.

To compensate for this reversal of his campaign promise, Clinton stepped up his efforts to find a diplomatic solution to the crisis. He met Aristide again in early March and declared that Haiti was being given 'top priority' status by his administration. He committed himself to taking stronger measures against the illegal régime and made it crystal clear that he would be working for the restoration of democracy and the reinstatement of Aristide. Indeed, he would be wanting to set a date for the Haitian president's return to office. This was an unambiguous commitment on Clinton's part and Aristide declared himself fully satisfied with the progress he'd made with his American counterpart.

At the very time these friendly moves were being made, however, another part of the American administration was embarking upon a radically different course of action. The Federal Bureau of Investigation was making rigorous enquiries into the circumstances surrounding the death of Roger Lafontant in September 1991. Captain Stagne Doura, governor of the State Penitentiary where the Macoute leader had died, declared that it was Aristide who'd telephoned him to order Lafontant's death. Every effort was made to underline the authenticity of Doura's statement, including the use of a lie detector. But Congressman Don Edwards, president of the judicial commission of the House of Representatives, considered the enquiry illegal on the grounds that it had been instigated for political reasons. And the New York weekly journal *Newsday* went further. It alleged that the enquiry was part of a deliberate attempt to discredit Aristide. Those conducting it were almost obsessively concerned to show that Aristide was responsible for Lafontant's death while taking no interest whatever in those who'd been responsible for the deaths of so many people since the *coup d'état*.

This incident is very revealing. President Clinton faced some powerful opposition from deep within the American security establishment from the very beginning of his time in office. He was bitterly resented by the US military for the fact that he'd dodged the draft during the Vietnam War. One of his early initiatives on taking office was to attempt to allow gay men to serve in the armed forces but this was resisted with venom by the military top brass, so much so that the president had to back down on this issue. His visits to army training schools and to meetings of war veterans were resented. And General Colin Powell wrote a fierce article in the *Washington Post* in which he made his view clear that, in the new post-Cold War order, as the United States sought to redefine its world role, the American president should be very wary indeed of assigning his military forces to UN operations and never even consider placing them under the command of a non-American officer. From these skirmishes, it became evident that there was a struggle for power going on between the new president's administration on the one hand and the Pentagon, Department of State, the CIA and the FBI on the other. These had worked hand-in-glove with George Bush who, as a former Director of the CIA, was definitely 'one of them'. But Clinton was an outsider and had problems.

The Haitian army had had long and close working relationships with the US military and its intelligence operations. Michel S. Laguerre has shown brilliantly, in his *The Military and Society in Haiti*, just how the Haitian army supplied its American counterpart with detailed intelligence on every aspect of Haitian national life. This intelligence operation continued unabated after the coup even though the Haitian army at that time, by their involvement in the reversal of constitutional government, had a clear conflict of interest. The intelligence they supplied after September 1991 was intended to paint the grimmest possible picture of Aristide and his supporters. It is quite incredible to mere observers and lovers of Haiti that those involved in the intelligence activities of the mightiest nation on earth seemed not to be intelligent enough to realize that they needed either to discover other, more objective, sources of information or else to adjust radically the highly biased material that was coming their way. But they did neither of these things. They simply accepted what they received at face value, ordered more, and then went on to use this 'information' in a concerted campaign of character assassination aimed against Jean-Bertrand Aristide. They were encouraged to do this by Republican leaders like Jesse Helms and Robert Dole. And they were conducting this 'dirty war' at the very moment when Bill Clinton and his team were making every effort to convince the world of their undiminishing support for Aristide and the re-establishment of constitutional government in Haiti. The United States government seemed to be speaking with two distinct voices. Cédras and his associates licked their lips at what they saw happening and sought to exploit it by every means they could in order to prolong their hold on power.

Meanwhile, in early 1993, the United Nations had added its strength to that of the Organization of American States. The UN Secretary General had appointed Dante Caputo, a former Argentine foreign minister, to act as Special Envoy to Haiti. It soon became clear that Caputo was not very blessed with the gifts of diplomacy; his public utterances were often rough and personal, as if he were attempting to shame the *de facto* leadership into a resolution of the crisis. There was one practical matter which faced him almost at once; this was the presence and deployment of a team of civilian human rights observers within Haiti. Their task was intended to provide more objective intelligence on the matter of human rights than the highly coloured information coming either from Jean-Jacques Honorat's Aristide-hating CHADEL or else from the intelligence units of the Aristide-hating Haitian army. The arrival of the UN team had been agreed by the Bazin government but obstacles had repeatedly been put in their way and no help given to them as they prepared themselves for their mission.

Their task was in no way made any easier by the fact that there were some substantial discrepancies between the terms agreed between the UN and Aristide on the one hand and those drawn up with the *de facto* leadership on the other. The main difference was the omission from the latter of any undertaking on the part of the military junta to ensure the security of those Haitians who ventured to give information to the UN team. This would hardly encourage local people to come forward to report instances of the abuse of human rights. Cédras and Bazin enjoyed this grey area, of course, and exploited it, indeed they were able to create all kinds of difficulties for the UN observers. It is little wonder that the report filed by those responsible for this mission carried the title: *Haiti: Learning the Hard Way*.

It was Aristide who'd asked for the UN team. He'd hoped it might total as many as 3,000, the sort of number who'd been present for the 1990 election. In the event the team never got beyond 270 observers. They were difficult to recruit and inappropriately equipped for their mission. They rode in expensive, air-conditioned, four-wheel-drive vehicles and were paid handsomely for their efforts. They were despised by most Haitians, even those who were looking towards 'the international community' to help resolve their problem. The Haiti mission was the third such operation (after Cambodia and El Salvador) undertaken by the United Nations and it exposed a number of blind spots.

Caputo was hated by the *de facto* leadership. He bullied and hassled them constantly. Indeed, he allowed them to stir up a great deal of public antagonism against him for his perceived 'imperialist' manner. But for all that, and supported by Haiti's 'Five Friends' (the US, Canada, France, Venezuela and Argentina), Caputo pushed the junta ineluctably towards a negotiated settlement. A special resolution of the Security Council, the imposition of UN-backed worldwide trade sanctions, the freezing of the assets (in US banks) of a number of wealthy Haitians, the cancelling of US entry visas—all these were among the measures it was necessary to adopt before Cédras and Bazin were prepared to come to sit at the table to discuss a settlement.

Throughout this time, Aristide played a fairly low-key role. He and President Clinton seemed to establish a good working relationship. Even though Clinton did not (was not able to) deliver the expected policy options on the matter of the Haitian boat people, Aristide refused to make capital out of this. He clung to Clinton as the one man who, in a longer perspective, could actually make things happen. His judgment was very astute on this point. When the OAS tried and failed it called in the UN. They pulled out all the stops but, as we shall see, got nowhere very fast. That left the United States government as the only serious player left. It took Clinton a little while to get the measure of how things worked in the area of foreign policy. In the end he grew more and more certain that he could force a way out of the impasse. He invested a great deal of personal commitment into 'solving' the Haitian crisis. And he needed to score a foreign policy success. He and Aristide had common enemies in Jesse Helms and Robert Dole and their Republican sympathizers. Very considerable efforts were made by these gentlemen and their associates to discredit both presidents. Somehow, their work succeeded only in forging a real personal link between the two men.

Aristide had consistently demanded the resignation of Cédras before he would sit down to negotiate with him. In the end, he dropped this demand. But his hatred for the army chief led to his refusing to sit in the same room with him. As he later put it:

> It did not strike me as unbearable to find myself face to face with a man who had wanted to kill me and who was now surrounded by criminals who'd betrayed me. What was much harder to take was the consideration that these were the executioners of four thousand Haitians and they continued to kill as they negotiated.

But, for all these difficulties, talks between the two sides did eventually open on Governor's Island, New York. The two delegations occupied separate buildings 100 yards apart with Dante Caputo, the UN Special Envoy, shuttling between them. It took several days of wrangling before Cédras was prevailed upon to sign an agreement. Aristide still hesitated and, in the end, was given until midnight that same day (3 July 1993, a week after the talks had begun) to add his signature. He did so under great duress. There were clauses in the agreement he was deeply unhappy about. But he did eventually sign and, from that moment on, the Governor's Island accord became the basis for the expected return to constitutional government in Haiti. Caputo hailed the agreement and suggested it would serve as 'a model for the future'. The Dayton discussions that led to a Bosnian settlement three years later were obviously based on this experience.

A ten-stage process was envisaged by the accord, a path that would culminate in the return of Aristide on 30 October, four months after the signing of the accord. The agreement stipulated that:

1) There would be a UN-sponsored dialogue between, on the one hand, representatives of all the political parties which had representatives in the Haitian parliament and, on the other, Aristide's 'presidential commission' which he'd established to defend his interests. This dialogue would lay down the critical path for the peaceful transition from existing realities to the return of constitutional government.

2) Aristide would name a prime minister.

3) Parliament would ratify the prime minister and endorse his entry into office.

4) The embargo would be lifted.

5) Foreign aid would start to flow for programmes to be carried out under the aegis of United Nations officials and aimed at the reconstruction of Haiti's shattered economy and the reform of the justice system, the army and the police.

6) Aristide would declare an amnesty. (No precision was given to this clause but it was widely assumed that the likely beneficiaries were army officers. This lack of detail proved one of the great stumbling blocks in later months.)

7) A civil police force with a commanding officer named by Aristide would be established.

8) Cédras would resign from his post as head of the army and Aristide would nominate a successor who would, in turn, name the members of his high command.

9) Aristide would be returned to Haiti. The scheduled date for this would be 30 October.

10) UN and OAS officials would monitor progress and verify each step.

Aristide had wanted the army chiefs to be sacked and banished from Haiti as soon as the new prime minister and his government began to function. He was implacably opposed to the lifting of the embargo before the departure of the army top brass. He suspected that they'd seize the opportunity to claim credit for the return to 'normality' and then seek to subvert the remaining clauses of the agreement. Aristide had also wanted to make his return on 15 August rather than late October.

It is clear that Haiti's *de facto* leaders came away from these talks with some very strong cards in their hands. Yet it was Aristide who was arraigned in the American press for his 'intransigence'. In the event, his understanding about the capacity of the accord to deliver the desired solution proved to be prophetic; things turned out pretty much as he'd suggested. But few remembered his prescience or were prepared to give him credit for it.

The new fact that everyone now had to contend with was that a firm commitment (with a date) had been given for the return of President Aristide. No longer were people jockeying for position on that question. Those longing for his return began to prepare for it. Those who didn't began to put out noises that expressed their pain and threatened a far-from-easy path towards the October date.

Quickest off the mark, in a speech made less than two weeks after the signing of the Governor's Island accord, was Cardinal Nicolas Lopez Rodriguez, head of the Roman Catholic Church in the Dominican Republic and president of the Latin American Episcopal Conference. He denounced the accord and called it 'a huge mistake'. He declared himself implacably opposed to the plan to bring Aristide back to Haiti. The deposed president, to his mind, was 'inexperienced in politics, insensitive and incompetent'. His return could well be considered a greater victory for the UN and the OAS and the international community than it will ever turn out to be for Haiti. The situation there might well get much worse. These remarks, offered gratuitously by such a senior church figure, goaded Bishop Willy Romélus of Jérémie, the one Haitian church leader who'd consistently supported Aristide's cause, to offer a passionate response. He dismissed the Cardinal's remarks, accusing him of being the mouthpiece of the Dominican government which had always been ready to show its implacable hostility towards Haiti. 'And in any case,' he added phlegmatically, 'there are plenty of other prelates who think that Aristide's return will indeed be the solution to Haiti's problems.'

A far more damaging development which took place in this transitional time between the signing of the Governor's Island accord and the projected date of Aristide's return came from a CIA report prepared for hearings of the Senate Foreign Relations Committee in early October. The purpose of these hearings was to underline American support and commit American forces to the implementation of the accord. The report was damning and its case rested primarily on an analysis of Aristide's personality.

At its heart it alleged that Aristide had undergone psychiatric treatment while living in Canada some years previously. It even named the Louis H. Lafontaine Hospital in Montreal as the place where he'd been treated for a condition which was said to be 'clinically manic-depressive'. Senator Jesse Helms, a conservative North Carolina Republican familiar with the CIA profile, described Aristide as a 'psychopath' who would execute his political enemies and return to his past criticisms of United States policies. 'Aristide is a killer. He is a demonstrable killer. I do not think we have any business whatsoever risking the life of one soldier or one sailor or any other American to put Aristide back in office,' he said (on the Senate floor) after reading the CIA report. On another occasion he declared, 'It is well known that Mister Aristide is a murderer. Yet somebody decided to return him to power at the risk, if necessary, of American lives.' The CIA's chief Latin American analyst, Brian Latell, was just as forthcoming. He said on one occasion, for the benefit of reporters, that Aristide had 'psychological disorders and has used thirteen kinds of medicine, especially Lithium and Haldol', before going on to allege that the deposed president, if returned, would rule with violence and settle old scores with brutality.

These allegations about Aristide's mental stability and

reliability were soon being widely reported. They were faithfully repeated by prestigious journals such as the *Washington Post* and on CNN television. The main point seemed to be clinched when General Brent Scowcroft, who'd been national security advisor to President Bush, stated his view that 'Aristide is probably a certifiable psychopath.' I was called on to make a number of broadcasts on radio and television at this time and found that those interviewing me inevitably wanted to concentrate on Aristide's state of mind rather than the prospects open to Haiti in the light of the Governor's Island accord. It was clear that the CIA report had shifted the focus of attention from the constitutional question of Aristide's return to the matter of his (psychological) fitness for office. I couldn't restrain myself from asking just how ex-president Reagan would have fared if questions had been raised about his psychological fitness for office. The spin being put on Aristide's character was very damaging at this crucial time when efforts were being made to follow the step-by-step process that was intended to prepare for his reinstatement.

Just a few weeks later, the CIA 'report' was shown up to be a tissue of lies. Christopher Marquis published a splendid article in the *Miami Herald* which exploded the CIA case once and for all. Marquis got Aristide to write a letter authorizing him to ask the Montreal hospital in question whether there was any truth in the reports that had been circulating. 'I take this opportunity to deny once again,' Aristide wrote, 'that I received psychiatric care while in Canada. These claims are garbage. In any event, you are hereby authorized to request any and all medical records that may exist.'

And, of course, the Lafontaine hospital reported that Aristide 'was never treated here'. Just to be sure, Marquis made a similar enquiry at three other hospitals which might conceivably have been involved. They too distanced themselves from such a possibility. Marquis went one step further. He secured from Michel-Ange Momplaisir, a Port-au-Prince neurosurgeon, a clear denial that he had ever written a letter which referred to his collaboration with a Montreal doctor in treating Aristide for a psychiatric condition. This 'letter' had been leaked to conservative US lawmakers and had turned out to be grist for their malevolent mill.

This incident did Aristide a great deal of harm. It seriously affected a delicate political process at a crucial time in its evolution. It allowed the deposed president's enemies to feel they could count on some sympathy from the world community if they continued to resist their opponent's return. But it also raised very serious questions about how the CIA gathered its information and indeed its very competence at this important time when the United States was redefining its role in the post-Cold War world.

When President Clinton was asked for his views on the CIA report he was categorical in his support for Aristide who, he stated, represented the best hope for political stability in Haiti and for ending the exodus of Florida-bound refugees. He said he was familiar with the CIA views, but, based on his own contact with Aristide, didn't believe them. 'I reviewed the CIA profile when I became president,' he said, 'and... worked through it and concluded it was not right. So what was I to do? Try to jam it? Eventually it would have to come out... Aristide is different. He has lived the life of an ascetic. He is not a Chicago pol [politician] or an Arkansas country judge. But if you look at what happened when he was in office, there was less, not more, political repression. He has done everything he said to us he would do.'

This remarkably generous statement from Clinton is one more proof of the huge gap that existed between him and the military/intelligence counter-culture in Washington at that time. The CIA report was hopelessly biased and this was in large part due to the agency's ties to the Haitian military. But it was also skewed because of the American perception that, in considering any potential threat to vital US hemispheric interests, there was one insidious body of opinion that was even more dangerous than conventional Marxist-Leninist communism, a way of thinking that had to be combated with resolution. The object of such paranoid and hysterical thinking was, of course, liberation theology whose proponents showed far greater likelihood of mobilizing the masses than traditional communists had ever been able to. And no one focused this ability more sharply than Jean-Bertrand Aristide.

An outburst by the church and a campaign of character assassination by the CIA represented two powerful reactionary attempts to forestall the Governor's Island agreement. Within Haiti a third force emerged, the *Front pour l'Avancement et le Progrès Haitien*, the Front for the Advance and Progress of Haiti. It was always better known by its acronym, FRAPH (always pronounced FRAPP), an ominous homonym for the French word *frapper*, which means 'to strike, beat, hit, hurt'.

In line with the Governor's Island agreement, Aristide had proceeded quickly to name a prime minister. His choice fell upon Robert Malval, a member of the mulatto business élite. He had a Lebanese mother and a father whose roots lay in Germany. He was one of Haiti's leading publishers and had dealt with Aristide, 'a combative alliance' he called it, when editing two of the ousted president's books. Mary McGrory, writing in the *Washington Post*, gave as concise a picture of Malval as anyone could. 'Robert Malval is all that the United States could ask for in a Caribbean leader,' she wrote. 'He is a rich businessman with a conscience. His English is excellent and... he has presence, dignity and humour.' Then she continued with undisguised irony, 'All he lacks is a clue about what to do in his tormented country.'

One of Malval's early initiatives was, in the name of 'reconciliation' and national unity, to issue a warm invitation to all Haitians living abroad to return home. He drew the line at no one and, in a newspaper interview, went as far as to say that even Jean-Claude Duvalier would be welcome. BabyDoc didn't take up his kind offer but many exiled Duvalierists did, people like ex-Port-au-Prince mayor Franck Romain and former president (1989–90), Prosper Avril. Their presence on Haitian soil at this sensitive time was bound to create difficulties. Soon, in a conspiracy with the Haitian army, they set up FRAPH as a paramilitary group with the clear objective of destabilizing Haiti and undermining the Governor's Island process. Well-armed FRAPH agents began their campaign of terror, bursting in on government ministers with threats and gunfire, disrupting public meetings, intimidating the poor quarters with night-time terror, calling 'strikes' and holding demonstrations, leaving the bodies of their victims on the streets as evidence of their impunity. They even abused Dante Caputo and demanded that he be sacked from his job as UN Special Envoy. Their methods and ethos greatly resembled those of the Tontons Macoutes. They returned Haiti to a state of terror just as it was supposed to be emerging towards a rediscovered constitutional rule.

Aristide followed the requirements of the Governor's Island accord scrupulously. He did flinch at the thought of declaring an amnesty that would allow people like Cédras and François to escape scot free; he clung to the distinction he'd previously made that an amnesty could only be offered to those who'd committed no offences against Haiti's civil code. But, this 'academic' distinction apart, Aristide stuck to the process even when Malval proved ready to criticize him fiercely in public. The three months following the signing of the New York agreement saw Haiti sliding irrevocably back into chaos. A particularly gruesome low point came when one of Aristide's most influential supporters, businessman Antoine Izméry, was dragged out of a church service being held to commemorate the Jean Rabel massacre. He was shot dead on the pavement outside the church in front of witnesses. People pointed the finger at police chief Michel François but no action was ever taken against him, nor was any real pressure exerted from any external quarter to bring him to book. He and his type acted in brazen defiance of the law. Nothing seemed to point to Haiti's emergence from what was fast becoming a dark and swirling abyss even when measured against its own standards. Against all these events, the lifting of the embargo seemed hardly likely to help; in the event it merely allowed the *de facto* régime to re-equip itself for a further round of attrition.

Throughout this time Aristide had become quite a celebrity. He ran his government-in-exile from a couple of rented

Georgetown apartments and was invited to a large number of social events. He was constantly on the interview-and-lecture circuit. He would at one moment be fêted at a party in Hollywood and the next acclaimed as a champion of democracy on Capitol Hill. He was able to visit President Clinton in the White House from time to time and they developed a good relationship. When such a meeting took place just after the Governor's Island agreement, the event was half lecture, half pep talk. Clinton wanted to help Aristide understand the need to become presidential, a figure who spoke about reconciliation and healing and rebuilding. He spent time with his Haitian friend urging him to begin to make the mental transition from president-in-exile to president. This little detail is as interesting for the light it throws on Clinton as it is for what it reveals about Aristide. Clinton was equally ready to bestow praise on his Haitian counterpart. He did so after a meeting in Miami which Aristide attended with Haitian business leaders, when, in a strong speech, he'd told his 180-strong audience, many of whom were among his strongest opponents, how 'Haiti must be reconstructed by its sons and daughters.' It was a moment so charged in emotion that when Aristide embraced Raymond Roi, a fierce opponent who was head of Haiti's Chamber of Commerce, the whole meeting erupted into a spontaneous rendering of the national anthem.

Aristide was ready to tell a startled reporter that the only word to describe his feelings for Clinton was 'love'. He was in regular touch with the American president and realized that 'there was a deep human vibration' in him. 'I felt that he really understood the reality,' Aristide said. He invited Clinton to visit Haiti when democracy was restored there.

The Haitian president learned a great deal from his regular contacts with world leaders through this frustrating time away from Haiti. And he made it clear that the Miami meeting with Haiti's business élite in July 1993 had persuaded him that their energies needed to be enlisted in the task of rebuilding Haiti. But their trust was just as important. He felt that Haiti's wealthy bourgeoisie was now realistic enough to recognize that the future lay with democratic and constitutional government. And they were pragmatic enough to co-operate with him. He felt equally positive about the re-establishment of good working relations with the Vatican and the Haitian bishops. He was hopeful of a better future. But he was unready to promise a miracle. He just wanted to provide some basic ingredients for the lives of his fellow-citizens. If they could 'eat the bread of security, enjoy freedom of movement, live without the fear of being struck down at any moment', if they could just savour these fundamental realities, they would in fact be taking the vital step that 'distinguishes utter misery from dignified poverty. And that one step is just about all I feel able to promise at this time.'

If there was one defining moment in the whole of the tentative Governor's Island process, indeed in the whole of the three-year period of Haiti's unconstitutional rule, it occurred on 11 October 1993. On that day the *USS Harlan County*, carrying 200 Canadian and US army instructors who were to help with some of the non-military aspects of Haiti's return to democracy, was turned back as it approached the Port-au-Prince harbour. The order for the turnaround came from the president of the United States of America himself who felt driven to take such a dramatic decision because of a noisy demonstration held at the Port-au-Prince dockside as the *Harlan County* began its approaches. At the very highest executive levels, therefore, the conclusion had clearly been reached that a 200-strong group of desperadoes, drunken thugs and ne'er-do-wells constituted a direct threat to the safety of the US personnel about to be disembarked. No doubt the stentorian calls of Jesse Helms that the Haitian crisis was 'not worth one American life' were ringing in Bill Clinton's ears. To be fair, eighteen American soldiers had been killed just a week earlier as part of a UN peacekeeping operation in Somalia. Even so, this decision was taken in panic and it served to fuel the Haitian crisis for a further year. I remember being in the United States at the time; the picture of the retreating *Harlan County* spread across the front page of the *Boston Globe* told a clear story of impotence and humiliation. Special Envoy Dante Caputo was as surprised (and angry) as anyone; he became aware of the pull-out only when he chanced to look out of his hotel window and saw the ship turn back to sea. The decision to retreat had been taken unilaterally by the US without a word to the UN or OAS. It was a pure and unalloyed capitulation, a cowardly abandonment of any commitment to the remaining shreds of the Governor's Island accord.

There was no way now in which Aristide could return on 30 October. A few days later, the UN voted to re-impose the embargo if Cédras didn't resign in forty-eight hours. He didn't, so trade restrictions were slapped on again. But this embargo was just like the previous one. No lessons seemed to have been learned. It took a long time to apply it and, even when fully operational, it was as porous as damp blotting paper. Oil tankers kept arriving with shipments supposedly targeted towards 'humanitarian' needs. The Dominican border became a smuggling zone of considerable importance. FRAPH intensified its purges of popular neighbourhoods, burning houses and killing known Aristide sympathizers. Its agents also burst into the parliament buildings making outrageous demands and threatening to kill FNCD members. On 14 October, the Minister of Justice, Guy Malary, the man charged with overseeing the formation of a civil police force and building a credible justice system in Haiti, was gunned down in broad daylight. He was killed by multiple shots fired into his body from automatic weapons at point-blank range. The gunmen then dragged his body out of the vehicle in which he'd been riding and arranged it carefully on the pavement for the scrutiny of the public. By now, the whole country was in turmoil.

Fifty Canadian police trainers and 270 UN human rights observers, the last vestiges of any active commitment on the part of the outside world, were withdrawn from Haiti on 15 October. This was the final sign of the utter failure of the international community to find a co-ordinated and consistent way of responding to the undoubtedly worsening crisis in Haiti. It also showed how the *de facto* leaders were able skilfully to play one party off against another in their efforts to survive. Thus they identified and exploited the different factions within the US administration, the split within the so-called 'Friends' of Haiti (a self-appointed group of nations—France, Venezuela, Canada, Argentina and the United States—who took a special interest in developments in Haiti) on the question of what kind of embargo to apply—the United States on the one hand and France and Canada on the other, the divisions between the US and the UN, the different operational roles of the UN and the OAS, the embittered hostility of the Balaguer régime in the Dominican Republic to any prospect of Aristide's return, and the moral boost given by the Vatican's appointment of a nuncio. In one way or another, the international community contributed hugely to Haiti's unhappiness by its ineptitude and downright stupidity.

I paid a visit to Haiti at the end of October. On the day when Aristide should have been back in Port-au-Prince under the terms of the Governor's Island accord, Haiti was in the worst state I'd known in the quarter of a century I'd been coming and going, and indeed worse than I'd ever read about in the whole of its independent history. The markets were empty of food, there was virtually no electricity, terror stalked the streets and the slums especially at night. I saw corpses lying on the sidewalk, some with their faces shovelled off. Emmanuel 'Toto' Constant, the FRAPH leader, was making loud noises about his own political ambitions. The Malval government was being intimidated to the point where its members no longer felt able to leave their own homes. Everything was very bleak indeed.

Aristide was thrown on the defensive by these developments. He addressed the General Assembly of the United Nations at the end of October, just two days before the date scheduled for his return, and made a strong plea for a total blockade of Haiti. He labelled the military repression as 'genocide'. He'd always been clear that the only way to get rid of the junta was by strong and determined means. But now his plea for total sanctions rebounded in his face. The *New York Times* published a front page story, supposedly based on a Harvard University study, claiming that the economic embargo was causing 1,000 extra child-deaths in Haiti each month. Even though a later clarification came to a different conclusion, 'that human rights abuses, mismanagement and the blatant corruption of the current and previous Haitian régimes—not UN sanctions—are the fundamental causes of the continued deterioration of health in Haiti', the original allegation continued to offer useful propaganda for anti-Aristide forces. Church and NGO (non-governmental organization) voices began to be raised in criticism of the deposed president's call for stronger sanctions. He was portrayed as heartless, self-seeking and arrogant.

A cartoon drawn by a Methodist missionary pictured Aristide stepping off a US navy gunboat onto Haitian soil. At the bottom of the gangplank, crawling out of fetid slum dwellings, are a couple of starving and disease-ridden Haitian children. They're on their bellies, they haven't the strength to stand. They can just manage to hold up a hand towards their president as he steps out towards them. The captain of the American ship, bluff and smiling, pointing towards the squalid children waiting for their hero, says to Aristide: 'Gee, look buddy, you got yourself a l'il ole welcoming party!' The caption under the cartoon says, quite simply, 'Aristide demands tougher sanctions.'

In December Prime Minister Malval resigned from office. He'd tried to get an all-party 'reconciliation conference' organized within Haiti in an attempt to unblock the dreadful situation. Aristide had vetoed this suggestion, choosing instead to call for a conference in Miami on the refugee question. Even though nine out of the ten cabinet ministers were also opposed to the prime minister's suggestion, Malval reserved his ire for Aristide. In his letter of resignation he listed a whole series of mean-minded actions and attitudes which Aristide had directed towards him during the 100 days of their co-habitation. It is clear that the president did everything he possibly could to undermine Malval whose appointment (part of the Governor's Island accord) he'd felt forced to accept. Aristide put one obstacle after another in Malval's way and showed a pettiness of mind that deserved the strongest criticism. Even so, the constitutional question remained: Aristide, for better or for worse (and this was about as bad as could be), remained the democratically elected head of state. Now his hard-heartedness in calling for tougher sanctions, together with his refusal to accede to Malval's call for a conference of national reconciliation, and also the determined way he'd set out to make life difficult for his prime minister, fed a determined anti-Aristide mood that was fast developing in Washington and elsewhere.

A leader in the 22 December number of the *Washington Post* well sums up the feelings that were taking shape. After accusing him of intransigence and political naivety, it called on him to work out his own salvation instead of relying on others in the international community. The piece ended with the following paragraph:

> If Mr Aristide continues to denounce and resist any further attempts at negotiation, he risks the fate of many exiles. In Haiti, a bad temporary situation will become a bad permanent one, hardly the first (or worst) in Haiti's long history, while the deposed president will continue to reside in Georgetown, the fading symbol of an outrage that most of the world will eventually forget. If Mr Aristide wants something better for his suffering country, he himself is going to have begin working energetically and skilfully with his enemies as well as his friends.

WASHINGTON POST, 22 DECEMBER 1993.

The Times added its own voice from London to this point of view. Its editorial of 17 February 1994 was entitled, 'Alas, poor Aristide: Haiti's robbed president must learn to compromise.' It argued that there were only three possible ways of solving the crisis. The first was an armed intervention which was completely out of the question. President Clinton could never gain support for such a proposal. Or else the world could impose tougher sanctions in line with Aristide's demands. But these would inevitably hit the wrong target; the poor would suffer far more than the rich. So all that remained was a negotiated settlement. And, on this matter, Aristide was showing an intransigence that was bound to be self-defeating. 'Mr Aristide's first duty,' argued *The Times*, 'is to the Haitian people. He must not let principles destroy his judgment.'

What was incredible in all this was the refusal of anyone to analyze the respective critical paths showing flexibility and readiness-for-compromise followed respectively by Aristide and the military leadership. The former had made concession after concession. His opponents had made none. Indeed, they'd tightened their oppressive control over a faltering Haiti, enjoyed a close working relationship with the CIA, managed to turn economic sanctions to their own benefit, and found huge amounts of extra resources from drug-running. They succeeded in all this without a hint of compromise, yet they had the satisfaction of seeing their arch-enemy pilloried for his 'intransigence' by an international community that had got tired of Haiti and just wanted to wash its hands of the whole affair.

In his New Year speech to the nation, Aristide spoke of the need to 'walk on two feet', the two feet of 'negotiation and mobilization'. He recognized that the year 1993 had been mainly about negotiation and promised that he was ready for much more of the same in 1994 if, and only if, he sensed it was all leading in an honourable direction. 'Moving forward doesn't mean much,' he declared, 'it's knowing the road you're on that matters far more.' If democracy wasn't returned pretty soon, he continued, then 'the Haitian people will no longer agree to cover their daily dose of misery with a sugar coating of patience'. Mobilization might then replace negotiation as the best foot to be put forward. He called on his people to reject Janus-faced politics that looked in two directions at the same time, to say no to negotiations that sold them short, and to condemn conspiracies that took place under the cover of an embargo. All these represented politics of betrayal, he declared, and called his people and their leaders to show the same courage that their ancestors had displayed when they wrenched independence from their colonial masters.

He came a little more down to earth in a speech he gave in New York in February 1994 to mark the third anniversary of his inauguration to the presidency. 'Just look at the kind of professional criminals we've got in power just now,' he said. 'Just look how they've killed so many innocent people in Cité Soleil with a savage arson attack. Just look how they killed more than a dozen youngsters in the course of this last week. Just think how the total number of their victims now exceeds 5,000.' He particularly wanted to draw attention to the crimes of his opponents because the Clinton administration was just tabling its latest 'peace plan'. Under its terms, a pathway to constitutional rule was being spelled out which, unlike the Governor's Island accord, made no mention whatsoever of a date for Aristide's return to Haiti.

In a long feature article which appeared in *Vanity Fair* at about this time, reporter Bella Stumbo made one point with great emphasis. Those who were saying that Aristide violated the Governor's Island accord (and, on those grounds, were now pressing for a modified agreement that would virtually obliterate the commitment to return him to Haiti) were quite simply wrong in arriving at such a conclusion. She quoted Aristide: 'We did everything we were supposed to do. Cédras and François are professional liars and murderers. According to the agreement, I had to grant an amnesty, and I did. It's they who have refused to comply with the accord. They want to falsify things so that they can go on in control.' The journalist had no hesitation in agreeing with Aristide's perception on this matter.

Stumbo found Aristide far more relaxed than she'd ever seen him before. 'His English is better, he laughs more easily, and he doesn't waste so much time picking precise, statesmanlike words.' All this despite the vicious personal attacks that were being made on him and all the 'frustrations of dealing with a world which increasingly seems only halfway committed to its pledges to him'. She described his rather ordinary one-bedroomed flat and the simplicity of his lifestyle. He'd recently been accused by high-ranking military officers in Haiti of wearing extravagant Armani suits. To the journalist's eye, the suit he was wearing that day seemed much more likely to have come from the J.C. Penney department store. Again and again in this report we meet unusual (and reassuring) verbs. Aristide is said to chuckle good-naturedly, to enjoy a joke, to grin spontaneously, and he laughs sardonically as well as easily. Indeed, he seemed in extremely good shape at what must have been the lowest point in his cycle.

But, for all that, he was showing signs of losing patience. A *New York Times* headline in April described the way things were developing in Haiti. 'A rising tide of political terror leaves hundreds dead in Haiti,' it read. And all the international community could come up with in the diplomatic effort to find a way out of the mess was a new plan that seemed to remove Aristide from the frame entirely. This suggestion was put forward by Ian Martin, who had been the deputy head of the United Nations human rights monitoring mission, and who suggested that the polarization of opinion in Haiti was so radical that the only way of accommodating both parties was by resorting to the notion of 'safe havens', carefully defined parts of the country earmarked for the different interest groups. The 'balkanization' of Haiti did seem a little far-fetched, but it also indicated the bankruptcy of ideas about how to solve the Haitian crisis. The army generals seemed safe for the immediate future. I found myself adding to the pessimism of the times by writing to Aristide in these terms:

Your excellency,
  I am more depressed at what I see in our beloved Haiti today than I've ever been. And I see you, my friend, being pushed further and further to the margins the longer this sorry tale lasts. I no longer believe that the international community possesses the wit, the will, or the wisdom to

help Haiti to return to constitutional rule.

So where does that leave you, my friend?

I'm wondering whether your continued presence in Washington is likely any longer to serve your cause. Indeed, I'm wondering whether anything will end this painful chapter short of your own physical presence on Haitian soil again. What do you think? You alone can raise the courage of your people and unblock the present logjam.

The US can't do it.

The UN can't do it.

The OAS can't do it.

The World Bank, the IMF can't do it.

Clinton, Mitterrand, Caputo can't do it.

Only you can do it. And you can do it only by being there, alongside your people to encourage and inspire them. This may sound like a counsel of despair but it doesn't seem to my gloomy mind that anything else will now work.

As I re-read these words I shudder to think just how dismal the prospects for Haiti seemed to have become in my mind. It really isn't in my character to advocate Castro-esque methods for solving political problems. The times were certainly grim.

Throughout the early months of 1994 there were constant reports of violence and destruction coming out of Haiti. Bodies were being found in Cité Soleil and other slum quarters almost on a daily basis. Scores of people were being reported 'missing'. Rape now began to figure in a systematic way in the armoury of repressive and intimidatory measures used against the population. In the northern town of Le Borgne hundreds of soldiers carried out a series of arrests, beatings and rapes in early April. A hundred homes were burned down there. Indeed, arson was a widespread tactic of the army through this period; it worked like a treat every time, spreading rapidly through the tin-and-cardboard shack townships that hang heavily like pus-filled boils on the edge of Haiti's main cities. Despair and terror were marching hand in hand through the lives of Haiti's poor people at this time. And all the outside world seemed able to do was huff and puff.

Aristide refused to follow my advice or indeed to bow to the pressures of the times. Indeed, he played the few cards available to him with great skill. In February, horrified by news and television pictures of the drowning of four Haitian refugees just a few yards off a Miami beach, he accused the American government of imposing 'a floating Berlin wall' on Haiti. And he hinted that he might suspend the 1981 agreement which allowed the US to repatriate Haitian boat people. US State Department officials said the president's remarks were 'mystifying' and 'peculiar'. In March, Aristide denounced the 'ambiguity and cynicism' of certain big powers. He also rejected a proposed Security Council resolution which would have given the UN Secretary General the power to lift the embargo if he felt the president wasn't taking steps towards the return to democracy. His outspokenness saw to it that the resolution was never voted on.

Later that same month (March) Aristide had extensive conversations with US Vice President Al Gore. Gore was working on the plan to establish parliamentary government in Haiti, a plan which gave no precise undertaking towards Aristide's return. The president countered this plan with one of his own in which Haiti's military, rather than himself, should be forced to make concessions. News of Aristide's proposal was leaked to the *New York Times* and used as further evidence, for those who needed it, of the president's 'intransigence'. When, a day or so later, Aristide rejected Gore's plan outright, the case seemed watertight.

In early April, Aristide wrote to the US administration announcing that he was suspending the 1981 repatriation treaty. He gave the US government notice that, from the following October, it would become illegal for them to resort to their automatic repatriation measures and he quoted violations of the agreement to justify his action. This was a very astute move on his part. The boat people represented the one aspect of the Haitian crisis that had impacted on the mind of the

American public. Fears of vast numbers of unwanted arrivals swarming across the beaches of Florida had given Haitian negotiators just about the only lever they'd ever had in talks about their country's future. And now Aristide was hoping to give that lever one last pull. And he intensified his pressure a couple of weeks later by denouncing US Haitian policy as 'racist'. In a press conference in Washington he declared that 'President Clinton has given no proof that he cares about Haiti... We've reached the point in Port-au-Prince where the bodies of those killed by the military are being dumped on garbage heaps and eaten by pigs. We're seeing photographs of people whose faces have been sliced off with shovels. How many people have to die before we can start talking of a holocaust? I keep on hearing fine words from American officials but I don't see much happening. Indeed, a few hooligans in Haiti are being allowed to give the impression that they are stronger than the most powerful country in the world.' This was fighting talk and it hurt. Clinton was languishing in the opinion polls at that time and Haiti, which he'd hoped would give him a foreign policy success that would help boost his ratings, was instead a source of great embarrassment to him. He was reaping the consequences of his pusillanimous decision to order the retreat of the *Harlan County* six months earlier.

This was a time of deep gloom. Every diplomatic ploy and peace plan had failed. The military and their FRAPH associates were acting with disdain for world opinion. The embargo was being flouted with impunity. The erstwhile friendship between the Haitian and American presidents was foundering. The American press had turned its ire on Aristide and its contempt on Clinton. Unknown numbers of people were being killed in Haiti. Tens of thousands lived in fear. And yet the oppressors' treasury was being topped up by an ample supply of drug-dollars that flowed from lucrative deals with Colombian barons glad to use Haitian soil as a staging post for supplying the American narcotics market. No one knew what to suggest; there was nowhere to turn, Haiti seemed to have reached its nadir point, the point of absolute impasse.

But this was not, in fact, the case. For those with very sensitive eyes there were signs that some tiny pinpricks of light were beginning to make their mark on the seemingly all-enveloping darkness around them. And these intimations of hope, present in such unpropitious times, are worth identifying. The first of these, wonderful to tell after its unremitting tragedy of errors, came from the Vatican.

When Prime Minister Robert Malval visited Rome in December 1993 he met, amongst others, Secretary of State Cardinal Angelo Sodano. The Cardinal declared his support for a plan to bring Aristide back to Haiti and went on to say that the Vatican had never questioned the legitimacy of his election even though 'they prefer a priest not to be a president'. These remarks were somewhat naive and raised as many questions as they answered but they did mark a change of tone towards Aristide. And, with public opinion beginning to look for an Aristide-free solution to the Haitian crisis, this hint at a possible new stance was most welcome.

More significant for the American administration, however, was the increasingly vociferous involvement of a number of Hollywood stars in the Haiti crisis. People like Robert de Niro, Paul Newman, Robert Redford, Julia Roberts, Spike Lee, Dustin Hoffman, Jack Lemmon, Bob Dylan and Jonathan Demme added their support to 'Artists for Democracy' and were prepared to speak out on Haiti. And, of course, they were never short of an audience. The Black Caucus in Congress was also increasing its pressure for a new look at the administration's Haiti policy. Jesse Jackson had taken a personal interest in Haiti from the very beginning of its *de facto* time. Now they began to press President Clinton for radical action to get rid of the military régime. The caucus announced a bill calling for the president to tighten the sanctions on Haiti, cease repatriation of refugees, and to seek actively the return of Aristide to his rightful position. Possibly the most eye-catching demonstration of solidarity at this critical time came from Randall Robinson, the director of the black pressure group TransAfrica, who went on hunger strike. Ten days into his fast, he accused President Clinton of being 'an accomplice in the assassinations taking place in Haiti'. He then rounded on Clinton for consigning so many boat people to their deaths. This was a cruel, immoral and profoundly racist stance, he said. 'The United States should be responding to these people with the same decency that we've shown in the past to other people fleeing from tyranny. But just now President Clinton seems to be without a moral compass.'

This pressure, together with Aristide's own increasingly open belligerence, and the worsening plight of the poor in Haiti, led Bill Clinton to see that his policies had run into the sand. He acted with resolution. In late April he sacked his top advisor Lawrence Pezzullo who had formulated the White House strategy of seeking a compromise with Haiti's military rulers rather than an all-out push to return Aristide. The sacking of Pezzullo represented a real change of heart on the Haiti crisis by the American president. This was confirmed when he was caught on camera after a taped TV interview about Haiti. 'They're chopping people's faces off now,' he was heard to say. 'We've just got to change our policy. It simply hasn't worked.'

Two announcements from the US government in May gave the first real sign of the direction in which Clinton's new policy might take. On 8 May, Washington announced a change in its Haitian refugee policy, saying that all refugees picked up at sea would be given a chance to apply for political asylum either at sea or 'in a third country'. Even though it added a rider that no more than 10 per cent would be accepted, this marked significant progress over the previous repressive Kennebunkport policy. Three days later, the State Department said, in what was a U-turn on all previous policy statements, that it was considering endorsing a UN Peace-Keeping Mission in Haiti. Direct intervention was being hinted at for the first time. The hints became shouts within a week when 44,000 American troops took part in a massive military exercise in the Caribbean. This was widely interpreted as a 'dress rehearsal for a Haiti invasion'.

At a press conference in early June, Aristide, sensing the

reactivation of commitment on the part of the United States government and hardly believing his luck, was pressed for an opinion on a possible invasion. This is always a particularly thorny question for any Haitian leader. Open support for foreign intervention would immediately brand him as a traitor in Haiti. This is the supremely sensitive issue for a country whose only fixed point of reference is the defeat of the French colonialist army in 1803. Yet Aristide had reached the point where he sensed that nothing other than a military invasion could possibly bring this long crisis to an end. So he weighed his words carefully. 'I don't want a military occupation,' he said, 'but I'm not going to waste time spelling out exactly what kind of action is needed right now since the international community knows precisely what it needs to do.' In an interview with the *New York Times* he was a trifle more focused. There he declared that 'the United States should envisage an intervention conducted with surgical precision and lasting a mere matter of hours. This would offer enough time to get rid of the criminals in charge and could save lives. It's been done in other countries. So why not Haiti?'

And that was now to become the leading, indeed the only, question as the end of Haiti's three-year period of anti-constitutional rule loomed into sight.

8 Operation Uphold Democracy

On 2 August 1994 I was invited to a high-powered meeting in the Foreign and Commonwealth Office in London. It wasn't my first visit, nor would it be my last. For some time past the head of the Caribbean section there had arranged occasional meetings with me to discuss the situation in Haiti. We'd try to read the signs together, to get behind the surface events, and to spot likely outcomes and trends, especially at critical moments. Whenever my Haiti Support Group had some distinguished visitor in Britain, we'd generally wheel him round for dialogue with F&CO officials. Thus Roman Catholic priest Jean-Marie Vincent, grassroots leader Jean-Baptiste Chavannes, Port-au-Prince mayor Evans Paul and even ousted President Jean-Bertrand Aristide himself, came and went. Similarly, Whitehall would let me know of any Haitian visitors who'd come to London under their aegis. Julio Larosilière, a member of the Senate, was one of these, I remember. And I was also called in on one occasion to help with the briefing of a new governor for the Turks and Caicos Islands, a tiny British dependent territory off the north coast of Haiti, a quarter of whose population are illegal Haitian immigrants. Through all these contacts, I'd become familiar with the Foreign Office working lunch. But this new summons was of a different order.

In a large and rather grim room which I'd reached as if following the rules of snakes and ladders I was introduced to William Marsden, Assistant Under Secretary of State (Americas). Haiti had never to my knowledge been treated with this degree of seriousness before. Even at the height of its most recent crisis, in the days following the September 1991 coup, it was considered only marginal to British interests and, therefore, never merited any serious or high-level concern. But the involvement now of an Assistant Under Secretary of State suggested that things had changed in that regard. I noticed that Marsden was holding a copy of the Roman Catholic weekly newspaper *The Tablet* and that it was open at a page bearing my latest article on Haiti. 'I've read what you have to say about Haiti,' he said, 'and I want you to know how much we respect your judgment on Haitian affairs. I've asked you here to give you advance news of the decision of the United States government to invade Haiti. The timing isn't yet certain but it's likely to take place in mid-September. What's more, our own government has decided to back the Americans. Our matériel support will not be enormous, some logistical and training input, but it commits us to Washington's line and gives us the possibility of making some input into the planning process over the next few weeks. I've asked you here because I'd be interested to hear your reply to one simple question, namely this. When the invasion takes place what, in your view, are we likely to expect and what mistakes should we avoid?'

A Methodist minister doesn't often find himself in a consultancy role for a military operation. I was determined to enjoy the experience and expressed my conviction that the American troops would be welcomed as a liberating force rather than an army of occupation. I was by now in full stride and enjoyed having the top brass as a captive audience for my views about the likelihood of American overreaction and the imperative need to respect Haitian autonomy. The conversation then went on to a more detailed analysis of a range of possible likelihoods. A little over an hour later I left Whitehall in possession of what was still, I suppose, a state secret. What was no secret at all was the way talk of a possible invasion of Haiti had been firmed up and turned into a formal commitment to go in. It had all sprung from Security Council Resolution 940 passed just two days before my encounter at the Foreign and Commonwealth Office. Having determined that 'the illegal *de facto* régime in Haiti had failed to comply with the Governor's Island agreement and was, therefore, in breach of its obligations under the relevant resolutions of the Security Council', SCR940 went on to authorize member states (under Chapter 7 of the Charter of the United Nations) 'to form a multinational force under unified command and control and to use all necessary means to facilitate the departure from Haiti of the military leadership consistent with the Governor's Island agreement'. It also promised 'the prompt return of the legitimately elected president and the restoration of the legitimate authorities of the Government of Haiti'. With the passing of this Resolution the way was opened for swift and conclusive action.

The Haitian army didn't appear to flinch at these developments. With its FRAPH associates it continued to suppress all evidence of popular support for Aristide and any public reaction to the increasing likelihood of an armed invasion. Indeed, General Raoul Cédras, a life-long Methodist, said on leaving church one Sunday morning: 'After this service, I have all the strength I need to defend the country.' The minister leading worship that day was the head of the Haitian Methodist church, the Rev Fède Jean-Pierre, an avid and outspoken opponent of the *de facto* government and an equally keen supporter of constitutional rule and the return of Aristide. When I asked Jean-Pierre just what he'd said that could have given such a boost to the self-confidence of Cédras, he smiled wryly and thought it might have been the prayer he'd offered 'for our legitimate rulers'. Cédras was so completely out of touch by this stage that he just might have thought the prayer was for him. The person offering the prayer, however, and almost everyone else in church would have known that that was far from the case.

As well as the thousands of anonymous victims claimed over the three years of unconstitutional rule, there were a few public figures like the Minister of Justice Guy Malary and the brothers Georges and Antoine Izméry, wealthy businessmen and outspoken supporters of Aristide. At the end of August another name was added to this list, that of Father Jean-Marie Vincent, one of the ousted president's closest friends. The 49-year-old Vincent was a Roman Catholic priest who'd been director of Caritas, an aid agency, in Cap Haitien and also a leading figure in the Catholic Church's literacy programme *Misyon Alfa*. He was deeply involved in community development as well as grassroots and ecological programmes. Twice he'd come close to death for his radical views, once in the Jean Rabel massacre in 1986 and the second time at Freycineau when Aristide and his party escaped assassination by the skin of their teeth.

Vincent stayed in our home when visiting London and spoke freely to me about both these events. He was a truly lovely man, dedicated utterly to the wellbeing and development of his people, unsparing in his efforts for justice. He was returning home on Sunday 28 August after the evening service. It was dark and someone called his name out quietly as he stood in the doorway of his home in Port-au-Prince. He turned towards the voice and was met with a long burst of automatic fire that killed him on the spot. His murderers roared away in a jeep. Vincent's loss was a great blow for the Haitian people and for their exiled president. Even for those of us who knew him less well, it was a terrible sadness. And yet, all this time after the event, I feel more and more honoured to have known such a man, a martyr and one of Haiti's heroes, who made the ultimate sacrifice for the cause he'd espoused with such nobility of spirit.

Throughout these months, with an invasion looming, Haiti lacked almost any constitutional legitimacy. After the collapse of the Governor's Island agreement, the country lost just about every semblance of due order. In May 1994, the military had named Emile Jonassaint, an 81-year-old former Supreme Court judge, 'president' of Haiti, but no other country recognized his position. It was only Robert Malval who offered a thread of legitimacy. He became a kind of 'acting prime minister' though it was far too dangerous for him to go out and about. So he remained at home in the heights above Port-au-Prince. Things had reached the point of absurdity now. There was no government of any kind on display.

Throughout September American rhetoric aimed at the Haitian military leaders became increasingly strident. They were 'illegal dictators', said Vice President Al Gore, who continued: 'They are a scandal to world opinion and, one way or another, they're going to have to go.' President Clinton called the Haitian generals 'brutal thugs'. He declared himself 'very angry indeed' at the terror they continued to inflict on their people. 'I don't want a confrontation with them,' he said, 'but if they don't get out they'll have to take what's coming to them.' A military invasion, however cool the American public might be on the matter, remained 'the most just solution' in Clinton's mind. And so the stage seemed set at last for action.

But not quite. Out of the blue, with no warning from anywhere, a very high-powered group of American 'negotiators', consisting of ex-president Jimmy Carter, former Chief of Staff General Colin Powell and Senator Sam Nunn, arrived for talks with the Haitian military leaders. These went on behind closed doors and continued virtually non-stop for almost twenty-four hours. Their aim seemed to be to persuade the Haitian generals to step down from office voluntarily in the interests of avoiding unnecessary bloodshed. Eventually, a deal was struck that surprised just about everybody. First of all, Carter and his colleagues came out of the talks referring to Cédras and his accomplices (who'd been 'brutal thugs' a few days before) as 'honourable men', 'co-operative', 'people with whom we can do business'. No longer was there an insistence on their immediate departure. Now they were free to remain in post until a general amnesty could be voted into law by the Haitian parliament 'or 15 October, whichever is earlier'. American troops would land on Haitian soil but their activities would be 'co-ordinated with the Haitian military high command'. The embargo was to be lifted without further delay and there was no mention at all of a date for Aristide's own return. This whole development was stupefying. It was followed almost immediately by the unopposed implementation of Operation Uphold Democracy which began on Monday 19 September when 21,000 American troops moved into Haiti.

The deal struck by Carter soon came under attack from human rights groups and many other quarters. And it produced the immediate resignation of UN Special Envoy Dante Caputo who accused the United States of elbowing the United Nations aside in the Haiti crisis. Caputo believed that Carter and his team should have simply delivered an ultimatum to Cédras and his accomplices rather than begin negotiations which, in effect, allowed the Haitian military leaders off the hook.

Caputo's anger was echoed by Aristide, but only after days of silence. Then he issued a statement which conveyed his support for the 1993 Governor's Island agreement from whose commitments, he said, the document signed by Jimmy Carter had wandered at several crucial points. He was furious that Cédras and his collaborators had been allowed to stay.

Once the American troops were duly installed in Haiti, however, it was clear that there was no future worth having for the Haitian high command. Michel François, the hard man in the junta, was attacked by his own men and soon took flight towards the Dominican Republic. It was clear that it was only a matter of days before Cédras and his third-in-command, Philippe Biamby, would be obliged to follow suit. The atmosphere quickened in Port-au-Prince as Aristide's return became the overriding topic of conversation. Work began on repairing his modest house at Tabarre on the northern outskirts of the capital, which had been pillaged and destroyed after the 1991 coup. Added to its simple amenities was a special surveillance unit with closed circuit television cameras and a round-the-clock guard. The destruction of his personal home was common knowledge but no one anticipated the wanton damage which his opponents imposed on the presidential palace. They tore out fixtures and defecated all over the toilet and bathroom floors, leaving the president's private quarters in a total shambles. For weeks after his return, Aristide slept on a camp bed and bathed out of a sink. But, for all this final flurry of hatred on the part of his enemies, at least now his return could be envisaged openly and joyfully by the people at large.

But who was the Aristide they were all waiting for? Was it the same man who'd left Haiti three years earlier? If not, how had he changed? Journalists were quite as interested in these questions as were the Haitian people. A number of percipient profiles began to appear in newspapers around the world.

Amy Wilentz's piece for *Time* magazine in September 1994 gave a nuanced portrait of 'the once and future president'. She described how he'd spent a great deal of his time in exile alone in his small Georgetown apartment, playing his guitar, taping weekly radio speeches and talking on the phone to friends near and far. Over the three-year period he'd been away from Haiti, according to Wilentz, Aristide had learned the need for cooperation and conciliation. As a firebrand priest, of course, he'd had opportunities to make a strong impression without carrying too much responsibility. He'd enjoyed a priest's immunity. He could indulge himself in strong language, so strong that it incited his hearers to passionate action and even brought danger to his own door. He'd had to learn the need for more moderate language. He'd always been very much an individualist rather than a team player, but in exile he made significant progress in the area of group decision-making and the taking of advice. Even so, he was never afraid of being his own man. The delay in backing Clinton's endorsement of the Carter agreement with Cédras was just one case in point. His readiness to condemn American policies towards Haitian boat people in the most forthright manner was another. He'd never become a cypher of the US administration; he remained a mystery to most of its members. What he managed specifically to do was to convince the Clinton government that without him democracy in Haiti had no hope at all.

To strangers, Aristide seemed 'wan, distracted... gentle-mannered to the point of caricature'. To his friends, 'he seems very open. He loves to joke and to make people laugh. When he feels secure, he opens up. When he's besieged, he shuts people out.' For Aristide himself, fascinated by his own ability to mystify commentators and gurus alike, his explanation was simplicity itself. To his mind, the deepest secrets of his mind were merely wrappings for his out-and-out commitment to the Haitian people. 'When I tell them I want justice for my people above all,' he once said, 'they look to me as though I'm crazy. But that is the one thing I keep in my mind all the time. Idealism is a bit alien to so many of them.'

There is a real paradox in the thinking of Aristide, one-time savage critic of American policies, returning to Haiti tied to the apron strings of the US ambassador. For the president, however, it was all part of a new attitude he'd cultivated, one that tirelessly invoked the language of reconciliation and the unity of all Haitians across the entire breadth of the political and social spectrum. By late September, Aristide was holding daily meetings with William Gray, Bill Clinton's special envoy, with senior officials from the State Department and with General John Shalikashvili, Chairman of the US Joint Chiefs of Staff. In the little sitting room of his Georgetown apartment, these officials went over details of the forthcoming invasion again and again and Aristide gave his own opinions as well as likely Haitian attitudes on the ground.

A very similar picture was painted in a long feature article in the 20 October number of *L'Express*. 'Titid has changed, he's learned, he's matured,' the author declared. Even so, he'd have to make very special offers of accommodation to Haiti's bourgeois élite who reproached him 'less for what he'd done than for what he was, a small-time black from the poorer end of Haitian society, venerated by domestic servants and barrowboys, but not one of them'. It was going to be interesting to see just how his experience of exile, which had broken his narrow parochialism and introduced him to the company of diplomats, investors and parliamentarians, would equip him for relating to those parts of Haitian society, especially its wealthy business class, that had always been at odds with him.

The writer of this piece in *L'Express* was sure that Aristide had had time to rue his errors. Amongst these were listed the appointment of René Préval as his prime minister, the sacking of General Hérard Abraham in favour of Raoul Cédras and the notorious speech in which he'd seemed to give his approval to the practice of necklacing. As a result of his time of enforced reflection, he'd learned how to sing in an entirely new key. 'In the president's pantheon, Martin Luther King, Gandhi and the South African Nelson Mandela have supplanted Robespierre,' the article continued. 'Now it's No to revenge, No to violence, Yes to reconciliation.' But it still remained to see whether all this would be enough.

Aristide's diminutive figure stood alone on the steps of the US government plane which had brought him back to Haiti on Saturday 15 October. His chest was swathed with a sash in the blue and red colours of the Haitian national flag. The national anthem was played by a military band and reduced the vast and seemingly uncontrollable crowd to an extraordinarily poignant silence. Two lads from *Lafanmi Selavi*, the orphanage Aristide had founded eight years previously, presented him with a bouquet of flowers at the foot of the aeroplane steps. He seemed impossibly distant from the enormous crowds who'd come to meet and greet their champion, their messiah. His speech was full of the language of reconciliation. He thanked his friend Bill Clinton and invited him to pay a visit to Haiti before too long. He assured people from every part of Haitian society that they had nothing to fear from him, that he wanted to be able to count on the energies of every Haitian for the rebuilding of the nation. Then, to the immense disappointment of the crowd who wanted a sighting of their hero, he was whisked by helicopter directly to the national palace. No security risks were being taken that day. And so it was that the three years and two weeks of exile were consigned to history. Cédras and Biamby were beginning a new life in Panama; François had reached the Dominican Republic; Emmanuel Constant, head of FRAPH, had sneaked away to the United States. The field now belonged once again to President Jean-Bertrand Aristide.

One of his very first acts, offered in the name of reconciliation, was to resign his priesthood. His letter to François Gayot, Archbishop of Cap Haitien and president of the Haitian Episcopal Conference, was dated 17 October, a mere two days after his return to Haiti. It didn't beat about the bush.

It read:

> Your excellency,
>
> You asked me to resign my priesthood so that harmonious relations could be established and improved between two heads of state - The Vatican Head of State and The Head of State of the Republic of Haiti.
>
> In the light of the events of 15 October 1994 when we saw flowers of peace, reconciliation and love bursting into bloom, I have decided, your excellency, to agree to your request.
>
> May the God of Love guide our steps for the salvation of our beloved Haiti.
>
> Warmly,
>
> JEAN-BERTRAND ARISTIDE.

This was followed up a few days later when, on a visit to Cap Haitien (and with news of his resignation from the priesthood still not released for general consumption), he embraced Monsignor Gayot publicly in an act of reconciliation that bemused, and angered, his supporters. Gayot, after all, had been one of Aristide's most implacable opponents for a number of years and this public gesture was too much of a volte-face for many. For the nuncio, however, it was cause for scarcely suppressed joy. In a statement he declared: 'The apostolic nunciature rejoices at the efforts deployed and initiatives taken to facilitate reconciliation and which will favour the democratic process and open the way for the reconditioning of the social fabric, for progress and for the well-being of the population.' Diplomats always seem to use six words where one would have done. This extraordinary sentence, when interpreted, surely means: 'Aristide's resigned his priesthood. Splendid. Now we can get on with things again. Hooray!'

The immediate task facing Aristide in the political arena was that of forming a government. He asked 57-year-old Smarck Michel, a dealer in rice and motor-fuel, to become prime minister. Michel was a known friend of the president's but hardly a lackey. A member of Haiti's bourgeois élite, he'd been Minister of Commerce in Aristide's first pre-coup government, an office from which he'd resigned over a difference that opened up between him and his head of state on the matter of a prices policy. He was acceptable to the Americans because of his business and political experience, and also because he stood a fair chance of winning the support of the business community. The other possible prime minister had been Claudette Werleigh, a long-time worker with peasant groups and a former director of the Catholic aid charity Caritas, but her known left-of-centre views ruled her out at a fairly early stage.

Michel's cabinet retained a number of those who'd held office under Robert Malval in the months preceding Aristide's return. All in all, it was a balanced team, one which couldn't by any stretch of the imagination be called (as had been the case with Aristide's first government) 'a cabinet of friends'. Indeed, a number of the president's oldest associates, including the left-of-centre weekly *Haiti Progrès*, dubbed Michel's list a 'macoute cabinet' to show their displeasure at the number of its members drawn from Haiti's traditional ruling class. The new prime minister announced his government's programme on the day he was sworn into office. He was concerned that Haiti should not lose what was clearly a historic opportunity. He foresaw the need to privatize bankrupt state-owned enterprises, to increase exports, to attract inward investment, to keep wage-levels down (this, he recognized, was what foreign entrepreneurs were looking for), and to allow exchange rates to fluctuate. He also declared his intention to reduce the numbers of those on the public payroll by as much as 50 per cent. This had already been done during Aristide's first term of office, of course, but panic measures resorted to during the Honorat/Bazin years had seen the return of old-style practices of state patronage and irresponsible staffing levels. Now all that pain had to be endured over again.

The new government staggered forward with its plans and programmes in a context of continuing street violence. The outlawing of FRAPH and the diminution of the powers of the army meant that large numbers of firearms were now in circulation whose only use was for personal security and as a potent means to self-enrichment. There was a crime wave, with a burgeoning of burglaries and assaults especially. This led to repeated calls by Aristide and others that the UN force should take measures to disarm those who continued to possess guns and other weapons. But these calls were just as consistently ignored.

Other key appointments awaiting Aristide's immediate attention were in the armed forces. After the departure of Cédras, the army was left under the command of General Jean-Claude Duperval. Just one day after the president's triumphant return there were persistent rumours that Duperval had attempted to assassinate him. This led to angry demonstrations on the streets of Port-au-Prince. Three days later, Duperval was sacked and replaced by Colonel Bernardin Poisson, head of the firefighting unit in the army and well thought of by the Americans. Colonel Pierre Neptune, who'd been head of the anti-terrorist service in Aristide's first administration (and who'd somehow survived the *de facto* years intact) was appointed head of the police force. These were supremely important posts in view of the president's frequently repeated determination to drive a wedge between the army and the police and to change the role of the latter so that it became a strictly civil body dealing with the enforcement of the law of the land and the maintenance of order on the streets. The Haitian parliament gave its early (and virtually unanimous) consent to Aristide's proposal to allow this separation to take place.

Everybody had ideas about the kind of police force they wanted. The refashioning of the army was harder to conceptualize. The debate about how best to do this was given a strange twist towards the end of November by an article which appeared in the *Washington Post*. There, the 1987 Nobel Peace Prize winner Oscar Arias, former president of Costa Rica, made a strong plea for Haiti to follow his own country's example (and that of Panama) in disbanding its army altogether. This was a very radical suggestion and gained enthusiastic support in a number of quarters in Haiti. It led Aristide, in a meeting with 500 trade unionists who pressed him to announce the abolition of the army, to deny any intention on his part to proceed in that direction. But his talent for speaking out clearly in a highly ambiguous way had not deserted him. He acknowledged that, throughout the *de facto* years, his audience (of trade unionists) had been a particular target for the repressive tactics of the armed forces. He promised that a number of soldiers would be brought to trial for their offences. Further, he sympathized with a great deal of the hostility that had been expressed by those who'd suffered so terribly at the army's hands. 'I don't agree with the army any more than you do,' he said, 'it's a cancer and I feel like a doctor who, when he discovers a tumour and before he operates, has to make tests and analyses. But you may be sure that I'm going to examine all available options in order to bring healing to the body of our nation.' Then he continued as if in an afterthought, 'But the Constitution spells out the need for an army and I've sworn to defend the Constitution. Therefore, I will resist calls for its abolition.'

Within weeks of this statement, and after so many reshuffles of senior and middle-ranking officers that no one any longer knew where they were or what was happening, Aristide's Minister of Defence, himself an army General, was declaring: 'There is effectively no army left and General Poisson (the new army chief appointed only a couple of months earlier) doesn't have a clue. He couldn't command anything anyway even if he wanted to.' At about this time too, Aristide decreed that the building which had housed the army high command in the centre of Port-au-Prince, a building situated directly across the road from the national palace, was to be turned into offices for the newly-established Ministry for Women's Affairs. This gesture added insult to injury. And meanwhile, what remained of the army, a force that was about to be reduced from 7,500 to a mere 1,500 soldiers, was to be stationed out of town along the border with the Dominican Republic.

After the army, the judiciary. In every sphere, Aristide was having to look at Haiti's institutional infrastructure with a very keen eye. He was aware of the extent to which the country's Supreme Court had undergirded the unconstitutional governments of the *de facto* years, giving them a veneer of legitimacy by offering them their judicial support. Indeed, they were so united in their opposition to the elected president that only one member of that body, Clauzel Debrosse, had supported the Washington accord of February 1992 which had stipulated the plain necessity for Aristide's return to power. The Supreme Court had even allowed one of its former members, Émile Jonassaint, to parade as 'head of state' in the latter part of the *de facto* period. For all these reasons, and with the reconstruction of Haiti's justice system one of the most pressing priorities facing him, Aristide now got rid of the whole lot of them save Debrosse on whom he conferred the presidency of a body of entirely new faces. He wanted a fresh start with judges he could trust.

When he flew out of Haiti on 8 December 1994 for a meeting of the leaders of OAS countries, he'd done enough to show that, for all the limitations under which he was undoubtedly working, there was no way he could be described as a 'lame duck' president. Aid was beginning to flow, his government was working reasonably well, the various sectors of Haitian society had come to terms with the need to collaborate with the new realities, the army had been re-jigged from top to bottom and put firmly in its place, the police force had been brought into being as a separate entity, a new raft of top judges had been sworn in, olive branches had been cast in the direction of the Roman Catholic hierarchy and he'd met a large number of groups representing various interests in Haiti's national life. His public discourse dripped with every conceivable use of the word 'reconciliation'. Even Hurricane Gordon, which left widespread damage when it struck in mid-November, didn't rock the ship of state. Aristide was lionized by those attending the Miami meeting. After all, Latin America was full of ex-presidents who'd been ousted by their armies. Not many of them had ever regained their positions in the way Aristide, a real come-back kid, had so recently done.

During these months I'd become president of the Methodist Conference, head of the British Methodist church. I was delighted that my year of office coincided with the return to constitutional rule in Haiti and I was determined to pay a visit to the land of my ordination and to a people to whom I owed so much. Aristide's entourage had invited me to fly to Haiti with the president when he made his triumphal entry on 15 October but my unyielding calendar had put that out of the question. But it *had* been possible to create some space in the period immediately following Christmas. This allowed me to be in Haiti over the New Year period and, since that included Haiti's national day, I hoped very much to be able to pay my respects to the president of the Republic and convey the love and good wishes of the Methodist people of Great Britain to a nation that had suffered so much in recent times.

The change of atmosphere was palpable. The last time I'd been in Port-au-Prince was just after Bill Clinton's fatal decision to turn the *USS Harlan County* around, a decision that made a considerable lengthening of the Haitian crisis so inevitable. On that visit, the gloom was thick and the people's suffering almost unbearable. Now, the usual busy-ness had returned to the thronging streets. I preached at the New Year's Eve service in downtown Port-au-Prince to a packed congregation of over a thousand. It was sobering to think that this was the first such service in four years when people had been able to gather without fear. They sang their hymns and anthems most movingly and, as midnight struck, I felt the surge of hope for a new year of grace that promised peace and progress in the place of oppression and tyranny.

The following morning, I went to the national palace for the thanksgiving mass on Haiti's Independence Day. There I met a number of Roman Catholic priests, most of them old friends of mine, who are very close to Aristide. They'd all been targeted by the military authorities and intimidated, insulted, and threatened in one way or another over the previous three years. They were delighted to greet another year with its hint of greener pastures. From there I headed back to the Methodist church where I led a vast congregation in the annual recitation of their covenant promises, a kind of New-Year's-resolution service. The familiar words of challenge took on extra meaning that particular day:

> Christ has many services to be done; some are easy, others are difficult; some bring honour, others bring reproach; some are suitable to our natural inclinations and temporal interests, others are contrary to both. In some we may please Christ and please ourselves, in others we cannot please Christ except by denying ourselves. Yet the power to do all these things is assuredly given us in Christ, who strengthens us.

The most moving moment of my time in Haiti was without any doubt my visit to Jean-Bertrand Aristide's home at Tabarre on the plain of Cul-de-Sac, a few miles north of Port-au-Prince. A small number of us formed an audience as the president made his televised 'state-of-the-nation' speech from behind his living room table. Then we stayed on for a small reception. When he and I were able to get near each other our embrace said everything I needed to know. He was back in harness and delighted—relieved—almost beyond words. It had been an enormous strain, he told me, but there was no going back now. He was convinced that the processes of democracy were irreversible.

I'd told Aristide on more than one occasion how worried I was about my best Haitian friend, Rosny Desroches. Rosny and I had shared the leadership of Nouveau Collège Bird in the 1970s, he as the headmaster and I as his assistant. He'd been a determined and outspoken opponent of Duvalier and was widely respected as one of Haiti's leading intellectuals. When political freedoms began to be enjoyed, he'd opted to give his support to the social democratic party of Serges Gilles (PANPRA). General Henri Namphy had invited him to become Minister of Education in 1986, a job he did for a few months before resigning when his freedom and integrity were undermined by some of the recidivist elements within the ruling junta. He'd become head of an educational foundation funded by the World Bank and which had responsibility for well over half of Haiti's schools. When he began to be critical of Aristide's populism and some of the policies he was putting forward, his views offended members of the president's entourage, making Rosny an object of vilification. I was (and remain) convinced that Rosny's views offered exactly the kind of fresh, intelligent thinking that's vitally necessary in a properly functioning democratic society. But in times of such severe polarization there were only two positions available, for or against Aristide. And if you dared to be against him, you were considered to be in favour of the military junta. Rosny had quite different views from Aristide and his *Lavalas* movement. But he was decidely not pro-putsch. I was so worried about how Aristide felt about the contribution of people like Rosny that I found myself asking him again and again just how he'd harness the energies of this kind of 'loyal opposition' when normality returned. I'd constantly urged him not to consider political opponents as being necessarily personal enemies. As we held each other in, I must admit, a rather long embrace, he indicated his desire to whisper something into my ear. Rather touchingly, I thought, and with everyone else wondering what on earth was going on, he told me that he'd heeded my words and that he was about to speak to Rosny on the question of how they might work better together. He was convinced that people like Rosny were essential for the building of Haiti's future.

A few months after this encounter, in the immediate aftermath of elections that saw both houses of the Haitian parliament completely dominated by Aristide's *Lavalas* party, the president was questioned about voting irregularities that had been widely reported. He said that he not only regretted these but utterly condemned them and wished the election had been better run. He also expressed sorrow at the likely absence of a coherent opposition in parliament. 'We must work actively for the participation of various political parties,' he said. 'We haven't any choice. One single party, the absence of an opposition, would be a death blow to our democracy. That's why I continue my dialogue with political leaders of all shades of opinion.' This kind of comment in a country that knew little about the role of an opposition struck an entirely fresh note and, if followed through, would represent new material with which to build a democratic future for Haiti.

With order restored in Haiti, the American administration sensed that the time was now right for one untidy detail to be cleared up to their advantage. 16,000 boat people were still being held in the US base at Guantanamo at the time Operation Uphold Democracy got under way. The Americans lost no time repatriating just about all of these; a final contingent of almost 4,000 was brought back to Haiti in mid-January 1995. They were induced to go back by offers of manual jobs and a cash payment of $80. Even so, large numbers went against their will, and human rights monitors criticized US immigration officials for the superficial way they'd screened applications for asylum. The blanket judgment had been made that the return of Aristide had made any further claims to be political refugees utterly and completely redundant.

The Clinton administration was beginning to gain political capital from the success of its Haiti policy. The number of American troops was steadily cut back until there remained a mere 3,000 by the end of March. These were joined by an equivalent number from other parts of the world and command passed over from the United States to the United Nations. Indeed, Bill Clinton came to Haiti himself to mark this moment of transition.

Shortly after the Americans had handed over responsibility for the Haitian operation, press reports began appearing which pointed to a direct US involvement in the setting up, arming and continued support of the paramilitary group FRAPH and its leader Emmanuel Constant. Constant had fled to New York where he was later arrested. He soon began spilling the beans to eager journalists. He admitted that he'd been on the CIA payroll and that starting in mid-1993, FRAPH had been launched on its reign of terror with secret shipments of US arms. Still-active FRAPH members, he maintained, had been used in very recent days in operations intended to further the aims of the US occupation. Some who'd been arrested by Haitian authorities had later been sprung from jail with Washington's help before being recruited afresh by the CIA and, as a matter of high-level US policy, allowed to keep their arms. Constant declared that he'd started the group that became FRAPH at the urging of the Defence Intelligence Agency, an account that was later verified by a US official who'd worked with him. But what was most astounding was that, even after the launch of Operation Uphold Democracy in September 1994, US forces continued to use FRAPH members for 'crowd control' and also 'to understand the neighbourhoods most loyal to Aristide'. American commanders in the field gave orders to 'come up off the FRAPH', to 'back off', and to deal with FRAPH as the 'loyal opposition'. And yet everyone recognized that FRAPH was not a military fighting force but rather a paramilitary group organized to kill unarmed civilians.

The main conduit through whom arms had been channelled prior to September 1994 was Colonel Michel François. Thousands upon thousands of arms—pistols, grease guns and hand grenades—had been supplied. At the height of the embargo, when US coastguard vessels were successful in keeping every tiny Haitian boat under constant surveillance, they were not only allowing huge oil tankers but also regular arms supplies to slip through their cordon with apparent impunity. Many arms were shipped via Jamaica, the Turks and Caicos Islands and the Dominican Republic. And when these weapons had reached their destination, they allowed FRAPH to impose its reign of terror on civilian populations throughout the land. These revelations shed some important light on the way the intelligence and military machine of the most powerful nation in the world went ruthlessly about the business of keeping powerless and ineffective countries like Haiti firmly in their place.

On the domestic front, Aristide was having to cope with the

resignations of a number of his ministers. In particular, he had to replace his Ministers of Justice and the Interior. The former was accused of being a Tonton Macoute at the heart of Aristide's administration while the latter, an ex-army General, was sacked in order to make room for another ex-army General of whom there were any number to choose from since the latest purging of the high command. In fact, by the end of February 1995 there was no serving officer left in the army above the rank of Captain. The Americans had repeatedly expressed their opposition to the abolition of the army but they seemed to have no answer to Aristide's brilliant powers of finesse. He was actually achieving the complete demise of his country's armed forces by a strategy of parry and feint; it was, in fact, death by a thousand cuts.

The marginalization of the army was not, however, an unmitigated benefit. Most of the responsibility for public order now lay with the new police force. This was asking a great deal of such an inchoate body. It was envisaged that the force would eventually comprise some 5,000 officers all of whom would have received a four-month crash training course either in the United States or, under the supervision of a very experienced New York officer, within Haiti. It would take two or three years to get the force up to full strength. It would draw its recruits, in roughly equal numbers, from former members of the armed forces on the one hand and, on the other, from those who'd attempted to escape from Haiti as 'boat people' during the *de facto* years. The hope behind this proposal was that the new police force would be seen to have a truly non-partisan role. Its lines of accountability would no longer run to the Ministry of Defence and the Interior but to the Ministry of Justice. On paper these proposals seemed sensible. On the ground they were extraordinarily difficult to develop.

The main problem encountered by those giving shape to this new police force was that they somehow had to create a brand new culture within a matter of weeks. To the Haitian man or woman in the street, the police had always been one arm of the state's unquestioned and tyrannical authority. Suddenly to trust this new body and to look to it for an objective and dispassionate approach to dealing with crime and injustice was asking rather a lot. The presence within the force of such large numbers of ex-soldiers would hardly have reassured many people either. And when, inevitably, a number of incidents saw inexperienced officers resort too readily to their weapons, or else take sides in a dispute, some of these fears were even further underscored. What's more, the biggest efforts to get things up and running in the early days were concentrated in the cities. The *chefs de section*, rural sheriffs, pillars of Duvalierist modes of law-keeping, kept their heavy hand on the administration of justice in the vast tracts of Haiti that lay beyond the urban centres even as public discourse was telling the population at large that they were finished, dinosaurs, gone for ever. Even when Aristide decreed an end to the rule of the *chefs de section*, it was always going to take time to replace the old order with the new. Over an extended period, the new police force could expect to gain the confidence of the public. In these first months of accountable government and law enforcement, however, it is hardly surprising that uncertainty reigned and that this left an unwholesome vacuum at the very heart of civil society.

Into this vacuum there rushed all kinds of evil spirits. There was wanton violence and there were many victims. In one week alone, thirty deaths were reported in the capital. They were all poor people whose savage end soon passed into oblivion. But one assassination grabbed the headlines. On 28 March, Mireille Durocher Bertin, an outspoken and brilliant lawyer, was gunned down in the streets of Port-au-Prince. Her death occurred just days after she'd formed a new political party and there had been clear hints and rumours that she was on somebody's hit list. Yet the authorities seemed powerless to prevent her killing. These bare details of Bertin's death seem to put her in the same category as Guy Malary, Georges and Antoine Izméry, and Jean-Marie Vincent who'd all met their end in a very similar way. But there was one significant difference in this case. Unlike all the others, Bertin was a very right wing ultranationalist. In the *de facto* years, she'd led a vigorous campaign to keep the international community out of Haiti and set out to prove that the various agreements being worked on in Washington and New York were illegal. She was a fierce opponent of Aristide and a tireless worker for her cause.

Her death was as regrettable as any of the others. But unlike the others, it was only her murder that kick-started the old right-wing double act of Jesse Helms and Robert Dole into another outburst of anti-Aristide rhetoric. They started a virulent campaign to withhold aid from Haiti until Aristide had found Bertin's killers or at least proved he'd pulled out all the stops in his efforts to track them down. In view of the state of justice in Haiti at this time these demands were, of course, somewhat utopian. But they also showed up these Republican politicians for what they were. They'd never invested an ounce of energy in demanding that the killers of any of the pro-Aristide public figures should be brought to book. Yet they seemed hungry for evidence that could help them prove to their electorate what a tyrant Aristide was and how unworthy of American interest or resource his government had revealed itself. Right to the end of Aristide's time in office they kept harping on these themes. It was as if, after their previous attempts at character assassination had proved so utterly ill-founded, they needed to find another way to destroy a man they'd come to hate obsessively.

In an interview he gave to the *Los Angeles Times* just a couple of days after Bertin's death, Aristide was up front about the delicate state of his country's health. 'My government has so far failed to provide justice or jobs in Haiti,' he said with disarming frankness, 'and these shortcomings are absolutely threatening to our national stability.' He deplored the wave of crime and violence that had broken out. He offered mild criticism of the United States (this was just a day before Bill Clinton's visit), especially its unwillingness to engage in law enforcement activities as well as peace-keeping. This extra dimension would fill the dangerous law and order vacuum and allow more time for the Haitian police force to get itself ready for the eventual shouldering of its full responsibilities. He saw three overriding needs just at that time: firstly, stability; secondly, the creation of a free-market economy with privatization of key government enterprises; and thirdly, a jobs programme aimed at bringing hope to many people who'd lived outside the money economy for far too long. He denied that his Interior Minister Mondésir Beaubrun had had any involvement in the killing of Mireille Durocher Bertin, as had been alleged by US military and diplomatic sources.

It is interesting to note the reference to the 'privatization of key government enterprises' in this interview. This was to become a major bone of contention and saw Aristide change his mind on formal commitments he'd made to the World Bank and the International Monetary Fund. It was to lose him his prime minister and leave an unholy mess for his successor.

While still in exile, Aristide had formulated a privatization programme that envisaged the selling off of all or part of nine state enterprises. These included the telephone company, the cement and flour factories, the Port-au-Prince port authority and two banks. Within a few months of his return to Haiti, he'd actually signed an agreement with a World Bank agency to deliver this programme. In late March, as the *Los Angeles Times* interview shows, he was still firmly in favour of this course of action. Prime Minister Smarck Michel was also fully committed but began to notice a waning of the president's resolve.

The argument in favour of privatization was simple. The state had no money to develop these enterprises. Selling them would bring new capital into Haiti and generate jobs and trade. It was envisaged that members of Haiti's business élite, who already owned the giant's share of every commercial activity in the land, would be prevented from bidding for these assets. It was new money the programme was hoping to attract; there was no desire to give the Haitian bourgeoisie an even more crushing stranglehold on the economy than they already had. Naturally, these plans didn't please the business class. So, strange to behold, they formed a coalition of interest with the leaders of popular and grassroots groups who, for wildly different reasons, were also objecting to this programme. This presented Aristide with a serious problem. He'd bent over backwards since his return to win the support of the bourgeoisie. What else had all his talk of reconciliation been about? But now they, together with elements from his own traditional support base, were voicing their strong opposition to the privatization programme.

The July parliamentary elections saw *Lavalas* candidates sweep the board and pack both houses of parliament with huge majorities. That, of course, made matters even more difficult. Now, the legislative arm of government was massively opposed to the planned sales to which their president had already put his signature. The whole debate intensified and it was clear that Aristide was backing away from his earlier position. In the end, this led to the resignation of the prime minister in October after heated exchanges with Aristide. The president replaced him with Claudette Werleigh, who was known to be an opponent of privatization. Meanwhile, international financiers were getting very irritated. 'The president isn't playing straight with us,' one of them was reported as saying, 'and that means that we're on a collision course.' And it is hard to find fault with this view. Initially, Aristide had referred to privatization as an act of 'economic democratization' that would strip the Haitian oligarchy of economic power and transfer it to ordinary people. But he never did anything to explain the advantages of privatization to his people.

By November USAID had suspended its aid programme because of its dissatisfaction on this issue. Meanwhile, there were demonstrations and strikes held by those who were violently opposed to what had become a very emotional matter; the selling of Haiti's assets to foreign investors was tantamount to treason in their eyes. Aristide's time in power was coming to its end. There was lots of talk about giving him three extra years to compensate for the time he'd lost in exile. He prevaricated and kept his own counsel on this question. In the end, at the last possible moment, he made it clear that he didn't intend to ask parliament for this extra time. He didn't want, he said, to act as so many of his predecessors had done in defiance of the

Constitution by making themselves presidents for life. He'd always said he'd honour the Constitution and he intended to do just that. He was going to step down and allow the people to choose someone in his place. Hearing Aristide take the moral high ground in this way, I must confess that I've wondered from time to time whether he might have been very interested indeed in taking the extra three years his supporters were begging him to accept if the question of the privatization programme hadn't reached such a perilous point. By getting out in the nick of time he could claim subsequently that it hadn't been he who'd sold the nation's silver.

René Préval, Aristide's first prime minister, was elected president of the republic in December. He got 82 per cent of the vote in a disappointingly low turnout, which amounted to a miserly 25 per cent of the electorate. It was only at the last minute that Aristide gave Préval his blessing. The new president committed himself to the privatization programme but 'in our own time, whatever the pressures put on us by foreign donors'. And so, for the first time ever in Haiti's history, one head of state elected by universal suffrage gave way to another.

There were two quite unexpected events announced by Aristide before he handed over power to Préval on 7 February 1996. On the very eve of his successor's inauguration, Aristide announced that Haiti had restored its diplomatic relations with Cuba, broken thirty-four years previously. He chose his moment to make this announcement in an attempt to save Préval from falling into Washington's disfavour on such a sensitive matter.

The second surprise was the news of his marriage. He informed the world that his intended bride was an American-born Haitian lawyer, 33-year-old Mildred Trouillot, the daughter of a steelworker and a hospital technician. His choice of a light-skinned wife caused some concern to a number of his followers. It reminded them too uncomfortably of Jean-Claude Duvalier. But far more importantly, the forthcoming wedding seemed to put his previous marriage (to the Haitian people) in question. Ms Trouillot was keenly aware of this problem, however, and was soon indicating her readiness to share her fiancé's struggle for the Haitian people. She promised to dedicate her efforts to working with Haiti's homeless and street children in the *Lafanmi Selavi* orphanage founded by Aristide. Michèle Bennett had never made such promises before or after her union with Jean-Claude Duvalier. In the presence of about 500 guests and with a minimum of ceremony, the marriage took place at the president's Tabarre home where the couple lived quietly together until Aristide's demission of office.

And so I draw to the end of this account of the first forty-three years in the life of Jean-Bertrand Aristide. In the course of it we've been able to consider the way in which this unusual man, in the tumultuous life he lived, seemed able always to make things happen around him. Indeed, there's no way that an account of Aristide's life could become the story of a dull second-rate man living in an even duller third-world country. Haiti has always intrigued. Aristide will go on intriguing too. He stands in the line of Toussaint Louverture, Henri Christophe, Jean-Jacques Dessalines, Alexandre Pétion, Faustin Soulouque, Lysius Salomon, Jean Price Mars, Etzer Vilaire, Carl Brouard, Jacques Roumain, François Duvalier—all Haitians who seemed larger than life and who, for better or for worse, left their mark on history. In the course of this narrative, Aristide seems to have forced himself on the world around him and given a sharp focus on otherwise confusing events and circumstances. Just consider:

American Foreign Policy

The deep involvement of successive United States governments in the shaping of twentieth-century Haiti has been well documented. But the story of Aristide has thrown light on the readiness of the CIA and the Pentagon to get involved in the drug trade, to take 'intelligence' from clearly prejudiced sources, and to arm fascist paramilitaries whose only objective was to terrorize civilian populations. American policies towards the Haitian boat people have verged on the racist and inhumane. The Aristide phenomenon has also shown up the deep cleavage between the Clinton administration and the American intelligence and military machine. The US president found himself up against the same reactionary characters in the unfolding Haitian crisis as he was fighting elsewhere in his political life and indeed, as far as the Whitewater investigation goes, in his civil life too.

The role of the United Nations and the Organization of American States

Here again, the Haitian crisis and Aristide's part in it has allowed a wide public to notice the strengths and, supremely, the weaknesses of regional and global bodies in handling situations of conflict. The OAS had promised direct action if confronted by a military takeover in any one of their countries. They refused to follow their own rhetoric when confronted by the Haitian crisis and opted instead for diplomacy and useless trade sanctions, which led to three years of utter misery and traumatic suffering for a whole people. One of the inconsistencies that came to light was the way certain articles of the Lomé convention (binding the European Union to a number of the world's poorer countries) could be invoked to break the embargo. And companies like Shell Oil showed no readiness to collaborate with the sanctions which, if they'd been rigorously applied, would have broken the back of the military resistance within a very short time.

It was only when the OAS handed over responsibility to the UN that real pressure was brought to bear on the Haitian junta. Even so, it was always Aristide who was expected to make concessions and, when he'd made them and found they were flouted by Cédras and his allies, was then expected to make yet more. The UN human rights monitoring force was a shambles and its report needs to be widely read. And the turning back of the *USS Harlan County* was one of the most shameful episodes in the whole of this sorry tale.

The Vatican and the Roman Catholic Church

The Roman Catholic Church is a big player in Haiti. Yet it showed itself inept through most of this story. In the early 1980s there had been so much promise. It all disintegrated after the departure of Jean-Claude Duvalier. Successive nuncios showed themselves utterly insensitive and far too much wedded to the triumphalist modes of a former era. It still beggars belief that a church that can sideline a progressive French bishop (Monsignor Gaillot of Évreux) when it suits them, will hang on to a reactionary Haitian archbishop (Monsignor Ligondé of Port-au-Prince) through hell and high water. It is also significant that a church which has learned to admit its complicity in the 'dirty war' in Argentina, where the bishops' conference there has published a self-critical document apologizing for backing the military junta, has not yet begun to face its not dissimilar responsibilities in Haiti. There's a lot of healing to do and it is good to note how, after the 1995 visit of Cardinal Etchegerey, head of the Vatican's Justice and Peace Commission, a more wholesome spirit seems to have been fostered and a new nuncio shows signs of enormous promise. Aristide has certainly focused the deep desires of people at grassroots level for peace with justice and, at the same time, he's shown up the instinctive sympathies of the church hierarchy within Haiti and in Rome for reactionary leaders and the status quo.

The IMF and the World Bank

The IMF and the World Bank were fashioned at Bretton Woods in the state of New Hampshire in July 1944. They were set up to help reconstruct a shattered world in the aftermath of the Second World War. They achieved this magnificently but the economies to whose aid they went were 'first world' economies about which some clear assumptions could be made. The lack of capacity (and will?) of these and other institutions to channel promised aid to Haiti with sufficient speed contributed materially to the downfall of Aristide's first government. The crude structural adjustment programme imposed as a condition for helping Aristide the second time round was so ill-judged from a psychological, historical and cultural point of view that it became a destructive pressure on the freshly restored democratic government almost from its outset. There has to be a less destabilizing and more sensitive way of organizing financial aid than this.

The Dominican Republic

Under the racist leadership of Balaguer, the Dominicans have exercised a key role throughout this crisis. They've offered safe haven to the vilest Haitian thugs, people like Franck Romain, Williams Regala, Prosper Avril, Wolff Ligondé and Michel François. Their treatment of Haitian workers on the sugar plantations has been widely criticized by human rights groups around the world. Their readiness to force the repatriation of tens of thousands of these during Aristide's first administration was one of the most serious and destabilizing problems he had to deal with. During the embargo, the Dominican border became the most reliable point of access for contraband goods. The story of Aristide has shown that a 'solution' to the Haitian crisis is going to have to include an island-wide strategy if it is to have any chance of succeeding.

The traditional power holders within Haiti

Until Aristide's arrival on the stage, Haiti's business élite and their puppet army could count on running their country with impunity. No one has ever pointed up their crass and greedy ways as Aristide has done. For a long time, members of this oligarchic bunch of Haiti's super-rich were referred to in the American press as MRE (the Morally Repugnant Élite). For the first time in Haitian history they've not been able to impose their own solution on the country's affairs.

The people

Haiti's illiterate and desperately poor people, scratching a living from unproductive soil or living in its cities' teeming slums, have played little part in the unfolding of their country's affairs. Throughout the 1970s, the 'conscientization' programmes of progressive priests across the land brought a number of grassroots organizations and the *Ti Legliz* (the Little Church) into existence. In Duvalier's last months, the people were ready to make their claim to a part of the action. Aristide arrived on the stage just as people's self-awareness was reaching its peak. He focused their energy, became their messiah-figure, enabled them to move forward. The synergy between Aristide and the people has been extraordinary. It remains to be seen whether his resignation from the priesthood, his marriage, and his 'more mature' self since returning from exile have destroyed this chemistry. But even if that turns out to be the case, the people will never again return to the passivity of their past. The genie has been let out of the bottle. Their interests will simply have to figure in any planning for Haiti's future.

Himself

Aristide has made his impact on all these external groups, from Haiti's humble poor right up to the might of Washington itself. It is more problematical to assess just how he's impacted on himself. At the close of this examination he continues to seem complicated and deeply mysterious. The fiery priest has become the measured statesman. Or has he? His repeated invocation of words like 'non-violence', 'reconciliation', 'transparency' and 'participation' have all, from time to time, seemed totally at odds with the violence his rhetoric seems to have incited, his capacity to polarize opinion, his secretiveness and his unwillingness to consult. Even so, it is not possible to write him off as a despot. He's quite right to point out that no one can understand him if they don't understand the symbiosis that exists between him and his people. And when the obstacles to a fair and decent future for Haiti's poor are so entrenched in its social stratification (to say nothing of the way the world works in favour of the rich and powerful), it is hardly surprising that there were times when he simply knew that 'sitting down to talk' would never get his people anywhere. It is highly unlikely that Aristide will bow out of public life now that he's no longer president. He'll want to throw his hat into the ring again in

December 2000 and be Haiti's head of state for the bicentenary of her independence in the year 2004. Or I'm a Dutchman.

Postscript

In an interview for the Créole-language newspaper *Libète*, given as he stepped down from office, Aristide looked back over the ten tumultuous years that had followed the departure of Jean-Claude Duvalier. The journalist was clearly moved by the whole event. He cited two slogans which had been painted on a wall in downtown Port-au-Prince. The first read: *Titid, ou antre ak lonè, ou soti ak respè*, Aristide, you arrived with honour, you're leaving with respect. This was a play on the delightful greeting exchanged when entering a Haitian home. The visitor knocks on the door and shouts *Honeur*, I honour this home, to which the host replies *Respect*, I respect your visit. The exchange completed, the visitor becomes, literally, the guest of honour. The second slogan ran thus: *Titid ale, pou Lavalas rete. Lavalas rete, pou Titid retounen*, Aristide is going but *Lavalas* remains; *Lavalas* remains so that Aristide can return.

I wrote to Aristide as he lay down his office. I felt I'd been very close to so much that had happened over the previous five years. My letter ran as follows:

February 1996

My dear friend,

Now you and I have one thing in common (apart from our love of Haiti, of course). That is, we're both ex-presidents!! I'm writing to wish you well as you hand power over to your friend and successor, René Préval. I hope the next few months will give you time for reflection, for spiritual refreshment and for travel.

I'm sure you'll be wise enough to keep a low profile and give your successor space to develop his own style and get on with things as best he can. No one knows better than you how miserable it can be to have someone else constantly breathing down your neck and undermining your best efforts to govern. Préval needs all the help he can get and you, I know, will give him precisely that.

Enjoy this time of less pressured living: may it be a time of deep inner peace and creativity. This comes with my warmest good wishes. The Lord bless you and bless you kindly.

The first indications following his laying down of power were that Aristide had no intention of following my advice. He has made it clear he will continue to stir the pot and influence events if he possibly can. But it is early days yet. Only time will tell.

Bibliography

ABBOTT Elizabeth. *Haiti: the first inside account: the Duvaliers and their legacy.* McGraw-Hill, 1988.
This account of the last days of the increasingly decadent rule of Jean-Claude Duvalier and the first attempts to govern Haiti after his departure is likely to remain unrivalled. Written by the sister-in-law of General Henri Namphy who headed the first post-Duvalier government, it is full of inside and personal knowledge that makes it a very readable book.

ARISTIDE Jean-Bertrand. *In the Parish of the Poor; writings from Haiti.* Orbis (New York), 1991.
This little book is beautifully translated by Amy Wilentz and is a passionate and poetic plea for justice for the Haitian people. The four sermons with which it concludes give something of an idea of Aristide's extraordinary oratorical gifts.
— *An Autobiography.* Orbis, 1992.
This is a sketchy run-through of the major events in Aristide's life up to and including the 1991 coup which ousted him from power. It avoids some of the crucial questions being asked (e.g. about whether he'd ever really advocated necklacing) and offers ample evidence of his somewhat whimsical and mystical style.
— *Dignity.* University of Virginia, 1996.
Not a very inspired account of Aristide's wilderness years. There's far too little personal recollection and colourful insight. Nor is there any balanced view of the total period of his presidency on offer here. On the other hand, there is plenty of steaming passion aimed against some predictable targets.

ARTHUR Charles. *After the Dance, the Drum is Heavy (Haiti: one year after the invasion).* Haiti Support Group (London), 1995.
A careful essay intended to educate people strange to the complications of the Haitian crisis. A very useful and encompassable guide.

ASSOCIATION DES AMIS ET AMIES DU PÈRE ARISTIDE À MONTRÉAL *Quelque chose a changé en Haiti.* CIDIHCA, 1988.
300 pages of newspaper cuttings, speeches, sermons, theological material relating to the explosive ministry of

Aristide between February 1986 and October 1987. It gives a clear picture of just how this man sprang from nowhere to grab the headlines.

BOUTROS-GHALI Boutros. *An Agenda for Peace*. United Nations, 1992.
The UN Secretary General sets out some of the main guidelines, as he sees them, for 'preventive diplomacy, peacemaking and peace-keeping', all roles to be espoused by the UN in the post-Cold War world. One of the first crises where some of this thinking was severely tested was Haiti.

COALITION NATIONALE POUR LES RÉFUGIÉS HAITIENS. *Un Besoin Prioritaire: Réformer la Justice en Haiti*. New York, 1995.
An essay that attempts to set out the case, amongst all Haiti's undoubted needs, for prioritizing the restructuring of its justice system. So little else can be expected to function without this important foundation.

CONFÉRENCE ÉPISCOPALE D'HAITI. *Présence de l'Église en Haiti: messages et documents de l'épiscopat, 1980-1988*. Éditions S.O.S. (Paris), 1988.
Key documentation of the church's thinking during the years when all its constituent elements were united in their struggle to unseat Duvalier and then build a new Haiti. The readiness of the official church to embrace the political options is clearly found in these statements. Aristide's arrival changed all that.

DEJEAN Paul. *Willy Romélus: L'Évêque-Courage*. Hurtubise (Canada), 1995.
A somewhat plodding and hagiographical account of the life of this brave bishop. It only comes to life towards the end with the bishop's personal account of the evolution of the Haitian crisis presented in a long letter to Pope John Paul II.

DIEDERICH Bernard and BURT Al. *PapaDoc: Haiti and its Dictator*. Bodley Head, 1970.
The classic chronicle by veteran Haiti-watchers of life under François Duvalier. No one has ever bettered this portrait of a dictator.

DUVALIER François. *Mémoires d'un Leader du Tiers Monde: mes négotiations avec le Saint-Siège ou une tranche d'histoire*. Hachette (Paris), 1969.
The opulently produced account of one of Duvalier's greatest

triumphs, the winning of the concession from the Vatican that allowed the Haitian head of state to nominate bishops to the various dioceses in Haiti. It took thirty years for Rome to win this right back again.

FARMER Paul. *AIDS and Accusation: Haiti and the Geography of Blame*. University of California Press, 1992. Farmer is a Harvard Professor of Social Medicine and also conducts research and medical practice in Haiti. His analysis carefully traces the progress of AIDS in the United States, Haiti, and the Caribbean, 'tracing AIDS in Haiti to, most probably, US gays who had sex with Haitian men during visits to the country'. He is scathing about persistent and wilful misunderstandings relating to the syndrome's supposed Haitian origins.
— *The Uses of Haiti*. Common Courage Press (Maine),1994. (With introduction by Noam Chomsky.)
A well argued account of the way Haiti has served the uses of third parties (especially the United States) over the years in providing 'myths' by which to justify themselves or else marginalize Haiti. Thus Haiti is thought of as a source of AIDS, its refugees are considered economic rather than political, Aristide is presented invariably as a fomenter of class struggle, and so on.

JALLOT Nicolas and LAURENT Lesage. *Haiti: Dix ans d'histoire secrète*. Éditions du Félin (Paris), 1995.
A racy account of the ten years following the ousting of Jean-Claude Duvalier. Its main interest lies in the face-to-face interviews conducted by the authors with some of the key actors in the Haitian crisis, especially the military and Tontons Macoutes. I'm not sure, however, whether they've quite made their case that Roger Lafontant was killed at the hands of French intelligence agents.

LAGUERRE Michel S. *The Military and Society in Haiti*. Macmillan, 1993.
This is a careful and indispensable account of the way the modern Haitian army developed in the aftermath of the US Occupation of Haiti (1915–34). Especially interesting is the section devoted to an account of the intelligence-gathering arm of the Haitian military and those to whom such information was channelled in the United States.

LAWYERS COMMITTEE FOR HUMAN RIGHTS. *Haiti: A Human Rights Nightmare*. New York, 1992.

A careful examination of the human rights situation in Haiti in May, June and July 1992. It reaches the conclusion that things had reached the lowest point in Haiti since the Duvalier era.

LIONET Christian. *Haiti: L'Année Aristide*. L'Harmattan (Paris), 1992.
The year in question is 1990–91, the year which saw Aristide's sensational rise to power. This is a detailed, chronological outline of the major events and an alphabetical list of all the major players with some excellent cross-referencing.

MOORE Brian. *No Other Life*. Bloomsbury, 1993.
This extraordinary novel is so 'in touch' with what was happening in the darkest times of Aristide's exile and has so captured the enigmatic nature of the Haitian president's character that it simply has to be described as a *tour de force*, as does its intriguing dénouement—which might well have been the way things eventually turned out.

NICHOLLS David. *From Dessalines to Duvalier: Race, Colour and National Independence in Haiti*. Cambridge University Press,1979.
This is the constantly re-issued standard reference book that gives the best overview yet of the historical, social and cultural developments since Haiti became an independent nation.

NICOLAS Mireille. *Jistis; murs peints d'Haiti* (Décembre 1990-1991) CIDIHCA, 1994.
A lavish book of photographs showing the wall paintings and public art which exploded throughout Haiti in the euphoric times surrounding the candidature and election of Aristide to the presidency. There's also a revealing Christophe Wargny interview with Aristide for good measure.

REMARAIS Georges and others. *La Presse sous la mitraille (Haiti: 30 septembre 1991)*. CIDIHCA (Canada), 1992.
A careful blow-by-blow account of the cynical way the leaders of the 1991 coup systematically targeted and intimidated journalists, destroying radio stations and beating and killing reporters as part of their drive to gain total control of the country.

RIDGEWAY James ed. *The Haiti Files: Decoding the Crisis*.

Essential Books (Washington), 1994.
A selection of documents and short articles which describe 'The Setting', 'The Players', 'The Crisis', and 'Chronology'. The third of these, 'The Crisis', breaks up into chapters on 'The Coup and US Foreign Policy', 'US Aid programs and the Haitian political economy', 'Drugs: the Haitian Connection', and 'Human Rights and the Refugee Question'.

THOMSON Ian. *Bonjour Blanc; a Journey through Haiti.* Hutchinson, 1992.
This is a remarkable traveller's tale from a young Englishman who spent three or four months footslogging his way through Haiti in the first months of 1990. His sense of the culture, his exposure to voodoo, his appreciation of the history, and his feel for the people in these extremely sensitive political days, make this one of the big travel books of all time.

UN/OAS: *Haiti: Learning the Hard Way (the UN/OAS Human Rights Monitoring Operation in Haiti, 1993-1994).*
A frank and dismal account of this understaffed and often insensitive effort to protect innocent victims of military misrule. The report expresses the hope that important lessons may be learned from this half-hearted failure. After all, this kind of operation may well continue to figure as one of the instruments resorted to in situations of conflict.

WARGNY Christophe and MOUTERDE Pierre. *Apre Bal Tanbou Lou (Après la fête, les tambours sont lourds).* Austral (Paris), 1996.
A little book that purports to unmask five years of American duplicity in Haiti during the years 1991–96. It tries to show how the rhetoric offered for public consumption was radically at odds with the way Haiti was being considered by American policy-making 'insiders'.

WERLEIGH Claudette. *Working for Change in Haiti*: CIIR Justice Paper No 12. London, 1989.
This was a speech given in London before the momentous events that brought Aristide to power. It was given by a woman deeply involved in Haiti's political life (she became prime minister a few years later) and has some shrewd analysis.

WILENTZ Amy. *The Rainy Season: Haiti since Duvalier.* Touchstone 1990.
This best seller was written by an experienced American

journalist who had unrivalled access to Jean-Bertrand Aristide in the months preceding the election that swept him to power. Many of its vignettes are moving and unforgettable. Her 'sense of Haiti' is excellent and her judgments sound. This book is a must for anyone reading the history of this period.

Index

Abraham, General Hérard 126, 144, 149, 196, 270

Adams, Alvin (American Ambassador) 124, 125, 173, 174, 202

Adrien, Antoine 85, 93, 126, 135, 191

amnesty 220, 222, 233, 241, 247, 255, 267

Amnesty International 217

ANDP (National Alliance for Democracy and Progress) 165, 195, 196

Arias, Oscar 274

Aristide, Jean-Bertrand
  birth in Port Salut 22
  his mother 22, 34-6, 41
  ordination 53, 56
  in Canada 54-6
  priest in Aux Cayes 65-6
  priest at St John Bosco 66ff
  assassination attempt at St John Bosco 109
  expelled from Salesians 118
  wins the election 145
  presidential inauguration156-163
  coup d'état 199-202
  return in October 1994 268
  resigns priesthood 271
  marriage 287

Aristide, Anne-Marie 22, 27, 46

army 20, 24, 29-30, 50-52, 60-61, 74, 82, 85, 93, 98, 99, 102-22, 126, 128, 131, 136, 141, 144, 146, 152, 161, 173, 175, 184, 185, 188, 196, 198, 199, 200-33, 236-38, 240-41, 242, 246, 249, 256, 257, 262, 264, 265, 274-6, 282

Athis, Louis-Eugène 102, 121

attachés 121

Avril, Prosper 108, 109, 117, 121, 122, 124, 125, 126, 189, 246, 291

Baker, James 212, 214

Balaguer, Joaquin 177, 178, 179, 180, 223, 251, 291

Barbarito, Mgr Luigi 153, 155, 162

Bazin, Marc 117, 145, 159, 165, 180, 188, 193, 224-228, 231, 238, 239, 273

Beaubrun Mondésir 285

Bélizaire, Déjean 196, 213

Bennett, Michèle 20, 51, 57, 58, 84, 131, 148, 288

Benoit, Victor 135

Bertin, Mireille Durocher 221, 283-5

Biamby, Philippe 268, 271

Bird, Nouveau Collège 20, 58, 278

Bishops' Conference 61, 63, 80, 87, 98, 103, 147, 150, 152, 229, 230, 290

Black Caucus 260

boat people 207-8, 234, 239, 258, 261, 269, 280, 282, 289

Bois Caïman 41, 167

Bosco, St John 36, 40, 43, 66, 69, 75, 87, 90, 91, 92, 109, 111, 112, 114, 115, 117, 119, 120, 138, 142, 162, 164, 211

Boyer, Hervé 76

Brouard, Carl 32, 33, 34, 138, 288

Brutus, Dully 195, 196

Bush, George 146, 208, 211, 213, 234, 235, 237, 244

Canada 54, 55, 56, 79, 125, 131, 172, 174, 184, 212, 239, 243, 244, 251

Caputo, Dante 238, 239, 240, 247, 250, 257, 268

CARICOM 180

Carter, Jimmy 17, 128, 133, 145, 159, 267, 268, 269

Casséus, Ernst Pedro 195

Cédras, Raoul 161, 196, 199, 200, 201, 202, 211, 212, 213, 216, 218, 220, 221, 223, 237, 238, 239, 240, 241, 247, 250, 255, 265, 267, 268, 269, 270, 271, 273, 289

CEP 86, 107

CHADEL 126, 187, 217, 218, 238

Chamberlain, Greg 170-1, 226

Charlemagne, Manno 204

Chavannes, Jean-Baptiste 108, 114, 115, 263

chefs de section 28, 283

Christophe, Henri 42, 288

CIA 30, 237, 243, 244, 245, 246, 254, 280, 281, 288

Claude, Sylvio Rev 103-4, 117, 146

Clinton, Bill 209, 233, 234, 235, 236, 237, 239, 245, 248, 249, 253, 255, 257, 259, 260, 261, 267, 269, 270, 271, 277, 280, 284, 289

Congress of Panama 176
Constant, Emmanuel (Duvalierist bishop) 51, 60, 61, 69, 89
Constant, Emmanuel 'Toto' (FRAPH leader) 51, 251, 271, 280-81
constitution 24, 29, 86, 104, 112, 132, 136, 148, 150, 154, 160, 173, 183, 184, 187, 197, 198, 199, 216, 275, 287
Créole 18, 19, 37, 38, 39, 40, 44, 60, 63, 82, 86, 87, 125, 128, 158, 166, 167, 205, 212, 225, 294
Cuba 104, 171, 208, 235, 287
Débrosse, Clauzel 276
dechoukaj 73, 74, 84, 96, 99, 100, 123, 134, 146
Dejoie, Louis 117
Desroches, Rosny 278
Dessalines, Jean-Jacques 15, 36, 42, 288
Dole, Robert 237, 240, 284
Dominican Republic 47, 59, 74, 102, 118, 150, 177, 178, 180, 181, 182, 205, 210, 214, 223, 229, 230, 242, 251, 268, 271, 275, 281, 291
Dufour, Jean-Raphael 202, 218
Duperval, Jean-Claude 274
Dupiton, Thomas Eddy 196
Duvalier, François ('PapaDoc') 17, 18, 20, 28, 31, 32, 37, 40, 44, 45, 46, 50, 51, 57, 58, 60, 61, 63, 64, 75, 76, 101, 102, 104, 108, 130, 164, 183, 199, 230, 278, 297
Duvalier, Jean-Claude 17, 20, 45, 54, 61, 71, 130, 131, 178, 207, 224, 225, 246, 287, 288, 290, 292, 296
  marriage 51, 57, 58, 63, 67, 68, 131, 148
  departure from Haiti 70, 71, 72, 75, 84, 98, 171, 294, 298

elections 9, 86,
  November 1987 101-5
  January 1988 107-8
  December 1990 125-9, 131, 133, 134, 141, 146, 147, 150, 151, 161, 195, 196, 225, 227, 232, 279
  December 1995 287
embargo 212-17, 219-20, 222-3, 231, 234, 241, 242, 247, 250-52, 255, 258, 259, 267, 281, 289, 291

FBI 237
Felix, Mgr Kelvin 143, 144, 154
FNCD (National Front for Change and Democracy) 135, 151, 164, 165, 183, 184, 195, 196, 227, 250

Fort Dimanche 40, 75, 76, 77, 79, 108, 121, 130, 166
France 23, 29, 81, 88, 108, 125, 127, 128, 152, 172, 174, 175, 184, 211, 239, 251
François, Michel 196, 199, 200, 201, 202, 203, 231, 247, 255, 268, 271, 281, 291
FRAPH (Front for the Renewal and Advance of Haiti) 14, 51, 168, 246, 247, 250, 251, 259, 265, 271, 273, 280, 281
Freycineau 93, 95, 110, 112, 163, 266

Gayot, Mgr François 20, 61, 67, 80, 98, 105, 127, 143, 147, 155, 271
Gilles, Serge 117, 124, 165, 227, 278
Governor's Island Accord 240, 242-4, 247, 250-52, 255
Guantanamo Bay 208-210

Harlan County 249, 259, 277, 289
Helms, Jesse 237, 240, 243, 249, 284
Honorat, Jean-Jacques 187, 217, 218, 219, 221, 224, 226, 228, 238, 273
Hurricane Gilbert 116

IMF (International Monetary Fund; see also World Bank) 166, 170, 180, 257, 290
Izméry, Antoine 204, 247, 265, 283
  Georges 265, 283

Jean Rabel 88, 89, 90, 92, 101, 110, 112, 121, 163, 186, 246, 266
Justice and Peace Commission 67, 147, 290

Kébreau, Mgr Louis 48, 49, 65, 103
Kennebunkport Order 208, 209, 235, 260

Lafanmi Selavi 81, 82, 85, 108, 111, 123, 146, 160, 164, 271, 288
Lafontant, Roger 129-134, 136, 142-3, 146-7, 149, 151-2, 167, 185-8, 199, 200, 201, 228, 236, 298
Larosilière, Julio 7, 263
Lavalas 33, 138-140, 216, 279, 286, 294
Liberation Theology 27, 45-7, 62, 64, 99, 158, 245-6
Ligondé, Mgr Wolff 49-51, 58, 60, 61, 66, 89, 115, 127, 147-50, 154-6, 159, 162, 231, 290, 291
literacy campaign (or Misyon Alfa) 39, 64, 68, 72, 73, 192

Madame Sara 34, 158 160

Malval, Robert 246, 251-253, 260, 266, 273
Misyon Alfa see literacy campaign

Namphy, General Henri 71, 72, 84, 97, 105, 107-9, 115, 117, 199, 278, 296
necklacing (also known as *le père lebrun*) 72, 74, 126, 127, 137, 150, 187, 188, 195, 199, 271, 296
nuncio 63, 70, 93, 109, 115, 118, 123, 127, 147, 148, 149, 150, 153, 162, 228, 229, 232, 251, 272, 290

Organisation of American States 159, 180, 211, 213, 233, 238, 289

PANPRA 165, 195, 227, 278
Paul, Jean-Claude 84, 108, 109, 117, 196, 200
père lebrun see necklacing
Péralte, Charlemagne 30, 32
Perez, Carlos Andres 142, 167, 202
Poland 24, 230
Pope John Paul II 25, 71, 142, 148, 151, 297
Port Salut 22-28, 35, 43, 65, 162
Powell, General Colin 236, 267
Préval, René 164, 169, 170, 173, 188, 191, 195, 270, 287, 294, 295
Puebla (Latin American Bishops' Conference) 64, 80

Quayle, Dan 195

rache manyok 87
Radio Cacique 48
Radio Soleil 54, 69, 70, 77, 88, 101, 119, 124, 131, 196, 229, 230
Radio Enriquillo 205, 223
Radio Vatican 230
Rodriguez, Cardinal Nicolas Lopez 242
Romain, Franck 76, 78, 112, 116, 121, 246, 291
Roman Catholic Church 20, 40, 44, 50, 51, 57, 60, 62, 64, 67, 68, 89, 98, 109, 144, 147, 151, 152, 153, 155, 192, 228, 231, 242, 290
Romélus, Mgr Willy 53, 61, 71, 79, 87, 98, 110, 133, 147, 151, 155, 159, 229, 232, 242, 297
Roosevelt, Franklin Delano 29
Ruelle Vaillant (massacre) 106, 107, 121, 128, 142

Salesians 35-7, 40, 41, 43, 49, 98, 114, 118, 119, 122, 191
Shalikashvili, John 270
Sodano, Cardinal Angelo 260
swine fever 59

Théodore, René 117, 220, 231
Ti (Kominote) Legliz 62, 67, 69, 71, 103, 108, 113, 119, 292
Tontons Macoutes 17, 20, 28, 40, 51, 69, 70, 86, 90, 93, 101, 102, 120, 136, 149, 154, 186, 199, 200, 247, 282, 298
Toussaint Louverture 15, 42, 94, 149, 288
Triest, Hugo Fr 230
Trouillot, Ertha Pascal 126, 128, 131, 133-4, 149, 152, 158, 167, 189
Trouillot, Mildred 287-8

United Nations 17, 146, 152, 159, 173, 179, 180, 181, 197, 211, 227, 233, 238, 239, 241, 251, 256, 265, 268, 280, 289, 297
United States Occupation 29, 30, 160, 281
USAID 60, 286

Vatican 50, 51, 63, 118, 143, 147, 149, 150, 152, 153, 175, 228, 230, 231, 232, 249, 251, 260, 272, 290, 298
Vatican Council 40, 44, 45, 46, 50
Venezuela 108, 125, 142, 146, 152, 159, 172, 176, 239, 251
Villa d'Accueil 222, 224, 227
Vincent, Jean-Marie Fr 7, 88, 89, 93, 262, 264, 266, 283,
Volel, Yves 53, 103, 121
voodoo 18, 19, 31, 38, 41, 57, 97, 98, 167, 300

Werleigh, Claudette 273, 286, 300
World Bank (*see also* IMF) 166, 170, 171, 172, 193, 224, 225, 257, 279, 285, 290